60 0077611 3

TELEPEN

KU-515-843

DATE DUE FOR RETURN

20. 03. 89		
09. FEB 95		
26		

This book may be recalled
before the above date

90014

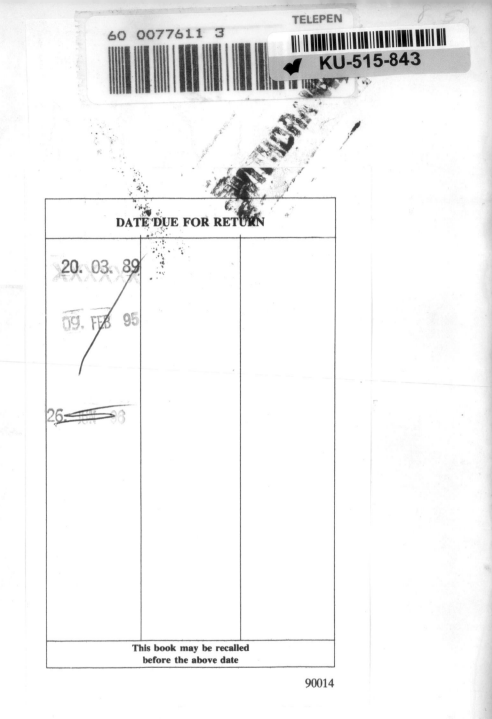

TRADE UNIONS AND
NATIONAL ECONOMIC POLICY

TRADE UNIONS AND
NATIONAL ECONOMIC POLICY

Jack Barbash
with the assistance of
Kate Barbash

THE JOHNS HOPKINS PRESS
BALTIMORE AND LONDON

UNIVERSITY LIBRARY
NOTTINGHAM
WITHDRAWN

Copyright © 1972 by Jack Barbash
All rights reserved
Manufactured in the United States of America

The Johns Hopkins Press, Baltimore, Maryland 21218
The Johns Hopkins Press Ltd., London

Library of Congress Catalog Card Number 75-173460

ISBN 0-8018-1342-5

TO THE UNIVERSITY OF WISCONSIN
FOR ITS COMMITMENT
TO THE PURSUIT OF KNOWLEDGE

Contents

Acknowledgments

The material in this project was prepared mainly under a grant from the Office of Manpower Policy, Evaluation, and Research, U.S. Department of Labor, under the authority of Title I of the Manpower Development and Training Act of 1962. Researchers undertaking such projects under government sponsorship are encouraged to express freely their professional judgment. Therefore, points of view or opinions stated in this book do not necessarily represent the official position or policy of the Department of Labor.

Supplementary support came from the University of Wisconsin Graduate School, a travel grant from the University's Western European Area Studies Program, incidental expenses from the University's Center for Vocational and Technical Education, and a consulting fee from the Office of Economic Cooperation and Development (OECD). Help far beyond the call of duty was rendered by Kenneth Douty of the Office of International Affairs of the U.S. Department of Labor and the American labor attachés, Dale Good in West Germany and Herbert Ihrig, Jr., in Sweden. The labor attachés and their staffs in all of the countries studied were uncommonly generous with their counsel, hospitality, and introductions.

To Gösta Rehn, head of OECD's Manpower and Social Affairs Directorate, we owe a manifold debt for making OECD materials available to us without stint, for granting us numerous interviews, for reading the Swedish chapter with care, and, most of all, for being a major innovator in his own right in the trade union relationship to national economic policy. Rudolf Meidner, Rehn's longtime LO colleague, now at the Swedish Labor Market Institute in Stockholm, also put his insights and knowledge at our disposal in reviewing the Swedish chapter. Allan Flanders of the United Kingdom's Commission on Industrial Relations, in both his writings and extended interviews not only imparted information but helped evolve a viewpoint. Our old friends Morris Weisz, Counselor of Embassy for Labor Affairs, U.S. Embassy, New Delhi; Joseph Mire, Director-Emeritus of the National Institute of Labor Education; and Joel Seidman, Professor of Industrial

Relations, University of Chicago, gave us the benefit of their insights and experience in foreign labor movements at various stages of this enterprise. Of course, none of these men nor anyone named below can properly be blamed for shortcomings.

The people listed below responded to our inquiry with unfailing kindness and information.

Sweden: Bertil Renberg, Swedish Labor Market Board; Arne H. Nilstein, Svenska Industritjänstemannaförbundet (SIF); Matts Larsson, Swedish Metal Trades Association; Lennart Bodström, Gösta Edgren, Sven Fockstedt, Stig Gustafsson, and Otto Nordenskiold, Tjanstemannens Centralorganisation (TCO); Birger Viklund, Metal Workers Union and Landsorganisationem i Sverige (LO); Tore Karlsson, Gösta Dahlstrom, and Einer Karlsson, LO; Bertil Ostergren and associates, Sveriges Akademikers Centralorganisation (SACO).

Austria: Paul Koch and Heinz Kienzl, Österreichischer Gewerkschaftsbund (ÖGB); Dr. Hans Reithofer, Dr. Milford, and Dr. Prager, Chamber of Labor; Kenneth Sullivan, Mrs. Langer, Anthony Geber, and John Rendahl, American Embassy; Drs. Choc, Ludwig, Steinbach, and Messrs. Illetchko and Ruhlke, and Franz Lenert, Austrian Federal Ministry for Social Administration.

The Netherlands: Harold E. Howland, American Consulate, Amsterdam; Joseph O'Brien and Mina Steiglis, American Embassy; Dr. Emile C. Sohns, Th. J. V. D. Peijl, Mrs. A. Oudkerk, A. B. Raven, and Dr. J. Groenendaal, Ministry of Social Affairs and Public Health; Dr. P. Pels, Foundation of Labor; Dr. J. Hollander, Employers Association; Ch. Buijtendijk and Dr. Engel, Social and Economic Council; R. Langebeek, Nederlands Vervond van Vakverengingen (NVV); G. Van Haaren, Nederlands Katholiek Vakverbond (NKV); G. Terpstra and P. Tjeerdsma, Christelijk National Vervond (CNV).

Germany: Rolf Weber, German Employers Confederation; Messrs. Zantman and Leverkurz, Ministry of Labor and Social Affairs; Walter Henklemann, H. Giersch, Messrs. Simon and Rosenberg, Deutscher Gewerkschaftbund (DGB); O. G. Schlatte, Federal Institute of Labor, Dusseldorf; Mr. Hofbauer, Erlangen; Mr. Komo, Nuremberg; Philip Heller, U.S. Consulate-General, Frankfurt; Mr. Nelson, U.S. Mission to Berlin; Hans Buttner, German Productivity Institute; Walter Schutz, Construction Workers Union; Dr. Günter Friedrichs and Hans Matthöfer, Metal Workers Union; Professor Necht and Professor Kurt Shell, University of Frankfurt; Mr. Potratz, President, Berlin Labor Office; Senator Baudin, Berlin Legislature.

United Kingdom: Professor Ben Roberts, London School of Economics; Thomas R. Byrne, Philip Kaiser, and Irvin Lippe, American Embassy; Mr. K. Dallas, National Economic Development Office; Alun M.

Morgan and D. P. Buckley, Department of Employment and Productivity; William Hughes, Ruskin College.

France: Irvin Lippe and Mrs. Bernard, American Embassy; Jacques Etevenon, David Christian, William Dymond, and Robert Smith, OECD; Charles Ford, Trade Union Advisory Committee to OECD; Seymour Chalfin, U.S. Mission to OECD.

Belgium: Professor R. Blanpain, University of Leuven; Heribert Maier and Morris Palladino, International Confederation of Free Trade Unions; Leo Slezak, American Embassy; M. J. Deroo, Belgian Bureau of Employment; Miss Nonon and M. Van Praag, European Economic Council.

Switzerland: David Morse, Paul Fisher, Robert Cox, Kenneth Walker, Johannes Schreglie, Aaron Warner, William Knowles, Mrs. Beguin, Mr. Watson, Mr. Fortin, Ralph Bergmann, Sven Grabbe, George Spyropolis, and Felix Paukert of the International Labor Office; John T. Fishburn, U.S. Mission to ILO.

List of Symbols

AEFU   Amalgamated Union of Engineering Foundry Workers (British)
AFL-CIO   American Federation of Labor–Congress of Industrial Organizations
BACIE   British Association for Commercial and Industrial Education
BDA   Bundesvereinigung der Deutschen Arbeitgeberverbände (Confederation of German Employers Association)
CDU   Christlich-Demokratische Union (Christian Democratic Union)
CEA   Council of Economic Advisors (U.S.)
CFDT   Confédération Française Democratique du Travail (French Democratic Federation of Labor)
CGB   Christliche Gewerkschaftsbund (Christian Trade Union Federation)
CGC   Confédération Générale des Cadres (General Confederation of Cadres)
CGT   Confédération Générale du Travail (General Confederation of Labor)
CNPF   Conseil National du Patronat Français (National Council of French Employers)
CNV   Christelijk National Verbond (Protestant Christian National Trade Union Centre)
DAG   Deutscher Angestellten-Gewerkschaft (Salaried Employee's Union)
DBB   Deutscher Beamtenbund (Trade Union Federation of Permanent Civil Servants)
DEA   Department of Economic Affairs (British)
DGB   Deutscher Gewerkschaftbund (German Federation of Labor)
EDC   Economic Development Committee (British)
FDP   Freie Demokratische Partei (Free Democratic Party)
FO   Force Ouvière (Workers Force)
ICFTU   International Confederation of Free Trade Unions

I.G. Bau	Industriegewerkschaft Bau Steine-Erden (Industrial Union of Workers in Building, Quarrying, and Public Works Contracting)
IGM	Industrie-gewerkschaft Metall (Industrial Union of Metal Workers)
ILO	International Labour Office
LO	Landsorganisationem i Sverige (Swedish Confederation of Trade Unions)
LO-Kartell	Federation of Civil Servants
NBPI	National Board for Prices and Incomes (British)
NEA	National Education Association (U.S.)
NEDC	National Economic Development Council (British)
NKV	Nederlands Katholiek Vakverbond (Netherlands Roman Catholic Trade Union Centre)
NVV	Nederlands Vervond van Vakverengingen (Netherlands Federation of Trade Unions)
OECD	Organisation for Economic Cooperation and Development
OEEC	Organisation for European Economic Co-operation
ÖGB	Österreichischer Gewerkschaftsbund (Austrian Federation of Labor)
RKW	Rationalisierings-Kuratorium der Deutschen Wirtschaft (German Productivity Center)
SACO	Sveriges Akademikers Centralorganisation (Confederation of University-trained Professionals)
SAF	Svenska Arbetsgivareföringen (Swedish Employers Confederation)
SIF	Svenska Industritjänstemannaförbundet (Swedish Union of Clerical and Technical Employees in Industry)
SPD	Socialdemokratische Partei Deutschland (Social Democratic Party)
TCO	Tjanstemannens Centralorganisation (Confederation of White Collar Workers)
TUAC	Trade Union Advisory Committee to the OECD
UAW	United Automobile Workers (U.S.)

TRADE UNIONS AND
NATIONAL ECONOMIC POLICY

CHAPTER ONE

Introduction

Trade union involvement in national economic policy in Western Europe and the lessons that it offers to the United States is the focus of this book. In American terms, it might be called a study in the structure of union responsibility—that is, in the sense of Arthur J. Goldberg's admonition that trade unions in formulating their wage and price policies and other policies "must look beyond the counsel of their tradition and out into the broad fields of modern economic realities both at home and abroad."[1] Structure in this context suggests that union responsibility requires more than an act of will; the act of will needs to be rooted in suitable policies, institutions, and environments.

Accordingly, this study delineates the policies, institutions, and environments which made trade union involvement in national economic policy—or union responsibility—feasible or unfeasible in varying degrees in Sweden, Austria, the Netherlands, West Germany, the United Kingdom, and France. The chapter on France highlights the circumstances of a trade union situation which seem to work against effective involvement in economic policy.

When this project was initially formulated, its major focus was to be trade union involvement in manpower policy. In an important sense, this is still true; union involvement in manpower policy as conventionally defined is probably treated in greater detail than is any other policy area. I found almost at once, however, that there was, in practice, no fixed boundary which marked off manpower policy from incomes policy, industrial relations, and economic planning. These policy areas did indeed have significant manpower ramifications which would have to be explored if something approximating a comprehensive account was to be rendered. There are aspects of economic policy that are treated only in passing, if at all, so that if this work were fully titled it might read: "Trade Unions and

1. Arthur J. Goldberg, Address to the National Academy of Arbitrators, January 26, 1962, Pittsburgh, Pennsylvania, U.S. Department of Labor Release 5015, p. 10.

1

National Economic Policy in Western Europe with Special Reference to Manpower Policy and with Implications for the United States."

The most prominent expressions of trade union involvement in economic policy have been the centralized bargaining system and the National Labor Market Board in Sweden; the Chambers of Labor, the Joint Council on Wages and Prices, and the Advisory Council on Economic and Social Affairs in Austria; the Foundation of Labor and the Social and Economic Council in the Netherlands; the self-imposed wage restraint, the Federal Institute of Labor, bargaining adjustments to technological change, the investment wage principle, and codetermination in West Germany; the National Economic Development Council, the EDC's, the Industrial Training Boards, and industrial relations reform in the United Kingdom; and the horizontal and vertical commissions of the Plan in France. Incomes policy was found to be least conducive to union involvement because it runs against the union's protective function. Economic planning was not conducive to union involvement because, except in rare situations, the union could be involved only at the periphery. Most conducive to union involvement was manpower policy because it is most compatible with the union's protective function and is capable of giving the unions an important role.

II

The trade union's ability to participate in national economic policy depends on the extent to which the trade union shares a core of common values with other elements in society and on the availability of mechanisms through which these common values can be converted into mutually acceptable policies and programs. This is called integration. Primarily it means the muting of ideologies which deny common purpose. Also included in the concept are institutions like centralized federations, centralized bargaining, industrial unionism, union-party alliances, and professionalized union administration able to produce a coherent union position in economic policy. Finally, integration means that the policy areas of involvement must in the long run be compatible with the union's protective purposes. Self-denial, in other words, cannot be a permanent feature of the economic policy in which the unions are involved.

The integration condition for high union involvement in national economic policy may conflict with other goals such as rank and file control, trade unionism as a revolutionary vehicle, and decentralization of power. No argument is offered that economic policy unionism is intrinsically superior to these other goals, although I believe that a case can be made—which I have not attempted to make—that, on balance, economic policy unionism in the manner suited to each society enhances the stability of the social order and the progress of unionism and its constituents.

In the following chapters, trade union involvement in economic policy is viewed in a specific historic context: namely, the period of post-full employment of the late 1950s and 1960s in Western Europe when "the main difficulty of the postwar economies was not slack demand, relative overproduction or insufficient investment, but an ungovernable tendency of demand to outrun the economy's capacity to meet it without inflation and price rise."[2] The European trade union movements were drawn into involvement in economic policy mainly to abate the inflation. When this study was completed, however, there was an escalation of inflationary pressures powerful enough to threaten even the Swedish and West German involvements—each in their different ways the most durable expressions of "union responsibility"—with rank and file disaffection in the form of an epidemic of unauthorized strikes.

III

Precisely because there is a close association between integration and high union involvement in economic policy, wholesale application of the European economic policy model of trade unionism to the United States is very unlikely and, at points, even undesirable. The fragmenting and decentralizing forces bearing upon American trade unionism are simply too powerful to permit the kind of high involvement exemplified in the Swedish situation. But if wholesale importation is not possible, partial application may be. The European economic and social council type of union involvement can have its analogue in the American type of national labor-management advisory committee, which lacks the authority of the European model but serves the same essential purpose of a meeting ground for unions, managements, and government policymakers. If an incomes policy approach is deemed necessary, it is worth exploring whether the European experience in *negotiating* that incomes policy has applications for the United States. This would require trade union research to be improved and expanded and to take a stronger analytic bent. Above all, the times and the great influence of the trade union movement appear to demand an attitude of "partial trusteeship for the system implying a responsibility to perceive the problems confronting the society and an obligation to *lead* [italics added] in their solution."[3]

2. M. M. Postan, *An Economic History of Western Europe* (London: Methuen, 1967), p. 19.

3. David B. Truman, "Labor's Responsibility in Public Affairs," in *Labor's Public Responsibility* (Madison, Wisconsin: National Institute of Labor Education, 1960), p. 11.

IV

The concept of integration provides the organizing principle for the European chapters; that is, each chapter is organized to demonstrate that effective trade union involvement in national economic policy depends on an integrated trade union-collective bargaining system and that conversely there is a relationship between decentralization and the inefficacy of involvement. The economic and labor market settings and the industrial relations context are treated only enough to provide a frame for the material on trade union participation in these areas. Hence, this report is not offered as a study in comparative labor movements or manpower policies; nor is it offered as an appraisal of the results of trade union involvement.

Some chapters have more detail than others. The Swedish chapter is the most detailed because the trade unions have been a central influence in manpower policy and administration and thus represent an "ideal type." The chapter on France is treated with the least detail because it was included as a point of contrast rather than as a potential example. The United States is treated with a bare minimum of background because it is assumed that the special contribution which this report could make to American readers is to give them not the detail of American programs but some main points of comparison with European ones.

CHAPTER TWO

Sweden: The "Ideal Type"

The Swedish case is significant in this study first because an active manpower policy formulated, implemented, and administered in part by the labor movement is the "centerpiece" of national economic policy. Sweden's active manpower policy evolved in the climate of a *post*-full employment economy in which "impulses to price rises in recent years . . . have to a high degree emanated from the labor market"[1] and in which economic growth objectives have taken on new force. Sweden is also significant because economy-wide collective bargaining is the major instrument of wage policy.

II

Swedish planning is a type of indicative planning midway "between the French system of highly centralized detailed planning and the 'mild' form of economic coordination used in the U.S.,"[2] employing the Keynesian battery of monetary and fiscal policy, augmented by Swedish innovations in manpower policy "raised from [an] earlier role of assistant to fiscal and monetary policy to an independent key role."[3] "The 'revealed preference' of the responsible government authorities seems to be a permanent excess demand pressure on the labor market; there should be more jobs than men."[4] Swedish planning is unaccompanied by sanctions except the sanction imposed by the force of economic intelligence and what Rehn once called "the dictatorship of circumstances."[5] Sweden's economy is "open."

1. Lars Jacobsson and Assar Lindbeck, "Labor Market Conditions, Wages and Inflation—Swedish Experiences, 1955–67," *Swedish Journal of Economics* (Stockholm), June 1969, p. 66.
2. Gösta Dahlstrom, "Economic Planning in Sweden," *Free Labour World* (ICFTU, Brussels), May 1964, p. 14.
3. Rudolf Meidner, "The Goals of Labour Market Policy," in *On Incomes Policy* (Stockholm: The Industrial Council for Social and Economic Studies, 1969), p. 191.
4. Erik Lundberg, *Instability and Economic Growth* (New Haven: Yale University Press, 1968), p. 257.
5. Gösta Rehn, "The National Budget and Economic Policy," *Quarterly Review*, Skandinaviska Banker, vol. 43, no. 2 (1962), p. 41, quoted in A. G. Gruchy, *Comparative Economic Systems* (Boston: Houghton Mifflin Co., 1966), p. 363.

Exports constitute about one-fifth of total production and one-half of industrial production. Imports are of the same order.[6]

The active manpower policy is perceived by Bertil Olsson, director general of the Swedish National Labor Market Board, as "ensuring a balance between manpower supply and manpower demand and measures increasing the level of employment by other than general economic methods."[7]

The new labor market policy, Rudolf Meidner reported in retrospect, evolved out of "the inner dynamics of the ideology of full employment."[8] The Swedish labor market policy "was launched," Meidner has said in another place, "as a reaction against the economic policy of the postwar years which created a situation of strong excess demand for the economy as a whole."[9] The Swedish labor movement was brought to a manpower policy by "worry . . . about the effect of a permanent over-full employment economy on the ability of the union organisations to act as free negotiating parties independent of the government. . . ."[10]

An OECD team has succinctly put the "basic principles" of Swedish manpower policy:

> A non-inflationary full employment economy cannot be maintained only by general fiscal and monetary means. To create, by these means alone, a level of demand high enough to eliminate all unemployment will unavoidably result in an intolerable overstrain of resources in broad sectors. A less inflationary level of overall demand will instead involve tendencies towards unemployment in some sectors and still mean excess demand in others. These partial imperfections have to be counteracted by a set of selective measures: on the one hand various stimuli towards occupational and geographical mobility of the labour force, so that the most expansive and productive industries can grow more rapidly, on the other hand job creation in surplus areas where an additional demand for labour can be established without resulting in overstrain. These measures are not to be regarded as makeshifts in an emergency but as permanent elements of economic policy aiming at a rate of growth high enough continually to absorb the whole labour force without utilisation of self-destructive inflationary stimuli or protection of sectors with low productivity. They have to be implemented

6. Gösta Edgren, Karl-Olof Faxén, and Clas-Erik Odhner, "Wages, Growth and the Distribution of Income," *Swedish Journal of Economics*, September 1969, p. 133.

7. Bertil Olsson, "*Active Manpower Policy in Sweden*," Official Memorandum for OECD Scandinavian Regional Seminar, National Labour Market Board (Stockholm), 1965, p. 2.

8. Meidner, "Goals of Labour Market Policy," p. 189.

9. Rudolf Meidner, "The Role of an Active Manpower Policy in Contributing to a Solution of the Dilemma between Inflation and Unemployment" (Paper delivered at the OECD International Conference on Employment Fluctuation and Manpower Policy, Paris, February 1969), p. 12.

10. Meidner, "Goals of Labour Market Policy," p. 189.

on a sufficiently large scale by a manpower policy administration entrusted with substantial financial and legal powers. This administration will have as important a task when external conditions promote a high level of economic activity as when recessionary tendencies prevail.[11]

Meidner has synthesized the task of "economic and particularly labour market policy . . . as bringing about a downward change of the Phillips curve [that is, the direct relationship between employment and prices] so that a given level of unemployment becomes compatible with a lower rate of price increase, and that a lower rate of price increase becomes compatible with a lower level of unemployment."[12]

The theory of the active manpower policy depends for its effectiveness both on the availability of a wide range of measures and the proper timing of their execution[13] and on procedures and organization which strengthen the labor market's institutions. On the labor supply side, the stress is on "mobility promoting measures" which facilitate the occupational and geographic movement of workers (for example, adult training and re-training, and relocation allowances).[14] Financial aid to workers undergoing training and/or relocation operates on the theory that individual risks for more efficient allocation of manpower are properly chargeable to social costs and, more particularly, that the system of financial aid ought to make mobility more attractive than subsidized unemployment. As an example of the latter, the subsistence allowance which an unemployed worker receives while undergoing training comes to about 80 percent of the working wage and is substantially higher than the unemployment compensation payment.[15] On the demand side, public works, public relief work, "tax allowances through anti-cyclical investment reserve funds," and industry location programs act as "employment creating measures."[16] For those unable to find employment there is unemployment insurance from union-sponsored benefit societies supported in part by government funds.

The Labor Market Administration—that is, the National Labor Market Board—together with its regional agencies, county labor market boards, and local employment offices and agents, forms and executes labor market policy.[17] The coordinated character of the National Labor Market Board enables it "to pursue a particular labour market policy quickly and effectively with no intervention on the part of other government departments

11. OECD, *Labour Market Policy in Sweden* (Paris, 1963), pp. 63–64.
12. Meidner, "Role of Active Manpower Policy," p. 6.
13. Olsson, "Active Manpower Policy in Sweden," p. 3.
14. National Labour Market Board, *Labour Market Policy, 1969–70* (Stockholm, 1968), p. 20.
15. OECD, *Labour Market Policy in Sweden*, p. 37.
16. *Ibid.*
17. *Ibid.*, p. 25.

or organizations."[18] "The employment service is the basis of all labour market policy. . . ." It must be highly flexible and be capable of "convert[ing] the principles of labour market policy into concrete action. . . ."[19] In keeping with this, the Labor Market Board is concerned with an advance warning system to make information on labor conditions readily available and with vocational guidance and vocational rehabilitation.

III

For our purposes the most significant fact about the active manpower policy is that the intellectual climate in which it evolved and the economic analysis on which it is based is largely a product of trade union economists and the experience of the trade union movement itself. The architects of this policy were mainly Gösta Rehn, the present director of Manpower and Social Affairs in OECD, Rudolf Meidner, now heading the government-sponsored Labor Market Institute (Rehn and Meidner relieved each other as heads of the LO research department), and a talented group of economists who were attracted to the LO, including Richard Steiner, Nils Kellgren, Per Holmberg, and Clas-Eric Odhner. Rehn has recently had an opportunity to review the events of this formative period and the review is reproduced here in some detail because it illuminates the interaction of ideas and forces and especially how economists in trade unions function as independent analysts, at times in disagreement with the leadership.

During the earliest postwar period Rehn and Meidner supported the policy of voluntary self-restraint and took a very active part in its defense against the attacks made by communists and others.

> During the war there was simply nothing else to do. We had to regulate on all points—prices, wages, etc. Anything that could disturb this would be dangerous, and the union members understood that. . . . When the war was over and we experienced the first rather over-optimistic outburst of free wages and prices the government reacted by urging a wage freeze. For one year we even supported this although we already had begun to see the need for another sort of stabilisation policy and had (already in 1946, with little success) warned the government against the consequences of a premature scrapping of some of the war-time taxation. But the historical truth demands that we must confess that we have to some extent still believed in the method applied as a guideline for wages policy: to figure out what is the probable room for a consumption increase and then to increase wages just the right amount to fit that. We had only begun to see the futility of that idea, even in a country where centralised wage bargaining or at least a morally persuasive influence from a trade union centre was so strong as in Sweden.[20]

18. *Ibid.*, p. 52.
19. National Labour Market Board, *Labour Market Policy*, pp. 14–15.
20. Gösta Rehn to Jack Barbash, February 26, 1970.

The trade union leaders had been scared by the inflationary wage-price picture of 1947–48 and by a severe deterioration of the balance of payments and had willingly accepted a prolongation of the collective agreements for 1949, although they had originally been signed for 1948 only. But when the government, worried by the balance-of-payments situation and the need for stability, asked for a second wage freeze, that is, for 1950, the LO economists reacted more definitely. There were rather dramatic debates with the prime minister in the governing body of LO. Although the president of LO at that time largely shared the economists' views, the majority of trade union leaders was uneasy and had no difficulty in siding with the experienced and responsible politicians against the young theoreticians. The main selling point of the politicians was the guarantee of one year's price stability through subsidization of certain prices.

This was precisely what the economists regarded as particularly odious. The subsidies would weaken the budget and increase the "inflationary gap." This would overstrain price control and put into motion an accumulation of suppressed inflationary forces. Their recommendation was rather to let the price increases which were due to cost increases and the devaluation (Sweden followed the British pound in September 1959) run their course, to let wages at least keep pace with them, and at the same time to lay the foundations for a better stability in the future. The government's policy of repressed inflation through wage, price, import, and building controls would not hold for any prolonged period, because (1) the unions would have difficulty in justifying a continuing wage restraint to their members with employer profits running high; (2) the heavy demand for manpower would result in substantial wage drift, creating internal inequities between the various groups of wage (and salary) earners; and (3) unrest generated by these factors would unloose a "wage explosion" nullifying the stabilization effect of the restrictive wage policy.

In a way, the early debating defeat of the economists laid the basis for a rather general acceptance by LO of their theories when their predictions materialized. True, the wage explosion, when it came in 1951, got a special impetus from the influence of the Korean War upon Swedish prices. But the issue was dramatized. The government, which had warned against a few percent price increases in order to get the trade unions to prefer the second prolongation of the agreements, now had to switch to the opposite line in a rather drastic fashion: in a so-called once-for-all inflation they really let prices run their course in the Korean scare (about 15 percent in 1951) and told the unions that they should use the high demand for labor, which the government policy deliberately upheld, to get adequate wage increases catching up with the actual and foreseen increases in the cost of living.[21]

21. *Ibid.*

As the inflationary effects of the immediate postwar period intensified "the theories and proposals presented by Gösta Rehn in 1947–1949 came to play a particularly important role in the debate about full employment and price stability."[22] It was in this period that Rehn developed the argument that the essential conflict between full employment and price stability could not be overcome solely by aggregate demand measures but required the kind of selectivity in manpower policy noted earlier in this chapter.

The trade union movement came to accept the Rehn-Meidner analysis and to elaborate it in a series of now classic LO reports. The way had partially been paved by *The Trade Union Movement and Modern Society* published in 1941. LO reversed an earlier stand and agreed to the appropriateness of the government interest in the labor market but sought to demarcate the lines between collective bargaining and public policy. LO also began hesitatingly to modify its negative attitude toward technological change.

Trade Unions and Full Employment presented to the LO Congress in 1951 represented the trade union movement's first major theoretical argument for full employment with stability. Government support of full employment cannot rest solely on "high demand for labour" which can only lead to "disruption of the wage structure and inflationary wage demands." On the other hand, heavy reliance on monetary and fiscal measures to limit demand would mean that "full employment would no longer exist unless government intervened and created a new demand for labour." The report recommended "a more vigorous labour market policy than hitherto, as complementary to general (preferably fiscal) measures to keep effective demand below inflation-creating levels." More specifically, selective measures to maintain a rapid adjustment between supply and demand—for example, removal allowances to encourage occupational and geographic mobility, and regional development—were urged. Labor market policy was said to be superior to measures of the "awkward negative type, always forbidding people to do things they want to do." Only as the prior condition of noninflationary full employment is fulfilled can the labor movement undertake to enforce wage policy by internal self-discipline. The wage policy should fairly reflect productivity gains and distributive justice in the form of the solidarity wage policy.[23]

Economic Expansion and Structural Change issued in 1961 is addressed to "the challenge which the Swedish economy will have to face from new

22. Assar Lindbeck, "Theories and Problems in Swedish Economic Policy in the Post-War Period," *Surveys of National Economic Policy Issues and Policy Research*, American Economic Review Supplement, June 1968, p. 19.

23. LO, "Trade Unions and Full Employment," mimeographed summary of report (Stockholm, 1953).

technologies and the associated requirements of more capital and increased adaptability, the integration of international trade policy in Europe, the industrialization of the underdeveloped countries, and the competition regarding economic expansion between the democracies and communist states." Labor market accommodation to the structural changes generated by these developments is advocated "on the basis of certain generally accepted values of the working class movement—freedom, democracy, security, greater equality, free choice for consumers, an improved social balance and international solidarity."

"Pure systems of economic policy" are rejected in favor of "a mixed economy characteristic of the present structure of our economy. . . . Various associations and organizations operate to balance one another as centres of countervailing power. Their interests differ so much that they provide a mechanism which almost certainly operates more fluently than competition. . . ."

The active labor market policy and regional development are the foundations on which the policies relating to credit, tax, international trade and competition, and prices must build. The labor market and location policy must in turn arise out of two conditions, the maintenance of full employment and the support of labor mobility as a social cost, not a private risk. "But this labour market and location policy must accept more explicitly the need for change and movement."

The role of the trade unions in this new environment is to pursue an active wage policy aimed at (a) "the creation of a 'rational' wage structure, i.e., a structure in which the wage differentials between different groups and individuals are determined by the nature of the input of effort"; (b) distributive justice, that is, "ensuring a reasonable share of the national product to wage earners as a whole"; (c) no obstruction to "economic equilibrium"; and (d) no obstruction to "the structural shifts in the economy which are the prerequisite of expansion."

The logic of the rational wage structure principle leads to the solidarity wage policy by which wages are determined not on the basis of the enterprise's capacity to pay, as businessmen advocate, but by "the nature of the input of effort." For weak enterprises, the effect of wage differentials as an allocative principle is to provide a " 'wage subsidy' by underpaid workers . . . and to preserve firms that are not profitable in the long run rather than to promote the exodus of labour to high wage enterprises." The upward pressure on wages exerted by wage solidarity will compel the enterprise "to rationalize and when these possibilities have been exhausted to close down." This method of transferring workers from less efficient to more efficient firms is probably more effective for optimum allocation than are wage differentials which operate slowly and within very broad ranges and which are subject to severe cyclical fluctuation. But the essential conditions of the solidarity wage policy are full employment and an active labor market policy which will provide worthwhile jobs for displaced workers, train them for these jobs, support them while in training, and relocate them to new jobs on completion of training.[24]

In 1961 LO also issued *Trade Unions and Industrial Democracy* which explores the shop floor implications of structural change and the role of workers in the management of the firm. This report provided the foundation for the revision of the agreement on works councils, to be discussed later.

In 1966 LO published *Trade Unions and Technological Change* which investigated the effects of changing technology on employment and working conditions and how efficiency may be made compatible with individual job satisfaction and adjustment to work. The report argues that "the capacity of our national labour market policy should operate as a constraint on the pace with which structural rationalisation is carried out in Sweden." The following deficiencies and needs hamper efficient labor market adjustment to structural change:

1. The inadequacy of labor market statistics relating to labor mobility, the search for jobs, the effectiveness of labor market measures, the occupational structure and its classification

2. The lack of adequate evaluation and measurement of labor market policy programs, for example, follow-up studies of plant shutdowns and large-scale redundancies

3. Deficiencies in forecasting for purposes of short- and long-term planning of training, prediction of technological developments in different sectors, and advance warning of large-scale redundancies and plant shutdowns

4. The minority of job changes in which the employment service is involved and the need for upgrading the employment service to become "the central job information service for the entire labour market, so that employers as well as job seekers [will] consult the exchanges as a matter of course for information and services"

5. The need for special measures for hard-to-place workers, including long-term rehabilitation

6. The widening educational gap between the generations, which requires expansion of adult education and training in the interests of a balanced labor force and social equality; "the requirement that only unemployed workers are entitled to subsidized retraining must be discontinued."

24. LO, *Economic Expansion and Structural Change*, ed. and trans. T. L. Johnston (London: Allen and Unwin, 1963), pp. 150–53 *passim*.

7. An inter-industry occupational classification system which will make possible job comparisons "from the individual's point of view," to implement the solidarity wage policy

8. The narrowness in scope and coverage of the existing redundancy payments: the workers who are inevitably displaced by rationalization should not "by themselves bear the risks of a drop in income. . . . Where there are no guarantees against loss of income innovations will naturally be met with greater suspicion." Older workers and low-wage workers especially are inequitably treated.

9. More data on how workers adjust to their work environment in respect to "bio-technical and health aspects, job enlargement" and "the overall work organization"

10. Reduction in hours not as work-sharing for full employment—only "a high level of effective demand" can achieve this—but to increase job opportunities for the part-time labor force

11. Collectively bargained "industry funds" to "facilitate the adjustment of the enterprise and the work force to changed technical conditions"; the funds will finance "research, market analysis, consultative activity, training and retraining programs, redundancy payments and pre-retirement benefits for elderly redundant workers."

12. The introduction of change according to a "careful strategy" worked out with "the participation of trade union officials, especially at the level of the works councils"[25]

IV

The leading role of the labor movement extends not only to policy-making but also to the administration of labor market policy in the National Labor Market Board which began its great expansion in 1958. The trade union representatives on the board—three from LO, two from TCO, and one from SACO—constitute the largest single interest group representation; the employers' confederation has three representatives and the director general and the deputy director general account for one vote each. There is general agreement that the main lines of labor market policy have emanated from the trade union side.

For the LO, interest representation on the Labor Market Board is an article of principle. "Coordination based on discussion and agreement is very much preferable to a more formal procedure. The parties are then prepared to accept their share of responsibility for events, something that can never be imposed upon them, measures can be adjusted more readily

25. LO, *Trade Unions and Technological Change*, ed. and trans. S. D. Anderman (London: Allen and Unwin, 1967), pp. 238–58 *passim*.

to suit changing circumstances, a mutual trust is established and contact with opinion maintained. . . . On the other hand, the possible results that can be achieved are naturally limited by what the parties consider or can be persuaded is in their own interests."[26] An LO economist has observed that "this representation undoubtedly contributes a great deal of insight from what might be termed the 'consumers' of labour market policy . . . and certainly opens up possibilities for the discussion and submission of proposals which would perhaps have been neglected. The representation of labour market organisations also constitutes a value in itself—a democratic guarantee and possibility of control."[27]

Labor movement influence in the administration of labor market policy via the Labor Market Board stems in the first instance from the facts that the labor movement has been the innovator of modern labor market policy and that with its political allies in the parliament and the Social Democratic Party, it continues to exercise the major initiating policy influence. The union representatives are also able to be effective in the give and take of detailed discussion because they know each other well enough to bring a problem-solving attitude without excluding the sectional interests which, as unions, they are bound to assert. The labor representatives, like their opposite numbers, are good working economists, even if not always formally certified, with a respect for labor market intelligence. There is a good informal relationship among the members. The associate director general observed, "When we deal with questions at our meetings there is much close contact among us. We get a great deal of information from each other. This participation goes deeply in our daily work."[28] One of the white collar labor members reported: "About once a year we have a meeting with the [director] and his staff and my staff and we go through the problems of the white collar workers in the industry. We have a meeting (including dinner and a sauna) and many of the ideas come out of these meetings. They last for about twelve hours."[29]

In the view of one employer member of the board, the immediate initiatives come from the director's "brains trust. There is always a play among the ministers and the parties. The spark may come from one of these contacts. And very often the director will try to get reenforcements from the unions or the employers." But the Labor Market Board is a "decision making board where the laymen actually take part and are responsible for decisions. . . . The problems handled by the board are

26. LO, *Economic Expansion*, p. 166.
27. Per Holmberg, "Final Report on the Seminar," *Active Manpower Policy*, OECD Scandinavian Regional Seminar, Manpower and Social Affairs (Paris: OECD, 1967), p. 15.
28. Interview with Bertil Renberg, Stockholm, August 12, 1968.
29. Interview with Arne H. Nilstein, SIF, Stockholm, August 12, 1968.

important problems for us as well as the unions. The board is not just a rubber stamp. And it should be noted that most activities in the [labor market field] have been launched unanimously."[30] In the view of a labor member of the board "very few things happen that are not OK'd by the unions."[31] There is common consent that the "great contribution of Bertil Olsson," the board's director, has been very important in implementing the active labor market policy.[32]

Tripartism extends to the administration of the twenty-five county labor market boards where the labor members also constitute a majority of the board. The greater routinization of the county board's work probably makes the labor members less important at the policy level in the county board than they are in the national board. Most of these labor members are not full-time union officers. The national labor centers undertake to train their representatives on the local boards. Some of the local board members have "felt they were just rubber stamps. The agendas were too heavy. There was not enough time to prepare for the meeting"—they did not get the agenda materials sufficiently in advance to come to informed judgments.[33]

Although there is the hazard, as an OECD examining group suggested, that the labor market organizations "have been put in a position to pursue their own policy," the government spokesmen on the board point out that the organizations "not only influence but also take responsibility for the efficient pursuance of the policies and measures decided upon."[34] From the government's viewpoint, "by having the cooperation of the parties in the detailed forming of the labour market policy, it is guaranteed that the decisions made are in accordance with their opinions concerning the current situation."[35]

There are occasional differences among the participants; these are as likely between labor members as between labor and employer members. Educational reform has divided the LO and the SACO representatives. The issue of foreign labor imports has divided the labor and employer representatives. The more restrictive union position has been based on housing inadequacies and overconcentration in particular areas. The unions have charged the employers with recruiting "foreign labour as an alternative to improving wages and other personnel conditions for the domestic labor

30. Interview with Matts Larsson, Swedish Metal Trades Employers Association, Stockholm, August 12, 1968; also Larsson to Jack Barbash, February 26, 1970.
31. Interview with Nilstein.
32. Meidner, "Goals of Labour Market Policy," p. 3.
33. Interviews with Stig Gustafsson, Otto Nordenskiold, Lennart Bodström, Sven Fockstedt, and Gösta Edgren, TCO, Stockholm, August 13, 1968.
34. OECD, Labour Market Policy in Sweden, p. 52.
35. Ragnar Thoursie, Labour Market Policy in Practice (Stockholm: National Labour Market Board, 1967), p. 8.

economy, and social insurance and welfare.[46] Several national unions also run their own education programs along these lines. The average union officer at the shop floor level and up has had a substantial diet of education and study.[47]

VI

LO wage policy has aimed at the following general objectives: "1. to assure wage earners a reasonable part of the national product; 2. to create 'just' and reasonable relationships between the various groups of wage-earners [the solidarity wage policy] ; and 3. to heed as far as possible, the demands of the national economy."[48]

The first objective—the demand for distributive justice—"is the foundation of all union activity and is often considered by the members as the most important."[49] The solidarity wage policy aims at distributive justice within a narrower scope—within the working class itself. It requires that "work of a similar nature should, to the greatest possible extent, cost the same for all employers. . . . The weighting of wages between different types of work should be effected with regard to the nature of the work, i.e. work contents [sic], work risks, the qualifications required from workers, etc. and not with regard to the various profitableness of firms and industries."[50] This carries with it the acceptance of technical systems of wage determination, that is, job evaluation, wage incentives, and merit rating.[51] The solidarity wage policy is "perhaps the most efficient tool in the hands of the trade unions with which they can put pressure on management to intensify their rationalisation efforts." If the weaker enterprises are forced to adhere to the same rational standards of wage determination as the more efficient enterprises, this will "compel firms to rationalise and, when the possibilities have been exhausted, to close down." In the setting of a full employment economy and an active labor market policy, the effect is to bring about "the transfer of labour to more productive enterprise than is possible through the creation of wage differentials."[52]

46. LO, *This Is the LO*, p. 26.

47. Herman Erickson, "Adult Education and Swedish Political Leadership," *International Review of Education*, June 1966, Reprint Series No. 163, University of Illinois, Institute of Labor and Industrial Relations, Champaign, pp. 136–37.

48. Rudolf Meidner, "A Coordinated Wage Policy," in *Trade Unions in Sweden*, p. 14.

49. *Ibid.*

50. *Ibid.*

51. Johnston, *Collective Bargaining in Sweden*, p. 326.

52. TUAC, "The Trade Union's Role in the Promotion of Innovation—Sweden," mimeographed (Paris, 1968), p. 9.

With respect to a wage policy geared to the "demands of the national economy ... the union movement certainly should not be forced, in a situation of economic imbalance, to restore the stability of the national economy by tempering its wage policy, but it cannot avoid taking upon itself a part of the responsibility for a policy aiming at maintaining a stable development of prices."[53] The instrumentality for achieving the wage policy is coordination by LO "based on moral authority and information, within the framework of the right to self-determination which the statutes give to the unions."[54]

The ability of Swedish trade unionism to act "responsibly" in economic policy rests on the assumption, as Meidner has pointed out, that the government is able to create "a state of economic equilibrium and moderates by selective manpower policy the tensions between sub-markets. This equilibrium has existed only at rare occasions during the post-war period in Sweden. Instead we have experienced an almost persistent inflationary situation which has caused a gap between the LO's willingness to accept the responsible role in wage policy and its ability to pursue such a policy. . . . The permanent inflation has successively eroded the concept of union responsibility and it is easy to understand why the unions have been so eager to support an anti-inflationary policy."[55]

"It is a controversial question," Meidner has said, "whether the solidarity principle ... has influenced the wage structure in any decisive way." At the most "it may have prevented a widening of income gaps among union members." While "the central agreements have gone in a leveling direction ... the local agreements have often restored the relations which existed at the starting point." The implication is that the solidarity wage policy is negated by "very disparate profitability conditions ... accentuated by inflation ... and despite all, [by] still weak contributions from labour market policy," particularly the inability to "eliminate the risks of negative consequences for employment."[56] Elsewhere Meidner has said, "We have to be a little more careful" about the consequences of "too tough a [rationalization] policy recommended by the economists fifteen years ago. We are now coming back to the automation position of the U.S. unions of some time ago. The handicapped, the older people, the ill-educated are being excluded" from the ranks of rationalized industry.[57]

53. Meidner, "Coordinated Wage Policy," p. 14.
54. *Ibid.*, p. 16.
55. Rudolf Meidner, Lecture given at the University of Wisconsin Industrial Relations Research Institute, April 19, 1970.
56. Meidner, "Goals of Labour Market Policy," p. 193.
57. Interview with Meidner.

VII

LO exercises considerable authority on the internal structure and organization of its thirty-eight affiliates who are subject to model statutes promulgated by the parent organization. The prevailing industrial union principle "is undoubtedly the form of trade union organisation which best facilitates a successive and smooth adjustment to changes in production."[58] LO has pushed a merger movement to implement the industrial union principle and is the final arbiter of jurisdictional disputes among affiliates.

Affiliates must adhere to specified standards of governance: "(a) The open union principle requires that . . . any worker with a clean record who is employed within the union's jurisdiction has the right to join the union, and (b) . . . a worker changing jobs between union jurisdictions has the right to transfer his membership from his former union to the new one and . . . the unions have the corresponding right to release and admit him respectively. . . ." The final authority to strike and to conclude a collective agreement must rest with the union's executive board which has the authority to override a membership vote on these questions.[59] LO exercises authority over the strike and bargaining authority of its constituent affiliates. If as many as 3 percent of the union's membership are likely to be involved in a strike, approval must be sought from the LO executive board at the risk of losing "the right to economic and moral support" from LO member unions if it refuses.[60]

The LO secretariat has the power to participate in the affiliate's collective bargaining negotiations and to present proposals looking toward agreement. If the affiliate rejects the proposal, it is subject to loss of financial aid in the event that ensuing "conflict causes or can be feared to cause considerable inconvenience for other affiliated unions, for the trade union movement as a whole, or for vital social interests."[61] The LO secretariat may also direct collaboration between unions in the same industrial field. Affiliates are bound to inform the secretariat on significant wage issues and disputes. Most important, the governing representative assembly of LO may authorize the executive board to conclude agreements with SAF and bind the affiliates to the results.[62]

Central wage bargaining has been subject to several kinds of internal strain: between the high-wage and the low-wage unions in LO, between the leadership and the local rank and file "who like the wage drift,"[63] between

58. TUAC, "Trade Union's Role in the Promotion of Innovation," p. 8.
59. LO, *This Is the LO*, p. 8.
60. *Ibid.*, p. 6.
61. Johnston, *Collective Bargaining in Sweden*, p. 40.
62. *Ibid.*, p. 41.
63. Interview with Birger Viklund, LO and Metal Workers Union, Stockholm, August 20, 1969.

LO's predominantly manual worker constituency and the white collar unions in TCO and SACO, and between the two latter with each other (this is discussed in more detail below).

VIII

The influence of LO and the affiliates extends into the local areas and factories through a system of branches, factory clubs, works councils, local central organizations, and local LO councils. The branch is the extension of the national union in the locality and engages in education, organization, collection of wage statistics, collection of union dues, and collective bargaining negotiations. "Branches have a certain amount of initiative in negotiating and concluding contracts at the local level"[64] subordinate, however, to the national union. The enterprise factory club is important when there are two or more firms, and in such circumstances it is the club which becomes the "effective local bargaining agency."[65] The grievance and complaint mechanism is administered by the shop stewards who are subject to branch or club control. The club also carries on educational activities. The local central organization is the mechanism for bringing together the branches of diverse LO nationals in any locality for education and propaganda, but not for bargaining.

Much discontent is currently expressed with the functioning of the union at the plant and shop floor level. Existing agreements make the employers' power almost absolute. The union's professional competence at the LO and industry level does not generally prevail at the worksite. "The union's negotiator is more of an amateur and he goes to the negotiation table often directly from his workplace."[66] The rank and file member has a distinct feeling of inadequacy in dealing with his employer.

A long wildcat strike in the publicly owned mining enterprise in the fall of 1969 dramatized several kinds of local disaffection: the remoteness of the union decision-making authority, the lack of an active union presence in the plant, "a union [which] doesn't work for the workers,"[67] the excessive leveling effect of the LO's solidarity wage policy, and the repudiation of the local union officials by the strikers. The higher union leadership discounts the abnormality of wildcat strikes and denies that an "authority crisis" is in the making.[68]

The works council role in Sweden differs materially from other Western European countries. Most significantly the employee members are by

64. Johnston, *Collective Bargaining in Sweden*, p. 262.
65. *Ibid.*, p. 57.
66. Meidner, Lecture, April 19, 1970.
67. "Swedes' Labor Stability Shaken," *New York Times*, January 7, 1970, p. 2.
68. Urs Hauser, "The Facts about Unofficial Strikes: 1, Sweden," *Free Labour World*, April 1970, pp. 11–12.

agreement elected from the union ranks in the plant with ex-officio membership by the factory club chairman. The works council thus exists within the union system, not outside of it as in prevailing European practice. But a clear line of demarcation exists between the union's collective bargaining functions, exercised at the enterprise level by the factory section, and the consultative, noncollective bargaining responsibilities of the works council. The Swedish labor movement has favored a consultation, not a codetermination, role for the works council although the industrial democracy doctrine is being advanced with increasing insistence.[69]

Under LO pressure, the 1966 agreement has attempted to reinvigorate the works council idea in the direction of "two fundamental objectives, . . . greater productivity and greater job satisfaction."[70] The original 1946 agreement gave the works councils the functions of improving, through consultation, production efficiency, employee understanding of the economics of the enterprise, employment security, health and safety, and vocational training. The 1966 agreement expanded the scope of the works council to provide for (a) greater flexibility in "organisational structures," (b) the designation of steering committees, (c) administration of social welfare funds, (d) administration of awards for systems suggestions, (e) more consultation with the firm's board of directors, and (f) the evaluation of personnel and the "effects of major technological change or serious decline" in the firm's business.[71] Later LO statements stress the special functions of the works councils in manpower adjustment—specifically, labour transfers, employee induction, retraining, training, and other labour mobility problems.[72] "Although some of the works councils function very well . . . many of them do not work satisfactorily."[73]

IX

Politics and ideology in Sweden have, on the whole, strengthened the integrative role of the trade union in the society and economy. "The enduring collaboration between the trade union movement and the political wing of the labour movement in the government" has been a unifying influence.[74]

69. Olle Gunnarsson, "The Demand for Industrial Democracy," *Free Labour World*, June 1968, p. 8.

70. TUAC, "Trade Union's Role in the Promotion of Innovation," p. 16.

71. Richard B. Peterson, "The Swedish Experience with Industrial Democracy," *British Journal of Industrial Relations* (London), July 1968, pp. 200-201.

72. LO, *Economic Expansion*, pp. 154-55.

73. Lars Ahlvarsson, "National Trade Union Reports—Sweden," (Paper delivered at Trade Union Seminar on New Perspectives in Collective Bargaining, OECD Regional Seminar, Paris, November 1969), p. 4.

74. LO, *Economic Expansion*, p. 154.

Swedish "middle way" socialism (a term which Swedish socialists seem to use approvingly) has not generated class polarization. The current terms of the party-union alliance provide for local branch—but not LO or national union—affiliation to the party with the right of individuals to contract out. Less than 1 percent of the members affected by affiliation have exercised that right. Approximately 60 percent of the LO members are also party members.[75] It may even be, in the words of a Swedish commentator, "anachronistic to use terms such as 'liberalism' and 'socialism' to characterize modern economic policy in a 'mixed economy' of the Swedish type, with an interventionist economic policy and a large sector for government services alongside with complete private domination in the field of industry and agriculture. . . . It does not seem to make much sense to argue whether strong government intervention to remove elements of rigidity constitute liberalism [or] socialism."[76]

The "highly practical and pragmatic character" of Swedish socialism has introduced what one commentary has styled as "functional socialism."[77] The key characteristics of functional socialism have been listed as "(a) belief in the balance of power, (b) dislike of violent solutions to social problems, (c) a pragmatic approach to the problem of free market versus state interference in the economic sector, (d) a realization of our basic beliefs and dislikes by functional socialism."[78] Functional socialism uses means "more sophisticated than . . . socializing all the means of production. . . . It is instead a selective socialization of some of the most important functions which we call ownership. We have limited the rights of the owners of the means of production to use their goods in an unsocial way."[79]

There are "components" of Swedish trade union policy which, Meidner points out, are "socialist" in a more traditional sense—income redistribution and economic planning.[80] Elsewhere Meidner has argued that there may have been "too much emphasis on strengthening the market forces" and insufficient awareness (as noted earlier in this chapter) "of the handicapped, the older people, the ill-educated" expelled by the market forces.[81]

The "functional" character of trade union socialism has reassured the employers that their partnership with unions in alliance with a socialist

75. See "Politics Are More Personal," *The Economist*, October 28, 1967, and "Organisation Men," *The Economist*, March 30, 1963.

76. Lindbeck, "Theories and Problems in Swedish Economic Policy," p. 79.

77. Gunnar Adler-Karlsson, *Functional Socialism—A Swedish Theory for Democratic Socialization* (Stockholm: Prisma, 1969), p. 9.

78. *Ibid.*, p. 11.

79. *Ibid.*, pp. 18–22 *passim*.

80. Meidner, "Goals of Labour Market Policy," p. 191.

81. Interview with Meidner.

government need not end in their own destruction. Indeed, "a socialist government may [even be] advantageous for big business since it is best fitted to put pressure on the trade unions in the bargaining process."[82]

A compatible union-party relationship gives the union reassurance that its self-denial in the general interest will not be used to weaken union institutional power. More than that, the party–trade union association has meant for LO that the "Swedish trade union movement has paid far more attention, and to some extent felt responsible for economic tasks than the unions in many other countries."[83] The corollary is that the socialist government has been willing to grant authority to the socialist trade unions in concert with employers to make wage policy on their own power which it would not have done if the trade union movement were neutral or hostile to the party.

The union-party-government relationship has given the trade unions a wider range of choice as to whether a particular union objective is more suited to the method of collective bargaining or legislative enactment—to use the Webbs' way of putting it. "By tradition," as LO president Arne Geijer has said, "the LO has accepted the necessity of legislation [in] social insurance and retirement pensions."[84]

In short, the compatible relationship with party and government has given the unions the power to influence decisions at critical points in the policy-making process from conception to legislation and administration.

X

SAF, the Swedish employers confederation comprising forty-three affiliated employer associations, has said that it was "formed in 1902, as a counterbalance" to the LO.[85] SAF's principal purposes are "(a) to consolidate employers and organisations of employers into one joint body; (b) to further good relations between employers and employees; (c) to assist affiliated employers or organisations of employers in negotiations with organised labour; (d) to compensate affiliated employers for damages caused by labour conflicts."[86] LO's extension of activities "outside the bargaining sphere" has also brought about a widening scope for the SAF interests, which now include the national economy and the labor market.[87]

82. Nils Stjernquist, "Sweden: Stability or Deadlock?" in *Political Oppositions in Western Democracies*, ed. R. A. Dahl (New Haven: Yale University Press, 1966), p. 131.
83. LO, *Economic Expansion*, p. 154.
84. Geijer, "Introduction," p. 1.
85. SAF, *Perspectives on Labour Conditions in Sweden* (Stockholm, 1962), Insert.
86. *Ibid.*, p. 5.
87. Matts Larsson to Jack Barbash, 1970.

SAF's strength derives in the first instance from its "fairly concentrated power. . . . Every labour contract must have SAF's approval, and members are liable to penalties if they ignore this rule or break the employer front in an open conflict by making a separate agreement contrary to the SAF line." SAF is represented at all key negotiations and gives financial aid in the form of a kind of strike insurance in the case of SAF-authorized disputes. The SAF probably—as SAF points out—wields more power over its employers than does the LO over its unions.[88]

XI

The Swedish collective bargaining system may be analogized to a species of bilateral or, in some significant senses, multilateral constitutional government. The multilateral parties are the trade union movement led by LO, the organized employers led by SAF, and the government which has, in effect, permitted the bargaining partners to exercise some part of its sovereignty over the labor market. The partners, in consideration of this conditional delegation of sovereignty, have in effect contracted with the government to stay within these constraints; as formulated by an ILO economist: "No unreasonable rises which would jeopardise foreign trade; no inflation which would lead to the same result; no disorderly movement of wages which would create inflation; and no dispute which would endanger the interests of the community."[89]

The word to describe Swedish collective bargaining is "coordination." Coordination operates both horizontally and vertically. Horizontally, the parties—government, labor movements, unions and workers, employers, and employer associations—have apparently regularized their role relationship to each other in the sense that everyone knows what is expected of him, the systematic procedures through which the expectation is to be fulfilled, and the power and influence which each of the parties brings to the bargaining process.

Specifically, with respect to what amounts to economy-wide bargaining, the "labor market partners" are fully aware that the delegation of responsibility for the determination of national wage policy is viable only so long as the policy is established "in the light of the government's overall economic policy."[90] And they have tailored a negotiations procedure which expressly injects the national economic interest as the major constraint on their settlement. Thus the quarterly review of economic trends by the National Institute of Economic Research and the annual

88. SAF, *Perspectives on Labour Conditions in Sweden*, pp. 24–26 *passim*.
89. Jean Mouly, "Wages Policy in Sweden," *International Labour Review* (ILO, Geneva) March 1967, p. 174.
90. Johnston, *Collective Bargaining in Sweden*, p. 335.

economic survey by the Ministry of Finance become important parts of the bargaining data as interpreted by the respective professional staffs of the LO and SAF. The initial frame of reference for negotiations is the economic situation in Europe and the United States and its likely implications for the Swedish economy. This analysis forms the basis for wage increase projections for the contract period ahead. An average percentage increase is determined by the parties and provides the wage fund out of which the wage increases negotiated in subordinate agreements will be financed.[91]

This then leads into what may be described as vertical coordination; that is, the negotiations at the level of industry and enterprise take their main cues from the "frame-agreement" negotiated by LO and SAF. With the wage policy agreed on at the LO level as a standard, "the percentage chosen represents for each particular industry, a percentage smaller or greater than that which would have been arrived at if the negotiations had not taken place at the outset on the national level. The workers in the more dynamic industries receive a lesser benefit than they would have doubtless obtained if they had negotiated on their own; conversely, those in backward industries probably get the benefit of a higher percentage than that which would have been conceded to them in the normal course of events."[92] Finally, as we have seen, coordination is extended to bargaining at the enterprise level between the branch or club and the employer. Both the union branch and the employer operate under rules carefully controlled from above.

Attempts have been made to introduce elements of flexibility into the coordinating system, particularly to provide some room for maneuverability at the subordinate levels. First, the respective LO-SAF national bargaining committees are constituted so as to include, on the union side, leaders of the major national unions and, on the SAF side, representative elements in the member federations. Second, provision is made for exceptions to industries which may be at some special disadvantage in respect to a preponderance of low-wage workers. Third, the agreement negotiated is a frame-agreement with "extremely brief" wage provisions,[93] which leaves much still to be negotiated at the industry and branch or enterprise levels. In particular, the commitment to the solidarity wage policy involves the application of work-centered standards, that is, job evaluation, incentives, etc., which do not lend themselves to centralized determination but invariably require a large degree of local self-determination. Fourth, additional flexibility is introduced by wage drift "measured by the in-

91. Mouly, "Wages Policy in Sweden," p. 177.
92. *Ibid.*, p. 178.
93. *Ibid.*, p. 175.

crease in earnings which is not due to negotiations."[94] Wage drift impairs coordinated policy but, contained within limits, it provides "give" without which the maintenance of the coordinated system becomes untenable. Fifth, the coordinated system provides means for participation and interpretation of LO and SAF officials in the supplementary industry and branch negotiations.

The constitutional government to which the Swedish system has been compared here has a highly formal "constitution" consisting of a basic agreement as amended and enlarged from time to time and a series of cooperative agreements. The organic document is the Basic Agreement of 1938. This agreement (1) commits the parties to the negotiation of labor-management disputes according to a specific procedure, (2) cites what in the United States would be called "unfair practices" by either employers or unions, (3) establishes a kind of due process which employers are obligated to follow in the layoff and dismissal of workers, (4) requires the referral of disputes which threaten essential public services to a joint committee called the Labor Market Council acting as a point of appeal.

In addition to the Basic Agreement which was amended in 1947 and 1958, there is a series of "cooperative" agreements. The Industrial Safety Agreement negotiated in 1942 and revised in 1951 establishes a Joint Safety Council and "general rules for the organisation of local safety services."[95] A vocational training agreement concluded in 1944 and revised in 1957, establishes a Joint Industrial Training Council with its own secretariat to develop and offer courses or programs for skilled worker training. The 1957 revision incorporates a standard agreement for vocational training in industry contracts between SAF and LO affiliates. Special panels are established to work out "guidelines,"[96] for the supervision of training and the maintenance of liaison with the public vocational schools. The model agreement recommends the appointment of one or more vocational stewards and sets up apprenticeship standards.

Union cooperation has contributed to an "exceptionally flexible system [of apprenticeship]. The unions do not enforce jurisdictional lines. . . . The three years training which is the formal qualification for skilled worker status is invariably waived if the worker demonstrates that he is capable of doing the work."[97] For example, the agreement between the metal workers and the metal trades employers specifies that the

94. SAF-LO, *Promoting Mutual Interests on Sweden's Labour Market* (Stockholm, 1961), p. 8.
95. *Ibid.*, p. 15.
96. *Ibid.*
97. Gertrude Williams, *Apprenticeship in Europe* (London: Chapman and Hall, 1963), pp. 156–57.

apprentice's "period of training is as a rule three years, though the vocational committee is empowered to vary this duration." The committee may also count previous trade training as training time under the agreement.[98]

The vocational training undertaking reflects a philosophy that "the traditional approach by which the entrant learns right from the beginning by taking direct part in production has become less and less feasible as specialisation has increased and costly machinery has become more common." But specialized training cannot be improvised; it requires professional training auspices, including "pedagogically qualified teachers,"[99] regular communication with the vocational schools in the preparation of training syllabi, and an industry responsibility to promote the training function in firms where it does not now exist.

The Works Council Agreement was concluded in 1946 and revised successively in 1958 and 1966, to promote collaboration for high production, to impart economic, technical, and financial information to employees, and to promote safety and vocational training. "The ceaseless rationalisation of production [as] a precondition of greater prosperity is something on which the parties are agreed."[100] On the initiative of LO, the revisions in 1966 brought the works councils more actively into the employment administration of the enterprise at the level of consultation short of co-decision.[101]

The LO and SAF undertaking on women is not formally a cooperative agreement but the product of a joint study. The major theme has been the equal pay principle which has been gradually introduced into the collective agreements. A Joint Female Labor Council has been established which has considered such problems as guidance in career choices, training, child care centers, "rationalising housework," closing hours, part-time work, and older women.

The Work Study Agreement was concluded in 1948. By work study is meant "systematic investigation of the interplay between human beings, materials and plant" and is practically applicable because "more than 60% of the work done . . . is paid for on a piecework basis." Work study is viewed "as an aid towards the rationalisation of the economy and thus to the achievement of improved living and working conditions." Work study is no longer a greatly controversial topic, but there is still a task "to overcome the dissensions which are still liable to occur here and there." The major form of local cooperation is the discussion of wage rate dis-

98. Agreement on Vocational Training, February 1, 1966 to January 31, 1969, Metal Trades Employers Association and Metal Workers Union, *et al.*, p. 3.
99. SAF-LO, *Promoting Mutual Interests*, pp. 16–17.
100. *Ibid.*, p. 22.
101. See Peterson, "Swedish Experience with Industrial Democracy."

putes. A Joint Work Study Council has been created to (1) promote "sound and appropriate conduct" in work study; (2) to act as an arbitration panel on work study disputes over interpretation of the work study provisions of the agreement ("it is gratifying to be able to state that the Work Study Council has so far [1961] never had to function as an arbitration panel"); (3) to promote training in work study; (4) to follow current developments in the science of work study; (5) to issue publications and studies which have dealt with such subjects as planning machinery, materials handling, standardization and specialization, design rationalization, method study and work simplification, supervisory efficiency, vocational training for productivity, and "ergonomics" or the science of work. All of this is based on the belief that "work study is one of the best instruments for increasing economic efficiency." But more than technique and methods, work study represents an unremitting effort at improvement in "working methods and product quality."[102]

Several industrial union affiliates of LO have been influential in inducing positive changes in their industries. The Building Workers Union has established its own research institute "to evaluate official statistics and findings as well as initiating complementary studies" in such subjects as the building industry credit market, wage system, "going over from specialised team work to collective team work with collective piecework payment for a whole group of workers . . . both unskilled and skilled."

In collaboration with LO and other unions, the Building Workers controls a construction company which it has utilized "to carry out experiments with new production techniques, planning methods and wage systems." In addition, the union is undertaking "the reform of the whole vocational training system." A number of joint committees with employers and cooperative societies have been established to deal with both the long-run problems and the day-to-day problems of efficiency. Regarding the latter, the union has promoted improved management techniques.

The textile and clothing industry unions have focused on industry rationalization, concentration, and expansion of markets to accommodate themselves to cheap imports and changing consumer tastes. The workers made redundant by these measures have been reemployed in other industries with "the active assistance of the labour market authorities," although there recently seems to have been a recurrence of difficulties. In the process the textile union has lost 35 percent of its membership in the period 1950-65.[103]

---

102. SAF-LO, *Promoting Mutual Interests*, pp. 29-33 *passim*.
103. TUAC, "Trade Union's Role in the Promotion of Innovation," pp. 13-15 *passim*.

The Metal Workers Union and its employers association negotiated a special agreement on vocational training which, among other clauses, establishes a joint industry-wide vocational committee to supervise and promote training. The agreement also provides for vocational stewards.[104]

The Metal Trades Employers Association operates an educational department, manned by engineers, instructors, and job analysts, which publishes training materials and engages in job analysis. "The Metal Workers' Union is constantly involved as consultants." The union member on the industrywide council "is constantly traveling to local units to see how the actual training is going on and to solve grievances."[105]

XII

Rationalization, to use a term which recurs frequently in Swedish industrial relations, comes closest to characterizing the style of collective bargaining. As used here, "rationalization is the making of . . . decisions through rules, organization and expertness rather than through trial by struggle, ideology and hit or miss. The alternatives from among which these decisions are made are more likely to be 'closely related to existing reality' than to revolutionary goals."[106] The powerful influence of rationalization on the collective bargaining style is indicated in the importance of policies and programs, economic research and analysis, and organizational innovativeness.

Collaborationist attitudes did not always exist. They emerged as a recoil from trials by violence and unrest in the depression of the '30s. The watershed year in which LO and SAF began to take stock of their critical situation was 1936 which "mark [ed] a milestone in the evolution of the trade union movement from a predominantly defensive collective bargaining agency to a mature and socially conscious power group."[107] "The habit of positive discussion" characterizes the communications process between trade unions and management.[108] The parties seem to have been able to exclude from the relationship rigid ideological positions which get in the way of practical accomplishment. The "spirit of Saltsjöbaden"—Saltsjöbaden is the locale where the Basic Agreement of 1938 was negotiated—symbolizes the attitude of compromise which the parties adopt toward each other.

The efficacy of the central bargaining system has recently been subject to mounting criticism. Lundberg has put the issues, as he has said, "very

104. Agreement on Vocational Training, pp. 2–3.
105. Interview with Larsson.
106. Jack Barbash, "American Unionism: From Protest to Going Concern," *Journal of Economic Issues* (Austin, Texas), March 1968, p. 45.
107. Johnston, *Collective Bargaining in Sweden*, p. 18.
108. *Ibid.*, p. 339.

simply. Labour costs (per hour) have been increasing by around 8-10% per annum during the last decade. The rate is more than twice the growth of labor productivity and it has been accompanied by a rapid rise of the consumer price index." The effects have been to put the level of Swedish wage costs "about 30-40% above the Western European average" raising "Swedish wages more rapidly than in the other countries compared."[109] Lundberg raises the question: "Why is direct government interference— when free collective bargaining has given results that fall outside a given region of tolerance—by means of compulsory arbitration considered to be an unacceptable device in Sweden? In Sweden there seems to exist more of a general feeling of the rights of freedom of the big organisations (especially the trade unions) than in other countries. But for an economist this is no real answer."[110]

A learned journal article authored in part by union economists has sought to demonstrate that lack of justification for the charge that the unions have "asserted themselves too strongly in wage negotiations and . . . thereby created the basis for price rises in the post-war economy. . . . The rise in prices derives from rises abroad, from the market mechanism and from strivings for equality in income. The latter factor operates because it has not been considered possible to tolerate a slower wage improvement for people employed in the sheltered sector, i.e. branches with low productivity advances," than in the international competitive sector.[111] In point of fact, "the actual increase in wages within the C-sector [that is, competitive] has . . . not been as much out of pace with economic development [as] has often been asserted."[112]

In 1967 SAF proposed a reorganization of negotiation methods and standards. The new procedure, as summarized by an employers association executive, would "start with a common appraisal of the economic factors by the economic experts from the top organizations. On the basis of that analysis a frame of the economic terms is fixed for economic policy as it is relevant to collective bargaining by a board of arbitration. Next step was to deduct from that frame the wage drift and the cost of social reforms."[113] As interpreted by LO economists, the intent was to "systematiz[e] consideration of economic balance and growth in wage negotiations without . . . increasing or formalizing the dependence of their wage policy on the economic policy of the government"[114]—in short, an

109. Erik Lundberg, "Incomes Policy in Sweden—Some Issues," in *On Incomes Policy*, p. 11.
110. *Ibid.*, p. 19.
111. Edgren *et al.*, "Wages, Growth and the Distribution of Income," pp. 154-55.
112. *Ibid.*, p. 146.
113. Interview with Larsson, p. 7.
114. Edgren *et al.*, "Wages, Growth and the Distribution of Income," p. 135.

attempt at rationalization of negotiated wage policy at the level of the economy.

The SAF plan, according to the chief LO economist, would have deprived both LO and SAF of "much of their raison d'etre" and in effect replace them "by a government control office for the determination of wages." Moreover, the employers' economic model was oversimplified, LO spokesmen argued, and would achieve the opposite of the growth and price stability effects intended, even if the statistical "exactitude . . . demanded by SAF proposals were available"—which they were not.[115]

XIII

If LO represents a national economic policy type of unionism in the sense of a commitment to enlarge the area of congruence between its own protective interests and the more general interest, TCO, the confederation of white collar workers, and SACO, the confederation of university-trained professionals, represent more sectional interests with structural features to match. "We are a smaller union," a TCO executive said, "and have to look after special interests."[116] "At the same time if you compare us to SACO there is a great difference. SACO looks *only* at the special interests. Our union looks at the general interest a little more." [117]

LO has a membership of 1.6 million or about 90 percent of its real potential. Some 70 percent of all nonmanual workers are in unions. TCO, with 529,000 members in its affiliates, has its main strength in the 170,000-member SIF. Other major TCO concentrations include unions of municipal and commercial employees, teachers, and civil servants. SACO, with 102,000 members, has also organized about 70 percent of its potential membership. Over three-fourths are employed in national, provincial, or local government, roughly in that order of importance. LO's affiliates are almost all industrial unions compared with TCO whose industrial union membership constitutes about 40 percent of the total; SACO affiliates are not only craft unions but SACO is committed to craft unionism as a principle of organization for professional employees. "Occupation and educational background provides a stronger foundation on which to build a community of professional and union interest." Industrial unions would otherwise "swallow up professional groups."[118]

SACO, as an association of highly differentiated professional craft unions, has no place for wage solidarity. "We have turned against . . . the

115. Claes-Erik Odhner, "The Government Agency for the Determination of Wages," in *On Incomes Policy*, pp. 240, 241.
116. Interviews with Gustafson *et al.*
117. *Ibid.*
118. E. M. Kassalow, "Professional Unionism in Sweden," *Industrial Relations* (Berkeley), February 1969, p. 122.

shallow oversimplification of the concept of 'general leveling' so commonly used in wage discussion."[119] SACO argues that "professional employees, because of high taxes and the inflation of recent years, were ... disadvantaged as compared to other groups." Because he has foregone earnings for the long years of secondary school and university training, the typical professional employee had poorer lifetime earnings than those in many other occupations.[120] SACO spokesmen charge that the bias favoring the manual workers extends to the tax system. "The cost of education is very high and there should be some reimbursement. The whole economy needs educated workers; otherwise the economy can't work."[121]

A major wage policy innovation is the job classification system of TCO's largest affiliate, SIF. The system's objective is the development of "a statistical reference system based on the grouping into classes of jobs with similar content as regards function and difficulty." By agreement with SAF it is used to compile salary statistics for white collar employees.[122]

The job classification system is, it should be stressed, a "statistical reference system" for classifying jobs, not a system-like job evaluation for determining remuneration. It may be used as one point of reference for salary determination but it does not itself relate jobs and salaries. Swedish practice negotiates salaries (as distinguished from wages) in industry and commerce on an individual basis without "restraints by way of fixed standard or minimum wages,"[123] but the system provides a base for introducing rationality into individual salary determination. For the union it makes it possible to compare "salaries which are paid to persons having either the same type of positions or different types." For the union member it answers the questions: "What salary may I reasonably demand to remain in my job knowing that it is possible for me to find another job? What salary shall I ask with a reasonable hope of getting it, when seeking a new position?"[124] From the management viewpoint, the job classification system "has helped firms in their personnel allocation planning ... to forecast ... salary costs under different assumptions."[125]

119. American Embassy, Stockholm, *Swedish Wage Negotiations*, Unclassified Reports (October 22, 1968; March 4, 1969; June 24, 1969), October 22, 1968, p. 5.

120. Kassalow, "Professional Unionism in Sweden," p. 130.

121. Interview with SACO officials, August 13, 1968.

122. Gösta Edgren, "The Role of the Job Classification System in Implementing TCO Wages Policy," in *Job Classification and Collective Bargaining* (Stockholm: TCO, 1966), p. 7.

123. *Ibid.*, p. 8.

124. Sven Jonasson, "The Labor Market Parties Classification System," in *Job Classification and Collective Bargaining*, p. 56.

125. K. O. Samuelson, "The Importance of a Job Classification System," in *Job Classification and Collective Bargaining*, p. 20.

In sum, the system makes possible "the very individualistic approach to salary fixing, which some white collar workers consider a pre-condition for joining a union without at the same time depriving the union of arguing on a collective basis. . . ," which Gösta Edgren, the TCO research director, considers a defect. Its usefulness "depends entirely on the relative strength of the negotiating parties in the establishment."[126] The essential function of the job classification system is to strengthen the information element in the white collar job market.[127]

SACO's concern with unemployment among college graduates is generating a craft-union type of restriction of entry. Unemployment among college graduates is "hidden"; since many graduates lack work histories, they are not eligible for unemployment compensation and are not taken into account in the statistics in the unemployment compensation reports. The unemployment is mainly concentrated among the graduates from the so-called "free" departments, that is, liberal arts and social studies, as distinguished from the restricted departments which limit enrollment. The "university students are increasing but the students can't get into the restricted department. . . . We [SACO] are advocating a policy of balanced growth in the universities." One solution is "to increase the capacity of the restricted departments . . . but the professions don't want the university doors opened widely." Another solution is to direct students to "occupations which do not require university education, for example, data processing, sales promotion. . . . But the government policy has been working against it."[128]

The center of power gravity in SACO and TCO is in the affiliated unions rather than in the confederation, although both bargain in behalf of the public employee affiliates in the national government and municipal government, respectively. Unlike LO, there is no centralized authority for coordination although each has some scope for intervention. The absence of coordinating authority may also have something to do with the almost guild-like demarcation which characterizes SACO affiliates; for example, there are research librarians, physiotherapists, military reserve officers, headmasters of education, architects, museum officers, archivists, pharmacists, taxation officers, masters of forestry, M.D.'s, dentists, veterinarians, and college-trained engineers. Again unlike LO, neither SACO nor TCO exercises control over the rules of internal union government that are operative in LO.

---

126. Edgren, "Role of the Job Classification System," p. 8.
127. See TCO, *The Wage Policy of White Collar Workers in Sweden* (Stockholm, n.d. [1962?]); see also SIF, *Position Classification Salary Surveys* (Stockholm, 1968).
128. Interview with SACO officials.

Both TCO and SACO have no formal commitments to the Social Democratic Party, and indeed both represent a source of strength for the "bourgeois" parties—rather more in SACO than in TCO, it would appear.

LO's right to speak for the trade union movement as a whole has been contested in both the 1966 and 1969 negotiations by union spokesmen for the sectional interests of the white collar and professional employees. The issue in dispute is the disadvantaged position of these groups compared with manual workers.

The 1966 and 1969 negotiations represented turning points from the "unwritten law" that TCO and SACO wage increases would adhere to the limits set by the LO-SAF negotiations. In 1966 the teachers' affiliate of SACO rejected LO's model settlement as "meaningless for large numbers of SACO members" and called the first major strike since the 1945 Metal Workers walkout. It argued that higher tax brackets, price increases, and the higher human resource investment of the professional workers entitled them to an increase larger than that negotiated by LO.[129] In 1969, LO's president Arne Geijer, applying his 1966 lesson, announced that "LO will under no circumstances conclude an agreement before other employee organizations."[130]

The issue in 1969 was the solidarity wage principle. "We cannot allow wages of low-income groups to lag behind," Geijer said, "merely to spare the high-income groups the pain of seeing prices rise." But LO has its pressures too. "LO's demands are higher than we originally intended because other wage earner groups were not moderate in their demands."[131] At any rate, after the 1969 negotiations, SACO warned that it was the last time it would accept LO domination.[132]

XIV

An environment of "permanent over-full employment"—what we call the period of post-full employment after World War II—is the context in which the Swedish trade union performance must be placed. For several reasons—noninvolvement in the war, the force of commitment to the Social Democratic Party's full employment goals—the Swedish economy and therefore the Swedish economists, including the trade union economists, were among the first to be exposed to the post-full employment stage of Western Europe's economic development.

Swedish trade unionism has achieved an essential, continuing, and legitimate role in the processes of economic government; an equal partner

129. Kassalow, "Professional Unionism in Sweden," p. 130.
130. American Embassy, *Swedish Wage Negotiations*, October 22, 1968, p. 7.
131. *Ibid.*, March 4, 1969, p. 3.
132. Interview with Meidner.

with employers and parliamentary government, it determines national manpower and wage policies. Economy-wide collective bargaining is, in effect, an economic parliament in which "questions about the distribution of national income between wages and capital income, the international competitiveness of the economy and the significance of wage developments for prices have become the central subjects of discussion between the parties of the labor market."[133]

There is what comes to a conditional delegation of authority by the parliamentary government to the social partners. Union power and influence are exerted along all points in the decisionmaking process of the economic government, from laying the theoretical foundation to routine administration.[134] The delegation of authority has lasted because it has acquired legitimacy; the performance of both partners has been widely recognized as enhancing national economic policy goals.[135] In particular, the trade union's central participation in economic policy is universally regarded as proper and useful. LO's credibility as a central participant in determining economic policy is based on the common assessment that the trade union movement has, in fact, practiced forbearance, and "does not," in LO's words, "restrict itself to the promotion of its narrow self interests."[136] That the unions do not drive the hardest wage bargain is not due to an abdication of their pressure group function but to a rational determination that there are limits beyond which an organization speaking for the majority of workers may not press its power. "The primary function of trade unions," a group which included trade union economists has said, "is to obtain as great a portion of the fruits of production as they can in negotiations. But with the strength which these unions now possess in Sweden, they must accept a social responsibility which goes beyond the primary function."[137] If they fail to make this sense of responsibility credible, the "strivings to avoid a national incomes policy with government involvement" will fail.[138]

The Swedish labor movement's ability to maintain over a long period the rank and file acceptance of continuous forbearance in wage policy is strengthened by the high visibility of the foreign trade balance and the general acceptance of the idea that a strong competitive position in the world economy is essential to Swedish growth and high standard of living.

The same sort of rational acceptance of the relationship between special and more general interests is evident in trade unionism's crucial role in

---

133. Edgren et al., "Wages, Growth and the Distribution of Income," p. 135.
134. TUAC, "Trade Union's Role in the Promotion of Innovation," p. 2.
135. LO, Trade Unions, p. 19.
136. Ibid.
137. Edgren et al., "Wages, Growth and the Distribution of Income," p. 154.
138. Ibid., p. 135.

manpower policy, but with this difference: the inducement to act does not spring alone from defense against imminent dangers but from a positive economic analysis initiated on the unions' own power. There is a defensive element, to be sure, insofar as the active manpower policy was originally designed to avoid—as we have seen in Meidner's observations—the impairment of "the ability of the union organisations to act as free negotiating parties independent of the government."[139] But the union response is noteworthy here because instead of saying "no," it offered a respectable alternative theory as better calculated to achieve the general interest in full employment, price stability, growth, and distributive justice. Sweden still has "the dilemma of reconciling full employment and price stability,"[140] but what we are emphasizing here is a trade union's intent and own image of itself, not its practical accomplishment.

Sweden's trade union movement represents the most advanced expression of labor's "will and ability"[141] to adapt itself to national economic policy goals. The characteristics or properties of this trade union economic policy "model" represented in the Swedish trade union situation are identified as follows. First, Sweden's economic development and circumstances of contemporary society have produced a stability and high degree of well-being that give the working class a powerful stake in the economic order. These circumstances of the Swedish environment are well known and need only to be itemized here: (1) the late and smooth take-off for industrialization, (2) the homogeneity of race and religion, (3) the availability of forest, water, and iron resources, (4) the avoidance of active military commitment in two devastating world wars, (5) the containment of change within a private enterprise market system thus minimizing ideological class warfare, (6) the public's high awareness of the economic implications of an economy open to the competitive forces of the international economy, (7) the absence of polarized great wealth and mass poverty, (8) a "stability and continuity of government power that can hardly be matched by any other democratic western country,"[142] and (9) the relative ease of communication, negotiation, and administration in the small-scale and compact Swedish economy.

In addition to the favorable circumstances, there has also been, as stated previously, a trade union "will and ability" to design methods and theories suitable to effective participation in shaping economic policy; these may be broadly enumerated as (1) integration of the industrial relations system, (2) an effective bargaining performance by the union in

139. Meidner, "Goals of Labour Market Policy," p. 189.
140. Lindbeck, "Theories and Problems in Swedish Economic Policy," p. 69.
141. LO, *Trade Unions*, p. 8.
142. Lundberg, *Instability and Economic Growth*, p. 193.

behalf of its constituencies, (3) the professionalization of union administration, and (4) a policy "mix" conducive to union participation.

The integration of the industrial relations system means the fashioning
of institutions and attitudes suitable to achieving a common purpose; and
acceptance of a common purpose mission is easier for LO because its
constituency "compris[es] the vast majority of Swedish workers." It
cannot, therefore, pursue a "narrow monopolistic policy" because the
"consequences will affect its own members to a very great extent." It must
"consider the total social and economic consequence of its wage
policy."[143] "Unions covering a minor sector of the economy," Rehn said,
"could safely pursue an efficient policy of 'group egotism.' " But this is
not possible "when two-thirds of the industries are unionized."[144]

Integration is also made possible by a favorable power relationship in
which, as SAF puts it, "management and labour face one another as two
strongly organized forces [in] a stable balance of power" at the national
level.[145] It is necessary to add that the stable balance of power functions
mainly at the national level. The constraining influence on the parties'
exercise of power is their sensitivity to the great risks which an economy-
wide strike—this is the effective scope of the bargaining unit—entails.
Geijer talked about the "grave danger of a national labor market conflict
during the negotiations for the 1969 agreement."[146] Another union
observer has argued that the union side has more to lose than the employer
because a strike could close down the country and cause the loss of its
foreign markets and the loss of the next election. "The employer knows
that the government and the unions have the main responsibility after all."
The union's strength does not lie in the general strike which is almost
unthinkable but in "the fear of the employer that he might have to work
without a contract."[147] But even when they are not considering an all-out
strike or lockout, the parties are, as we have seen, fully aware of what the
meaning of their negotiations is for the economy.

Conducive to the maintenance of an integrated industrial relations
system for common purpose is the absence of an influential socialist or
communist ideology which denies the legitimacy of common purpose areas
between unions and management. Replacing class-struggle socialism as the
policy doctrine of the past is the "class-collaboration" or the "classless"
ideology of the neo-Keynesian "socialism."

143. Edgren et al., "Wages, Growth and the Distribution of Income," p. 199.
144. Gösta Rehn, "Unionism and the Wage Structure in Sweden," in The Theory
of Wage Determination, ed. John T. Dunlop (New York: St. Martin's Press, 1957),
p. 229.
145. SAF, Perspectives on Labor Conditions in Sweden, p. 21.
146. American Embassy, Swedish Wage Negotiations, October 22, 1968, p. 8.
147. Interview with Viklund.

The mechanisms of the industrial relations system have been efficiently designed to coordinate, that is, to integrate at various points, the diverse interests which make up the system. These coordinating or integrating mechanisms are (1) industrial unionism to minimize the fragmentation of worker interests, (2) centralization of collective bargaining power and influence in LO, (3) unification of the union line of authority from the federation to the national union, to the area organization, to the shop floor works council, (4) exculsive bargaining—one union to an industry and the absence of rival unionism, (5) an economy-wide wage bargain between LO and SAF as the frame-agreement for bargaining at the level of industry and enterprise, (6) a compatible union-party relationship, (7) employer acceptance of the legitimacy and desirability of union function and presence, and (8) established mechanisms for employer–trade union relationships with government.

The national economic policy appeal of the union is credible to its constituents only if the union has in the first instance proved itself as a protective organization in their behalf. Swedish trade unionism's ingenuity has consisted not of abandoning the protective function but of demonstrating that, in Meidner's words, trade unions "have adjusted their methods to be congruent with [the] larger interests of the society, with economic and social development, with equality and all the tendencies in the modern welfare state."[148] This implies an antecedent condition, namely that the Swedish unions have been able to demonstrate their ability to produce for their members, because collective bargaining more than state intervention regulates labor conditions.

Effective performance of the trade union protective function has been enhanced by the rationalization of union administration evidenced in the importance of research and education. The trade union respect for professionalism has made it possible for the union to more than hold up its end in the negotiation of the increasingly complex general interest issues; this in turn has made trade union employment attractive to the professional, especially the economist.

Union respect for professionalism has made possible an unprecedented development of a trade union theory of the role of labor market policy in national economic policy. This theory has been noteworthy for several reasons: first, a trade union movement confronted urgent problems analytically rather than polemically—an approach usually not taken by unions; second, the movement not only formulated a theory but earnestly carried it through to policy formation and administration; third, this theory formulated under the auspices of a socialist labor movement has

148. Interview with Meidner.

taken the efficiency of the market system as given and has sought to make the market "work under competitive conditions which do not come about automatically but must be created";[149] fourth, the theory has embodied more than theoretical wisdom; fifth, the theory has been continually subject to internal criticism, reappraisal, and redefinition.

Some general interest policies are more compatible with the protective function of unionism than others. Wage repression was rejected by the unions precisely because it could be sustained for a certain length of time—if at all—only at the enormous cost of weakening the rank and file's commitment to the union as an institution. By contrast, the active manpower policy in its general outline is not only compatible with the union's protective function but clearly enhances it by the improved worker productivity which it makes possible and which in turn provides the basis for negotiating a higher "real" wage. The solidarity wage policy reflects the redistributive bent of socialism, and although it is protective for the low-wage worker, it risks division within the working class on the issue of the proper allocation of the wage increase fund.

Continued and accelerated inflation is making Sweden's national economic policy unionism more difficult to sustain against the interests seeking special protection. Wage increases averaged about 10 percent in 1970, most of which was wage drift resulting from increased piece rates and from employers bidding up wages in a tight labor market. The anti-inflationary effects of the active manpower policy as projected in theory have not been fully realized because only in the last few years has the policy been given substantial scope.

Meanwhile the inflation is reinforcing the protective stance of sectional interests within the trade union movement. The white collar and professional unions contend that the redistributive policies of the largely blue-collar LO, and, for that matter, of the Social Democratic government have gone too far and they are demanding a reversal. The wildcat strikes are being interpreted as a strong bid for more local authority, as well as a demand for a more active union presence in the plant.

In theory, the active manpower policy should enhance the efficiency of the labor market in dealing with readjustments due to technological change and plant shutdowns and thereby minimize the need for special protection for the groups disadvantaged by these readjustments. But the labor market has not worked that smoothly and, consequently, the security needs of workers are being voiced with increasing vehemence. "There is a growing demand for more fixed forms of wages" rather than piece rates.[150] The number of "hard-to-place" workers—the aging, the

149. Gösta Rehn and Erik Lundberg, "Employment and Welfare: Some Swedish Issues," *Industrial Relations*, February 1962, p. 4.
150. *IMF News*, April 1970, p. 3.

handicapped, the ill-educated—as Meidner pointed out earlier, is increasing and there, too, special protective measures to compensate for the malfunctioning of the market are being urged.

National economic policy unionism which is based on a narrowing of particular and general interests is, in short, being subjected to strains which, for the moment at least, appear to be widening the gap between particular and general interests.

Supplementary References

Anderman, S. D. "Central Wage Negotiation in Sweden: Recent Problems and Development." *British Journal of Industrial Relations*, November 1967, pp. 322–37.

De Schweinitz, Dorothea. *Labor-Management Consultation in the Factory*. Honolulu: University of Hawaii, Industrial Relations Center, 1966.

Faxén, K. O., and Pettersson, E. "Labour-Management Cooperation at the Level of the Undertaking in Sweden." *International Labour Review*, August 1967, pp. 194–202.

Kassalow, E. M. *Trade Unions and Industrial Relations*. New York: Random House, 1969, pp. 31–34 and 72–76.

LO. *Labour Market Policy: A Swedish Trade Union Programme*. Stockholm, 1967.

Nilstein, Arne H. "Sweden." In *White Collar Trade Unions*, edited by Adolf Sturmthal. Urbana: University of Illinois Press, 1966.

Ramstein, Neil. "Works Councils." In *Trade Unions in Sweden*. Stockholm: LO, 1961.

SAF. *The Swedish Employers Confederation*. Stockholm, 1961.

Shonfeld, Andrew. *The Changing Balance of Public and Private Power*. London: Oxford University Press, 1965, pp. 199–211.

"Sweden—Strikes Disrupt Labor Force." *Labor Developments Abroad*, March 1970, pp. 7–9.

Viklund, Birger. *Trade Union Educational Work*. Stockholm: LO, 1969.

CHAPTER THREE

Austria: The Negotiation of Economic Policy

The Austrian trade union experience represents the evolution of a movement from ideology and "class struggle" to pragmatism and "social partnership."[1]

Structural change is the dominant theme of current Austrian economic policy. The major sources of structural strain are (1) the insufficient diversification of industry and the failure to modernize for the changing world situation; (2) the large number of small units in the processing industries—old-fashioned, inefficient, family-managed—that survive because they are sheltered from competitive forces by subsidy, cartelization, and tariffs; and (3) the inefficiencies of state-owned industry arising out of political management and lack of foreign capital sources.[2]

The structural deficiencies are evidenced in the slowing down of Austria's growth and export rates and in the increasing share of imports that could be seen in the 1950s and 1960s. The government has been fully aware of the problem and the Koren Plan seeks to improve the adaptability of the economy through the Labor Promotion Act, investment funds programs, review of efficiency needs in the nationalized sector, a ban on resale price maintenance in certain household goods, and tax inducements for company mergers.[3]

Austria's performance in postwar reconstruction has been regarded as "outstandingly successful."[4] Major structural shifts are in process in the composition of GNP and in the allocation of the labor force away from

1. Dennison I. Rusinow, *Notes Toward a Political Definition of Austria*, American Universities Field Staff, Reports Service, New York, 1966, p. 3, "Socialists in Crisis and the End of Coalition," p. 5.

2. Interview with Anthony Geber, Economic Counselor, American Embassy, Vienna, July 11, 1968. Largely a summary of the interview supported by OECD, *Manpower Policies and Problems in Austria* (Paris, 1967) and OECD, *Economic Surveys—Austria*, Paris, May 1968 and July 1969.

3. OECD, *Economic Surveys*, July 1969, p. 29.

4. Andrew Shonfeld, *Modern Capitalism* (London: Oxford University Press, 1965), p. 192.

agriculture and forestry to industry, handicrafts, and services—tourism being especially important here. "A very diversified set of policy instruments" has been utilized, including government subsidies, depreciation allowances, credit inducements, export credit arrangements, private investment guarantees, and, discussed in greater detail later, a comprehensive scheme of wage and price regulations.[5]

By mid-1970 OECD reported: "It is the outstanding feature of the present upswing that it was combined until now with a large degree of wage and price stability and with a sizeable improvement in the relative cost position." But the period of stability seems to be about over since "inflationary pressures have become more pronounced."[6]

II

Labor market policy must switch from "concentration upon static protection against awkward changes," as a team of OECD examiners put it, to "a dynamic stimulus of productive adjustment to changing conditions."[7] More concretely, "the anti-productive forms of security of employment and the non-productive forms of assuring income during unemployment are being or can be made less necessary by manpower policies designed to promote the most productive utilisation of Austria's manpower resources without imposing undue sacrifices upon individuals or groups."[8]

Tariffs, direct subsidies to private industrial enterprise, and indirect subsidy to nationalized industry shelter enterprises from "changing market conditions or technical and organizational progress." Workers are sheltered by unemployment insurance with benefits at 60 percent of their income. Although it fulfills income maintenance purposes, the social insurance system does not sufficiently serve the objective of enhancing the individual's incentive "to adjust himself to the changing manpower needs of the economy."[9]

If growth, rather than static protection, is to be the goal, the public employment service will need to be reoriented from unemployment toward promotion of occupational and geographical mobility essential to basic structural change. The Employment Office is strong in vocational guidance for young workers, but weakness in "systematic forecasting" hinders its fullest utilization. The office's activities in mobilization of marginal labor reserves—married women, the handicapped, older workers—are concerned more with welfare than with labor market objectives. This also holds true for the office's promotion of winter building and jobs in development areas.

5. OECD, *Manpower Policies and Problems in Austria*, pp. 32–33.
6. OECD, *Economic Surveys*, June 1970, pp. 5–6 *passim*.
7. *Ibid.*, p. 35; OECD, *Manpower Policies and Problems in Austria*, p. 35.
8. OECD, *Manpower Policies and Problems in Austria*, p. 39.
9. *Ibid.*, p. 11.

Mobility is hindered by housing shortages and an inadequate vocational training system. For young people, vocational training focuses too narrowly on apprenticeship in small enterprise; for adults, it is restricted to the unemployed and therefore not available for upgrading and training the underemployed.[10]

Apprenticeship, with its many shortcomings, is still the major resource for trained manpower, but most of the adults are not using the skills for which they have been schooled. Nevertheless, "the complete lack of restrictive attitudes among the work force and trade unions with respect to entrance to crafts, monopolies for specific crafts for certain work and demarcation lines between skill levels has favoured occupational mobility."[11] There is a need for coordination of the manpower functions that are now distributed among diverse agencies in a way to achieve "an integrated system where the relevant authorities on central and local levels can make a rational choice between various instruments for action—whether for the elimination of growth-hampering shortages or of wasteful underemployment."[12]

The momentum initiated by an OECD investigation of Austrian labor market policies resulted in the passage of the Labor Promotion Act in December 1968. The act stresses financial inducement for occupational and geographic mobility, including income protection for workers undergoing retraining and travel and resettlement assistance for workers who are relocating. Other provisions provide for financial assistance to workers disemployed because of changes in technology or demand pattern. The employment service is strengthened by additional support for research, data collection, and forecasting. A new Central Council for Labor Market Policy organized on a tripartite basis is established at the level of Ministry for Social Affairs and also at regional levels. Subcommittees for statistics, labor market research, occupational and geographical mobility, and seasonal fluctuations are being organized.[13]

III

The major participants in the making of economic and labor market policy are the labor movement, ÖGB, and the chambers—that is, the Chambers of Labor and the Chambers of Commerce and Industry, and their allied organizations. ÖGB membership, which is about 1.5 million, represents approximately two-thirds of the 2.4 million in the labor force in a population of about 7.3 million.[14]

10. *Ibid.*, based on pp. 9–40.
11. *Ibid.*, p. 327.
12. *Ibid.*, p. 18.
13. "New Legislation to Promote an Active Manpower Policy in Austria," *OECD Observer* (Paris), April 1969, pp. 10–11.
14. ÖGB, "The Austrian Trade Union Federation," mimeographed (Vienna, 1968).

ÖGB is possibly the most "strictly centralized" confederation to be found in any nonauthoritarian society, in the extent of its control over affiliates.[15] "This kind of organization was made possible by the fact that in the vacuum left by the National Socialist dictatorship the trade union movement had to be rebuilt from the ground up."[16] The small size of the affiliates makes it doubtful that, except for the Metal Workers, they could make it on their own.[17] Membership dues are forwarded directly to the federation which defrays the expenses of the affiliates. The 20 percent of the dues which goes to the affiliate pays for social programs, rest homes, and supplementary welfare benefits. ÖGB controls a central strike fund which enables it to regulate strikes by affiliates.

Collective bargaining negotiations are carried on mainly by ÖGB's sixteen industrial union affiliates, "but the agreements themselves may be concluded only by the union itself as an organ of the federation, failing which they would have no legal validity."[18] In practice, individual unions carry on their own collective bargaining except for "basic social policy matters" on which the confederation speaks for the whole labor movement.[19] Internal coordination in wage policy is achieved through an ÖGB Working Party on Wages Policy which "deals not only with the level of wage demands . . . but also attempts to set and realize common objectives of wages policy," exemplified in the drive for one month's bonus each for Christmas and annual leave and in systems of wage determination.[20]

Subordinate bodies of the federation are the provincial Landesexecutiven which in turn oversee local bodies. The industrial unions are organized in subordinate bodies according to "trade group, sections, branches, and factory groups."[21] The works council system in the enterprise is formally not part of the union structure but strong informal ties bind it to the unions in ways that are discussed later.[22]

The infrastructure of the ÖGB is marked by ideological fractionalization and organizational departmentalization. *Proporz*, the term used to

15. Fritz Klenner, *The Austrian Trade Union Movement* (Brussels: ICFTU, 1956), p. 111.

16. Ernst Lakenbacher, "Austria," in *White Collar Trade Unions*, ed. Adolf Sturmthal (Urbana: University of Illinois Press, 1966), p. 47.

17. Interview with Paul Koch, ÖGB Secretary for International Affairs, Vienna, August 18, 1969.

18. Klenner, *Austrian Trade Union Movement*, p. 116.

19. Gerhard Weissenberg, "Social Policy Experiences of an Austrian Trade Unionist," *International Institute for Labor Studies Bulletin* (Geneva) November 1967, p. 37.

20. *Ibid.*, p. 39.

21. Klenner, *Austrian Trade Union Movement*, p. 116.

22. ÖGB, "Austrian Trade Union Federation"; see also ICFTU, *The European Trade Union Movement within the ICFTU* (Brussels, 1964), pp. 30-32.

describe "the proportional distribution of public positions according to party strength,"[23] is also the principle applied to the distribution of positions in the unions. It has undoubtedly done much to normalize the political relationships within the trade union movement. Accordingly, ÖGB is not so much a non-party as a "tri-party" organization with the Socialists occupying the dominant role.[24] The Socialists—so far the largest with about two-thirds of the membership—the Christian-Social Party (15 percent), and the Communists (10 percent) each have their own fractions within the ÖGB. The ideological divisions which before World War II, in the case of the Socialists and the Christians, functioned through separate federations were brought together with the Communists in one federation because "the tremendous difficulties of the first post-war years . . . could be overcome only by hard work and joint effort."[25] During normal times, political alignments were once again asserted but this time within the organizational umbrella of the ÖGB. This is generally regarded "as a favourable development" making for "greater clarity, and in many important questions it has been found quite possible to come to an agreement which satisfies all three [fractions], though when the Communists in the Federation pursue political aims, as they so often do, agreement is impossible." [26]

The fractional alignment permeates the union structure from the federation to the national union to the local union and, additionally, to the works council and the chamber where candidate slates are drawn up according to party lines. The fractions each have their own instruments of government, newspapers, and international affiliations.[27]

The ÖGB organizational infrastructure consists of staff departments for various functions complemented by the staffs of the labor chambers. The Social Policy Department in the ÖGB is serviced by a staff of six and also by a larger staff in the chamber. The main jurisdiction of the department is the development of new legislative projects, labor law, collective agreement policy, social insurance, labor market policy, international social policy, and social statistics. "Leaving the details" to the Chamber of Labor, the department works out the broad outlines.[28] It also advises the works councils in these areas. ÖGB operates three residential schools and an additional number with the Chamber of Labor.

23. Kurt Shell, *The Transformation of Austrian Socialism* (New York: State University of New York Press, 1962), p. 48.

24. *Ibid.*, p. 63.

25. Klenner, *Austrian Trade Union Movement*, p. 123.

26. *Ibid.*, p. 125.

27. Walter Galenson, *Trade Union Democracy in Western Europe* (Berkeley and Los Angeles: University of California Press, 1961), p. 20.

28. Weissenberg, "Social Policy Experiences," p. 34.

IV

"A major Socialist success following World War I was the establishment of the Chambers of Labor."[29] Their present form dates from 1954. The special stamp which Austria has given to the role of the social partners in the management of the economy and labor market is the legalized chamber system which establishes formal vehicles through which the interest groups can assert their interests. The major chambers are: Industry and Commerce, Agriculture and Forestry, Handicraft, and the Chamber of Labor and Salaried Employees. The Chambers of Labor are established by law with compulsory membership and compulsory deduction of dues—0.5 percent—from the workers' wages. There is a Chamber of Labor in every province coordinated through the Federation of the Chambers of Labor. More than the others, the labor chamber "has the function of promoting its members' interests, its economic weight lying principally in its force of argument and its cooperation with the trade union movement."[30] The highest body in the chambers is an assembly elected by wage earners from slates drawn up by the political fractions in the trade unions. The assembly in turn elects the president and the executive committee. The officers of the chamber are all active trade unionists who hold high office in their respective organizations.

The chamber is also manned by "a staff of highly qualified experts" advising internal policy committees dealing with white collar employment, unemployment insurance, labor law, education, budget, women workers, international trade, youth and apprenticeship, price policies, public service, social policy, statistics, social insurance, and transportation.[31] The chamber also represents workers' interests through representation on many external committees: the most important are the Joint Wage and Price Council and the Advisory Council for Economic and Social Questions, which are treated later.

The Chambers of Labor perform these major functions: (1) review of and research in labor and social legislation; (2) economic advice to the labor negotiators with employers and government; (3) representation of workers in their individual claims under labor and social legislation; (4) vocational education for youth and adults; (5) propaganda and education in social and economic policy; (6) consultation with works councils in social policy matters; (7) representation of trade union interests before public agencies; (8) promotion of workers' cultural, recreational, and educational interests; (9) compilation of statistical data; and (10) protec-

29. Shell, *Transformation of Austrian Socialism*, p. 79.

30. Anton Proksch, "The Austrian Joint Wage and Price Council," *International Labour Review* (ILO, Geneva), March 1961, p. 232.

31. Federation of Austrian Chambers of Labour in Austria, *The Chambers of Labour in Austria* (Vienna, 1967), p. 8.

tion of apprentices—the Chambers of Labor advise the Chambers of Commerce on apprenticeship duration, ratios, and examinations.[32]

The Vocational Promotional Institute of the Chamber of Labor offers several thousand evening courses mainly for the retraining of and as supplementary training for employed adults. Training for semi-skilled and skilled occupations is available. A remarkable expansion program is under way for the establishment of training centers. The deficiency in the chamber programs found by the OECD team were (1) the lack of coordination in respect to facilities and evaluation of results with the Economic Promotions Institute, which is a Chamber of Commerce vocational training undertaking, and with the government training programs; and (2) the fee requirement which, although it is small, may act as a disincentive to training.[33]

The Chambers of Labor "are not a substitute, but a suitable complement of the unions."[34] The unions are "mainly organised to conduct wage and other struggles" while the chambers "are institutions of public right."[35] Or, as cited in another source, "while the trade unions are primarily the source of motive power the Chambers of workers are mainly responsible for the scientific principles governing this force";[36] this presumably means that the chamber staff provides the technical expertise.

The chambers are able to "remain more independent of the special interests of the members in the different branches than can trade union headquarters." The larger affiliates are likely to be the most influential in the federation and hence to "put their special interests first concerning economic legislation."[37]

V

The principle that trade union power also carried with it economic responsibility was early established by Johann Böhm, ÖGB president until 1959. In Böhm's view, the labor movement had to look beyond its bargaining power to the needs of the larger community.[38] More specifically, the ÖGB "has advocated a cautious wage policy ever since its inception," with the understanding that "the ability of Austrian exports to compete internationally is very much dependent upon the fact that wages are relatively lower than they are in Western Europe generally."[39] The

32. Interviews with Chamber of Labor officials, Vienna, August 19, 1969.
33. OECD, *Manpower Policies and Problems in Austria*, pp. 72–73.
34. *Chambers of Labour in Austria*, p. 7.
35. *Ibid.*, p. 58.
36. Weissenberg, "Social Policy Experiences," p. 33.
37. Lakenbacher, "Austria," p. 75.
38. Proksch, "Austrian Joint Wage and Price Council," p. 234.
39. H. Kienzl, "Prices Policy and Incomes Policy in Austria," in OECD, Manpower and Social Affairs Directorate, *Non-Wage Incomes and Prices Policy* (Paris, 1965), p. 56.

current ÖGB president Anton Benya puts it: "The trade unions . . . do not
simply raise demands, . . . they also contribute actively to all measures
necessary for reconsolidation of our economy."[40]

Between 1947 and 1951, five general wage-price stabilization agreements were negotiated among the ÖGB, the labor chambers, and the trade
and commerce chambers. "Whenever the prices of basic consumer goods
were to be raised it was decided on the basis of a cost of living index that
wage increases would have to result, and these were put into effect
together with the price increases." The agreements became increasingly
unpopular "as the workers learnt by experience that the employers did not
or could not always keep their part of the bargain regarding prices."[41] The
1950 agreement was the leverage used by the Communists in their unsuccessful attempt at a takeover. By 1951 "inflation was under control and a
period of stable growth set in."[42]

In 1957 inflationary pressures reappeared. A Joint Wage and Price
Council—the Paritetic Kommission, known by its German initials PK—was
established on Böhm's initiative. The Joint Council was chaired by the
federal chancellor and included as members the presidents of the ÖGB and
the chambers. A price subcommittee was organized at once; a wage subcommittee was set up in 1962 to review applications processed by ÖGB.

"Before a trade union begins negotiations with the employer . . . it goes
to the federation and says we want to make this wage claim. It has to be
based on the guide-line which we developed in the ÖGB. Then the general
secretary of the ÖGB negotiates a claim with the Chamber of Commerce.
If it's agreed then they go to the Joint Council."[43] In the Joint Council
the claim is reviewed on the basis of forecasts of wage, price, and productivity trends. The council has no authority of its own to compel submission of increases claims or to secure enforcement of its decisions. It
may, however, recommend sanctions to the Ministry of the Interior; but
this is rare. The main result of the Wages Subcommittee's review is to
delay the timing of wage increases rather than to deny them altogether.
Sometimes the award is in "two tiers": a higher increase for the low-wage
workers and a smaller increase for those who have already benefitted from
wage drift. On price policy the union and chamber representatives undertake to act in behalf of the consumer interest.[44]

40. Anton Benya, "The ÖGB—25 Years On," *Free Labour World* (ICFTU,
Brussels), July–August 1970, p. 4.
41. Proksch, "Austrian Joint Wage and Price Council," p. 235.
42. H. A. Turner and H. Zoeteweij, *Prices, Wages and Incomes Policies in Industrialized Market Economies* (Geneva: ILO, 1966), p. 102.
43. Interview with H. Kienzl, Economic Policy Advisor, ÖGB, Vienna, July 11,
1968.
44. OECD, Manpower and Social Directorate, *Non-Wage Incomes and Prices
Policy* (Paris, 1965), p. 142.

In 1963 the Joint Council established an Advisory Council on Economic and Social Affairs (Beirat) as a committee of experts to consider economic issues from a larger time horizon. "The structural weaknesses of the Austrian economy and its worsening competitive position were becoming plainer for all to see," a trade union publicist said in 1964. The Beirat was necessary to consider "long-term economic problems which could not be resolved with short-term palliatives."[45] Beirat working parties, frequently extended to include representatives from universities and research institutes, have made many studies and recommendations on economic and social questions, specifically on prices and incomes, budget, capital markets, labor force forecasts, construction industry stabilization, "gray" markets, part-time employment and hours reduction, and medium term forecasting.[46]

In general, the OECD reports, "the trade unions are satisfied with the system" preferring it "to an open competitive system."[47] The trade union movement recognizes that the system is "contrary to the concept of a market economy." But it is essential as a public "counterweight" to the monopolistic forces at work in the tariff protection system, the close price cooperation encouraged by the Chamber of Commerce, and the "inherently inimical" attitude of the Austrian employer to competition.[48]

Wage restraint is acceptable to the unions only if the latter can be sure "that exactly the same thing . . . happen[s] to prices as to wages." Yet the unions understand that "the ability of Austrian exports to compete internationally is very much dependent upon the fact that wages are relatively lower than they are in W. Europe generally."[49] Price control "may be a valuable instrument for ensuring stability, expansion and wages policy, providing that the government uses such methods as part of a thoroughly thought-out and rational overall policy and that the trade unions have the right of codetermination with regard to prices and wages policy; but if this is not so, government price fixing may have adverse effects."[50]

From a larger vantage point, the social partners, including the government with or without coalition, utilize the Joint Council and Beirat to negotiate national economic policy. "A new approach to incomes policy was made last year," OECD reported in May 1968. "An understanding was reached between the government and the monetary authorities on the one hand, and the representatives of the central labour market organisations on the other, whereby the latter consented to exercise restraint in their wage

45. Fritz Klenner, "Half Way," *Free Labour World*, March 1964, p. 4.
46. OECD, *Manpower Policies and Problems in Austria*, p. 107.
47. *Ibid.*, p. 143.
48. Kienzl, "Prices Policy and Incomes Policy in Austria," pp. 55–56.
49. *Ibid.*, p. 56.
50. *Ibid.*, p. 63.

and price claims in return for tax cuts and measures of monetary relaxation."[51]

In 1961 Anton Proksch, the Socialist Minister of Social Administration, characterized the Joint Council as "an experiment without parallel in the industrial countries that subscribe to the principles of a market economy. . . . No attempt has yet been made on so broad a scale to consult workers' organisations on price policy and to frame policy with a view to economic growth. . . . One of the reasons for this is the high degree of organisation of both employers and workers and the major role of the Federal Government in economic policies." Nevertheless, the Joint Council is "only a step albeit a considerable one towards the creation of an economic committee in which the workers' organisations would have full powers of joint decision in economic matters and through which they could avail themselves of all existing economic instruments to play an important part in determining prices and the general economic development of the country."[52]

The ability of the unions to find common ground with employers also says something about the change in employer attitudes. Employers in the Second Republic differ from those in the First. In the earlier period the unions dealt with antiunion employer organizations. Now the unions deal with an employers' chamber organized into a statutory body which "reaches into every aspect of economic policy" and in the process "naturally develops a different style."[53] The nationalization of much of large-scale industry after World War II has also acted to moderate management's attitudes toward unions.

VI

Austria is still in the emerging stages of an active manpower policy in the OECD or Swedish sense. The new Labor Promotion Act represents the current phase of development. The trade union influence is very great in the field of manpower policy. In 1959 the ÖGB first raised the issue and became the driving force behind the introduction and realization of an active manpower policy. The idea was further developed in a circle of socialist economists who cooperate closely with the trade unions. Then it was brought to the government by Socialist Minister Proksch.

There is vigorous support for the idea of industrial modernization. Union economists see the mass of small enterprises with their inefficiency and reliance on low-cost labor as a major stumbling block to structural change.[54] A Chamber of Labor economist observed, "The Austrian

51. OECD, *Economic Surveys*, May 1968, pp. 21–22.
52. Proksch, "Austrian Joint Wage and Price Council," pp. 244–45.
53. Lakenbacher, "Austria," p. 58.
54. Interview with Koch, July 8, 1968.

economy is changing; its structure is not the best one. Many enterprises are not profitable. It would be necessary to facilitate mobility from these enterprises to others. This is a regional problem as well as structural."[55] An active manpower policy stressing mobility through retraining and security against the risks of mobility is urged as the method of achieving the restructuring of the economy. Labor movement spokesmen note three obstacles in the way of achievement. First is the jurisdictional or "competence" problem—that is, which agency shall direct the program; at the time of the coalition, this was basically a political problem, inasmuch as the system of *Proporz* would have forced the program either into a People's Party ministry or a Socialist ministry. Second is the resistance of smaller enterprises relying on low labor costs who would be most likely disadvantaged in a program of retraining of the employed for more productive jobs. Third is the absence of adequate benefits to finance mobility and training; this was partially remedied in the 1968 legislation.[56]

The Chamber of Labor experts criticize apprenticeship in Austria as being obsolete and "not suited for a modern society. The apprenticeship law is from 1859; the list of professions is from the 19th century. There is a good deal of waste in that many of the apprentices do not go into the trade in which they were trained" and in most cases are used "as a source of cheap labor." In respect to training, generally the Chamber of Labor is proposing a new training law which would include financial subsidies to people in training and to the enterprises to encourage training programs.[57]

Regarding technological innovation, the ÖGB holds that "the scope for union responsibility and initiatives is . . . very limited" even though "the Government or the employers have failed to keep pace with requirements of up-to-date technological standards" in many industries. The major concern of the trade union movement is not with the "promotion of technological changes" but with the identification of the possible "negative consequences . . . on employment and the social and economic status of individuals and the promotion of a system of benefits, services and techniques for adjustment and protection." What the trade union movement can do affirmatively to advance technological innovation is to "contribute to the information of their members about the nature of, and need for, impending changes and . . . overcoming their resistance to change through stimulation of adjustment techniques to be developed by Government and employers in close cooperation with the unions."[58]

55. Interviews with Chamber of Labor officials, July 9, 1968.
56. Interview with Koch, July 8, 1968; interview with Kienzl; interview with Franz Lenert, Deputy Director, Federal Ministry of Social Affairs, Vienna, July 8, 1968; interviews with Chamber of Labor officials, July 9, 1968.
57. Interviews with Chamber of Labor officials, July 9, 1968.
58. TUAC, "The Trade Union's Role in the Promotion of Innovation," mimeographed (Paris, 1968), p. 1.

Several ÖGB affiliates have been concerned with greater efficiency in their respective industries. With the parent organization, the Wood and Building Workers' Union has urged "the transformation of the building trade into a building industry," singling out construction technology, utilization of manpower, organization of work at the building site, winter building, and planning. In food processing, the union has proposed legislation to reduce the number of "uneconomic small units" by compensatory benefits to the owners and displaced workers. The Metal Workers' Union has been trying to convince its membership in uneconomical enterprises to "promote rationalisation rather than to fight for maintenance of jobs."[59]

VII

Only the German labor movement has historically represented a comparable ideological tradition uniting the political party and the trade union movement—"the Siamese Twins" Victor Adler called the relationship.[60] The Austrian Social Democratic Party "was more than a political organization"; it was also an ideology, "interest groupings and manifold ancillary party organizations."[61] The party was "a state within a state."[62] Before World War II this subculture produced "Austro-Marxism" which took "a middle road . . . between . . . the extremes of Revisionism and believers in 'catastrophic socialism.' "[63]

Since World War II major changes have taken place in socialism's ideology and politics. "Comprehensive socialist theory" has "totally disappeared" and there is an "almost complete loss of interest on the part of those calling themselves Socialists in the reestablishment of a coherent system of socialist thought."[64] The prevailing economic theory is a kind of mixed-economy Keynesianism for full employment—"extreme full employment" is disavowed—combined with a general socialist commitment.[65] "The trade union's legitimate goal is to weaken, and eventually abolish altogether, the specific legal basis for economic production and distribution of products which characterises the capitalist economic order."[66] "Keynes' teachings and the practical demands of the American 'alliance' " have combined to undermine "the view that capitalism and crises were twins."[67] With the decline of ideology the ÖGB has replaced the party as

59. *Ibid.*, pp. 3–4.
60. Klenner, *Austrian Trade Union Movement*, p. 9.
61. F. C. Engelmann, "Austria," in *Political Oppositions in Western Democracies*, ed. R. A. Dahl (New Haven: Yale University Press, 1966), p. 262.
62. Shell, *Transformation of Austrian Socialism*, p. 9.
63. *Ibid.*, p. 191.
64. *Ibid.*, p. 139.
65. *Ibid.*, p. 192.
66. Gerhard Weissenberg, "The Role of Free Professional Associations in Present Day Democracy," *Free Labour World*, September 1969, p. 7.
67. Shell, *Transformation of Austrian Socialism*, pp. 192–95 *passim.*

the senior partner in the labor movement.[68] Ideology has also given way to the need for social stability marked by the Socialist willingness to enter into a government coalition with the People's Party—a lineal descendant of the pre-war Christian Social Party whose leaders handed the government over to Hitler in 1934. The SPÖ-PP coalition lasted for twenty years until 1966 when the People's Party eked out a slim absolute majority.

Despite official political neutrality, the main vehicle for the effectuation of ÖGB interests in public policy is the interlocking leadership between ÖGB and SPÖ. Many of the top ÖGB leaders are simultaneously Socialist members of parliament as are some of the Christian leaders. "A certain number of seats on the Party Directorate are tacitly reserved for trade union representatives."[69]

The fundamental transformation that has taken place in the postwar years is that "the working class," as Karl Renner, the outstanding Socialist theoretician observed, "is no longer that incoherent sum of helpless individuals who are exposed to the storm of economic crises and the arbitrary rule of rulers as the desert sand is exposed to the elements. It is no longer the proletariat of 1848, but a powerful, confident, well-organized member of society. It is this member position which gives it power and often more power and security than the possession of private wealth."[70]

Marxist feeling still runs deep, especially among the working class core, and there are some important leaders who feel the need for a strong socialist identity in the party and the labor movement. Moreover, the Communists, while relatively unimportant in their own right, are nevertheless marginally significant as additions to the socialist vote although the ambivalence of the Socialist Party in accepting Communist Party support has been interpreted as having been a factor in the Socialist parliamentary losses in the 1966 elections. "The strategy of eroding Communist voting strength . . . is a primary reason why the Austrian Socialist Party has had to retain more social radicalism, more ideology in its posture than, for example, the German Socialist Party."[71]

A unified labor movement must also reckon with its conservative People's Party component. The People's Party is a federation of three interest groups: the Peasant League, the Economic League of Entrepreneurs, and the Workers' and Employees' League, with a noticeable shift of power in the direction of the last-named and a shift of tactics "to concede principles in order to win daily successes."[72] Even though

68. Rusinow, *Political Definition of Austria*, pt. 3, "Socialists in Crisis and the End of Coalition," p. 6.

69. Shell, *Transformation of Austrian Socialism*, p. 63.

70. Quoted in Engelmann, "Austria," p. 278.

71. Rusinow, *Political Definition of Austria*, pt. 2, "Black, Red and Brown beside the Blue Danube," p. 10.

72. *Ibid.*, p. 6.

"ideological differences have subsided—in 1945 the Church left politics"—the two groups (that is, the People's Party and the Socialists) "remain socially and psychologically separated."[73] The Christian presence in the trade union movement does not seem to have seriously inhibited the policy objectives of the ÖGB except perhaps in the "purely political" issues, for example, state support for Catholic schools. Otherwise the position of Catholic trade unionists is substantially in agreement with that of the Socialists.[74]

VIII

The national or industry branch collective agreement is mainly a wages document; legislation regulates social insurance and labor standards in detail. In fact, the agreements are "mainly an expert codification of improvements which have already been achieved in the majority of enterprises."[75] Social legislation establishes old age pensions, workmen's compensation, health insurance, unemployment insurance, family allowances, rehabilitation, retraining, mobility aid, and bad weather compensation for construction workers. Labor legislation regulates maximum hours of work (currently forty-eight); paid holidays; dismissal notice requirement; severance pay for salaried, public, and domestic employees; apprenticeship; collective agreement procedure; and works councils.[76]

The characteristic distinction between workers' conditions determined by collective bargaining and by law is not fully valid in the Austrian situation because "the trade unions look upon social security as their own creation" with "a real say in the way it is administered." The unions "played an active part in the shaping of the new social security machinery."[77]

The ÖGB aim in collective bargaining is not "so much with achieving apparent, but relatively short-lived successes, but rather with effecting permanent structural changes." Thus the additional week's leave is equal to about a 2 percent wage increase, but unlike a wage increase it cannot be "easily eroded in a very short time by developments in the economic sphere. Structural changes of a much more sweeping nature can obviously affect the whole basis of the economic system."[78]

The major field of collective bargaining action on manpower is through the enterprise agreement between management and the works council.[79]

73. Engelmann, "Austria," p. 167.
74. Shell, *Transformation of Austrian Socialism*, p. 65.
75. OECD, *Manpower Policies and Problems in Austria*, p. 113.
76. *Ibid.*, pp. 107–15.
77. Gerhard Weissenberg, "Social Security in Austria," *Free Labour World*, December 1961, p. 511.
78. *Ibid.*
79. Weissenberg, "Social Policy Experiences of an Austrian Trade Unionist," p. 34; OECD, *Manpower Policies and Problems in Austria*, p. 114.

The works councils, elected by workers in the enterprise from slates prepared by the political fractions, are technically independent but a network of informal relationships establishes strong ties with the unions. The unions provide the supporting technical data and information so that council representatives can hold their own in dealing with management.[80] Most importantly the works councils relate to the unions by overseeing the enforcement of the collective agreements, in fixing piece rates, and by establishing work rules.[81] The councils also perform some of the more classic functions of works councils, including suggestions, consultation, etc.

Collective agreements are almost silent on manpower planning and readjustment. In collective bargaining at the national and industry level, measures for assisting manpower adaptation to change are not usually discussed.[82] Manpower adjustments to change have to be made at the plant works council level and even there "an unparalleled history of almost permanent insecurity over the past 50 years" has generated a "concept of permanent and total job security ... [as] the main determinant of manpower policy in both the public and private sectors." Moreover, guaranteed job security has come more and more "to mean a guarantee of holding the same job." [83]

But manpower adjustments nevertheless get made. The legal right of the works council to review dismissals and transfers is a kind of job security substitute. The council has frequently "softened resistance" by individual workers who have "to feel assured that their interests are well represented. . . . Apart from a few exceptions which received too much public attention workers' resistance was soon overcome once the decision for change had been taken."[84]

Consultation or codetermination on innovation is not required under the Works Council Act, but in practice the works council chairmen have "wide scope for participation" as "partners in innovation." This is "most advanced" in large enterprises in metals, bread, tobacco, construction, the nationalized Post, Telephone and Telegraph Service, and the railways. [85]

IX

The trade union movement has approached "the economic sphere not as a pressure group attempting to extract economic benefits for its members but as a participant shaping its decisions."[86] This enlarged role is

80. OECD, Manpower and Social Affairs Directorate, *Adjustment of Workers to Technological Change* (Paris, 1967), p. 304.
81. OECD, *Manpower Policies and Problems in Austria*, p. 113.
82. *Ibid.*, p. 35.
83. OECD, *Adjustment of Workers to Technological Change*, p. 322.
84. *Ibid.*, p. 344.
85. TUAC, "Trade Union's Role in the Promotion of Innovation," pp. 4–5.
86. Shell, *Transformation of Austrian Socialism*, p. 66.

a natural outcome of a union membership base that is almost coterminous with the working class itself.

The commitment to the general interest first came about as a defense against common adversity but has proved hardy enough to be stretched to the more positive and sophisticated needs of price stability, growth, and structural change in the era of post-full employment. The major economic policy concern has been incomes policy, but more recently manpower policy has also come to the center. Incomes policy is normally a hazardous commitment for trade unions but it has proved to be supportable in the Austrian case because of a widely shared understanding of the country's economic needs, the central role of the trade union movement, the inclusion of price control, as well as wage control, and the rising level of general economic well-being.

The highly structured mechanisms for general interest involvement—the chambers, the Joint Council, and the Beirat—are essentially bilateral insofar as the critical decisionmaking power is in the hands of the trade union movement and business although government is, of course, represented. The initiative and innovation seem to come mainly from the professionals in the unions and in the Chambers of Labor, especially in the case of manpower policy.

The road to central involvement in national economic policy required a major ideological reorientation on the part of the unions which evolved out of the ordeal of civil war, occupation, devastation, and neutralization. Austria's rich tradition of Marxist theory has given way to an ideologically low-keyed Keynesianism cum nationalization—the nationalization reflecting not so much socialism (it was voted by a National Assembly controlled by the People's Party) as literally the national interest in assuring domestic control over basic industry. The trade union movement for its part of the ideological reorientation abandoned a long-standing anticlericalism to unite with the Catholic labor elements; the party dampened its anticlericalism, antiemployerism, and antilandlordism to join with a political movement representing all three, in a government coalition which was to last for twenty years.

The Austrian labor movement also took steps to prepare itself organizationally to influence economic policy; specifically, these steps were (1) a highly centralized and politically unified trade union federation, (2) the institutionalization of political fractions within the federation, (3) the integration of authority from federation to works council in one union system, (4) industrial unionism, (5) the Chamber-trade union relationship and the resulting professionalization of union administration, (6) the Joint Wage and Price Council and the Advisory Council on Economic and Social Affairs—for the negotiation of economic policy, (7) the conversion of employers from antiunionism to union recognition, and (8) a viable trade union-party relationship. These arrangements add up to a good deal of centralization compatible with a democratic order only in a relatively small-scale economy and society.

"The champions of conservatism," according to trade union spokesmen, are threatening the trade unions with total "integration into the overall constitutional and legal scheme of things; . . . this applies not only to their organisation but also to their tasks and their rights in official decisionmaking on all state bodies." The trade union movement "rejects the idea of making trade unions into legal institutions" and charges that the aim of the conservatives is "to stem the impetus of trade union progress" because they see the union as aiming "to change the whole face of society."[87]

The trade union movement has, in brief, become a major "source of political authority"; because of its importance, there has been a major shift of power "from parliament to the political parties and from the political parties to the decisionmaking centers of the corporate interest groups behind them, in particular to the Trade Union Federation, the Labor Chambers, the Economic Chamber, and the farmers' organizations."[88]

87. Weissenberg, "Role of Free Professional Associations," pp. 7, 8 *passim.*
88. Rusinow, *Political Definition of Austria*, pt. 3, "Socialists in Crisis and the End of Coalition," p. 23.

CHAPTER FOUR

The Netherlands: Rise and Fall of National Wage Policy

The Netherlands' experience, representing the rise, decline, and fall of a trade union commitment to national wage policy, must be viewed against the background of the World War II and postwar economy which evolved from devastation, austerity, and reconstruction to economic growth, and from mass unemployment to labor scarcity. In less than twenty years after the war—which had destroyed 30 percent of its national wealth—the Netherlands' economy changed from one based predominately on agriculture to one based on industry.[1] Between 1947 and 1960, the working population declined from 20.2 percent to 12.2 percent in the primary sector, increased from 34 to 40.7 in the secondary sector and from 41 to 44.8 in the tertiary sector.[2] "Except for very small countries such as Luxemburg, the Netherlands are by far the most open industrialized economy in the world."[3] In 1964 imports of goods and services constituted 63 percent of GNP at constant prices, rising from about 46 percent in 1950.

The critical instrument of public policy has been a high degree of public regulation notable for "the uncompromising method of direct wage control," buttressed by an "extreme readiness to use price control."[4] Public regulation in the Netherlands represents the most "sophisticated methods of short-term forecasting and . . . refined ways of planning policy measures" to be found in any Western country.[5] Shonfeld analogized the wage control policy "to the traditional case for protecting infant industries. Only in this instance instead of providing shelter for these industries by a high tariff wall, it was to be supplied by putting an artificially low ceiling on wages."[6]

1. OECD, *Manpower and Social Policy in the Netherlands* (Paris, 1967), p. 32.
2. *Ibid.*, p. 33.
3. Erik Lundberg, *Instability and Economic Growth* (New Haven: Yale University Press, 1968), p. 262.
4. Andrew Shonfeld, *Modern Capitalism* (London: Oxford University Press, 1965), p. 213.
5. Lundberg, *Instability and Economic Growth*, p. 264.
6. Shonfeld, *Modern Capitalism*, p. 212.

The basic manpower problem confronting the labor market of the Netherlands is the "transition from a state of general labour surplus to that of labour stringency both on a local and general basis,"[7] and transition "from the care of the unemployed and prevention of unemployment to assuring competent and adequate manpower resources for the economy, particularly for the growth sectors."[8] The need is for the development of "new sources of manpower . . . to attain the nation's economic growth objectives." This requires (1) augmenting the labor force by foreign labor, women with children, and disadvantaged groups and shifts toward higher productivity occupations; (2) "upgrad[ing] the quality of the labour force" toward the higher intellectual preparation required in the modern industrial economy; (3) reorientation of labor market administration and organization to working "as active intermediaries rather than awaiting requests"; (4) economic protection during job shifts sufficient "to sustain [the employee's] human and potential economic quality."[9] On the credit side, several programs have been singled out for commendation as having "reached such a stage of maturity and effectiveness that they can serve as guides for other countries"; specifically, these are "regional development, supplementary unemployment programs, social employment, . . . seasonal stabilisation of the construction industry and consultation with interested groups."[10]

Some members of the Social and Economic Council secretariat say, however, that "if you are talking about labor market policy we don't have it. We take an estimate here and an estimate there and we try to do something." The reason for the absence of a labor market policy has been the relatively low unemployment. "But now because of the influence of the European market the feeling is changing."[11]

II

The labor movement, like other aspects of society in the Netherlands, is divided on religious and ideological lines into the socialist-oriented and nondenominational NVV, which is the largest federation, with a membership of about 550,000 and 19 national union affiliates; the Catholic NKV with about 420,000 members and 34 national union affiliates; and the Protestant CNV with about 240,000 members and 25 national union affiliates. Another 100,000 members are in unaffiliated unions. Approximately 40 percent of the 3.5 million wage and salary earners are in unions.

7. OECD, *Manpower and Social Policy*, p. 15.
8. *Ibid.*, p. 180.
9. *Ibid.*, p. 179.
10. *Ibid.*, p. 15.
11. Interview with members of the Social and Economic Council secretariat, The Hague, August 9, 1968.

Although divided into three centers, the Dutch trade union movement, since World War I, has nevertheless been able to develop viable means for collaboration through "a consultative organ which tries—usually successfully—to reach agreement on important social and economic questions." Informally, "personal relations between the leaders of the different centres are particularly cordial. In negotiations at the national level the president of NVV usually acts as spokesman for the whole trade union movement."[12] Aside from fundamental doctrine and ideology, "the three federations are becoming ever more similar to one another in outlook, policies, structure and government."[13] A recent attitude survey showed a substantial majority in the federations favoring a unified trade union movement.[14]

NVV describes itself as a "highly integrated" organization;[15] this is also applicable to the other two federations. External circumstances, particularly the need for centralized union authority to negotiate and participate in the permeating system of controls, have shaped the integration process—to the extent that there have been deliberate constitutional changes. But even under integration, the national unions are important organizations: they constitute the sources of financial support for the federations; they carry on collective bargaining with employers associations; and their agreement is indispensable to a unified federation front. The liberalization of controls very likely increased their importance. Integration of another kind is achieved through industrial unionism which is the prevailing union structure, especially in the NVV.

Below the level of the national union, the roots of union organization are not firmly established. The local union is not generally considered an effective body. The Metal Workers observe, "With the growing distances between home and place of work it is . . . becoming more and more difficult to organise members' meetings in separate companies through the channels of these sections."[16]

The major worker organization at the plant level is the works council which has no formal union identification. There is a "lack . . . of a body on the shop floor to shape the union's will."[17] The unions criticize the works council's isolation from the workers and its "actually slight influ-

12. D. Roemers, "Trade Unions in the Netherlands," *Free Labour World* (ICFTU, Brussels), June 1965, p. 3.

13. John P. Windmuller, *Labor Relations in the Netherlands* (Ithaca: Cornell University Press, 1969), p. 143.

14. NVV, "Labour Market Council," *Informationbulletin* (Amsterdam), no. 98, August 1969, p. 8.

15. NVV, "Trade Unions in the Netherlands," mimeographed (Amsterdam, n.d. [1967?]), p. 3.

16. C. Poppe, "Trade Union and Company," *Bulletin of the International Metalworkers' Federation* (Geneva), August 1967, p. 29.

17. *Ibid.*, p. 28.

ence is accompanied by excessive readiness to fit in with management's views."[18] There is general agreement that the works council system needs strengthening at specific points: (1) legal protection for council members, (2) easier access to expert advice, (3) closer contact with the unions, (4) timely consultation with management, (5) joint consideration with the management Board of Supervisory Directors of the annual report, and (6) participation in trade union training courses.[19]

Full-time officers are elected by the members but only after they have survived a selection process by the incumbent officers. One NVV officer justified this method on the ground that "the average member is as a rule not able to appreciate the job qualifications which leaders in important positions must meet." The fact that a candidate is a good speaker or writer and is generally popular is not itself an indication that "he has the other qualifications to fill the particular positions." The judgment of who has the qualifications "can be made in the trade union movement only by a small group of knowledgeable persons, for they alone are conversant with the factors necessary to reach a decision."[20] Windmuller concludes that the willingness of Dutch leaders "to shape an interpretation of the [public interest] . . . at odds with the short term interest of their members" may be decisively attributed to the "procedure for selecting and promoting union officers."[21]

III

The formal doctrinal loyalties of the three federations seem to be sufficiently strong to rule out merger but not strong enough to rule out close collaboration and joint action programs. NVV is a socialist movement in origin and its closest relationships are with the Labor Party. Its leaders frequently serve as Labor members of parliament and, in several instances, as members of the cabinet, as have leaders of NKV in the Catholic People's Party. The socialism of the Labor Party does not have a strong revolutionary tradition and, in the pre–World War II period, represented "plan socialism" more than class-struggle socialism.[22] Prior to World War II, one of the socialist leaders observed that "many of our old theses and dogmas which had unrivalled value in bringing the working class to consciousness

18. *Ibid.*, p. 32.
19. Consultative Body, NVV-NKV-CNV, *Programme of Action* (n.p., 1967), pp. 2–3.
20. C. Lammers, quoted in Windmuller, *Labor Relations in the Netherlands*, p. 212.
21. *Ibid.*, p. 221.
22. Hans Daader, "Opposition in a Segmented Society," in *Political Oppositions in Western Democracies*, ed. R. A. Dahl (New Haven: Yale University Press, 1966), p. 211.

and organization have now become a liability for future growth of the socialist movement."[23] In 1946 the party name was changed from Socialist to Labor.

The nonrevolutionary bent of NVV is observed in the recognition that class or sectional interest may have to give way to the national interest. "We shall have to expect the state to restrict our power," the NVV president has said, "as soon as the market mechanism tilts the wages balance in our favor to an extent that would endanger the national economy and prejudice the interests of third parties." If, however, the market mechanism discriminates in favor of the employer, "the trade union movement similarly expects the state to take the necessary corrective action." Moreover, "positive aspects of the employer's production methods" are recognized. "We no longer see the employers as representatives of a system doomed to failure by its internal weaknesses," the NVV president has said. "Public control and powerful trade unions can effectively knock off the sharpest corners of the capitalist production system." Union tactics have been accordingly modified by a shift in emphasis "from the traditional trials of strength in favor of joint consultation."[24]

Unlike the NVV and their Labor allies, the Catholic and the Protestant federations do not have well-articulated *labor* ideologies. The Protestants are more likely to be sympathetic to the idea of unity of employer and employee interests and, like the Catholics, are less sympathetic to state intervention. But these are shades of difference and probably no greater than the range of ideological difference *within* the respective federations. Coalition politics which the governments have had to pursue in the absence of a clear majority for one party have "contributed to a lessening of socioeconomic tensions." The religious parties with their "heterogeneous" following have been drawn toward "a centrist position" and the Labor Party is a "catch-all type."[25] In the more recent period, however, the era of relatively good feeling among the classes has, as we shall see, deteriorated. The union temper has become less conciliatory, more militant, and more self-assertive in behalf of the workers' special interests.

Codetermination comes closest to being a classic ideological issue affecting union policy. "If the unions fight for participation in decision-making . . . at [the] firm and plant level it is not only because they want to defend the interests of their members but also because they wish to have their share in the running of the enterprise. . . . This claim is less the expression of a demand for power than of a sense of responsibility for

23. J. W. Albarda, quoted in *ibid.*, p. 212.
24. A. H. Kloos, "The Frontiers of Trade Union Power," *Free Labour World*, December 1965, pp. 9–10 *passim*.
25. Daader, "Opposition in a Segmented Society," p. 220; see also Windmuller, *Labor Relations in the Netherlands*, pp. 133–43.

economic and technical progress and higher efficiency."[26] The union objective is to "review the acts of management" and to establish "a board of trustees for checks and balances. This cannot be done through collective bargaining."[27] The Metal Workers, on the other hand, would prefer "to give the union such a firm hold in the plant that it would have genuine opportunities to exercise control" and therefore to obviate the need for statutory codetermination.[28]

More recently, trade union disaffection is eroding the atmosphere of collaboration. There is, specifically, union discontent with the uncertain status of the strike weapon which "has virtually no parallel among industrialized democracies."[29] The joint consultative body of the trade unions has demanded that "strikes called out and/or led by an incorporated trade union organisation [should], in principle, not [be] illegal and participation in such a strike [should] carr[y] no personal responsibility for the worker, as long as the court has not passed judgment of conviction."[30] The Social and Economic Council with some reservations has "advised the Government to enact the right to strike" and the government with further reservations has concurred.[31] Only if the strike is appropriately legalized can the labor movement "play the game again as an equal opponent and not feel like a paper tiger any longer."[32]

IV

On the employer side, collective bargaining and government relations are the functions of an intricate network of employers associations organized essentially along denominational lines. Personnel and plant management are the functions of the individual employer. Some of the larger enterprises like Philips and Hoogovens do their own collective bargaining. Government intervention in the economy and centralized union power have probably enhanced the importance of the employers associations for the individual employer.

Employers resist the union presence on the shop floor "to safeguard control over company affairs against all interlopers, whether they be

26. TUAC, "The Trade Union's Role in the Promotion of Innovation–The Netherlands," mimeographed (Paris, 1968), p. 6.

27. Joint interview with R. Langebeek, NVV; G. Van Haaren, NKV; G. Terpstra and P. Tjeerdsma, CNV, Utrecht, August 6, 1968.

28. C. Poppe, "On the Road to Codetermination," *Economic and Social Bulletin* (ICFTU, Brussels), September–October, 1966, p. 15.

29. Windmuller, *Labor Relations in the Netherlands*, p. 319.

30. Consultative Body, *Programme of Action*, p. 17.

31. NVV, "Bigger Say for Workers in Important Decisions," *Informationbulletin*, no. 96, July 1968, p. 3.

32. A. H. Kloos, *Het Achterste Van De Tong* [From the Back of My Tongue] (The Netherlands: Paul Brand Bussum, 1969), p. 102. I am indebted to Mrs. Iefke Goldberger for translating the quoted portions.

unions, works councils, stockholders or administrative agencies of government."[33] Nevertheless, they concede the legitimacy of the union as the spokesman for an interest group—or even a class—in the regulation of employment terms at the level of the industry or the economy, even as they reject the union role in the individual enterprise. Strategically the enterprise is seen by employer groups as their last bastion of undisputed power; politically, "the unions are very well represented," as one association representative expressed it, "but management has only one party. . . . We feel that we have to protect ourselves in the collective bargaining field, for by parliament we will be forced to do more or give more away."[34]

In contrast with the unions who use their professionals in negotiating sessions, one nonpartisan observer has noted, the employers "do their own negotiating. That is why they were afraid of a free collective bargaining policy. . . . All marginal industries were in favor of a government wage policy because they could not handle the unions themselves. The unions agreed to it because they had their communications and alliances and fusions, because they could protect their flanks on the political side."[35]

V

The Foundation of Labor, in theory, is a private organization established in 1945 by employer and union leaders in the Dutch underground during the Nazi occupation, to engage in "joint consideration of social affairs at the industrial, provincial and national levels" with the objective of "ensuring permanent social relations in industrial life by means of organised cooperation between employers and workers." The foundation represents "a bipartite 'summit council' for industry" providing "representation on the one hand for the central industrial employers associations, the 'middle class' and the agricultural employers organisations, and on the other hand for the three big central workers' organisations."[36] The board of the foundation consists of eighteen representatives, nine each designated by the employer and union associations with the internal partisan representation weighted according to relative membership. A foundation secretariat is appointed by the board.

The foundation has gone through two main stages of development. In its first period, from 1945 to 1950, it was the main source of policy on wages, social insurance, industrial councils, and vocational training. In its latter period, which continues to the present, the foundation scope has

33. Windmuller, *Labor Relations in the Netherlands*, p. 240.
34. Interview with J. Hollander, Council of Netherlands Industrial Federations, The Hague, August 7, 1968.
35. Interview with members of the Social and Economic Council secretariat.
36. P. S. Pels, "Organized Industry and Planning in the Netherlands," *International Labour Review* (ILO, Geneva), September 1966, p. 3.

been narrowed to more concrete and "day-to-day" concerns in collective agreements and social insurance. The Social and Economic Council, established in 1950, took over the broader responsibilities (these will be indicated later), and the foundation became "the place where a joint labour-management view is evolved for presentation to the Council which bears the responsibility for reconciling the sectional attitudes with the national interest in the formulation of wage (and other) policy suggestions to the Government."[37]

The foundation operates in two main areas. Its major field has been the review of wage agreements through a permanent Wages Committee. "Wage questions of principle and social problems of a general character are handled by the Board of the Foundation."[38] The developments of the mid-1960s, including the general labor disaffection with wage restraints, have considerably diminished foundation influence in wage determination. The foundation also handles social insurance; it designates participating representatives in the administration of the various insurance programs.[39]

The Social and Economic Council was established by law in 1950 on a tripartite basis with thirty to forty-five members. The "third" group is composed of independent experts rather than government spokesmen. The council was conceived as a consultative organ for social and economic policy and as a regulating agency empowered to direct a complex of industry syndicates. On the latter, "there is well-nigh universal agreement that [it] . . . has been a dismal failure."[40] In the former function, the council issues recommendations requested by the government on national economic policy, social security, wage policy, and industrial relations.

The process by which the council considers its economic forecasts has been described by its director. "We get the figures first from the Central Planning Bureau. At the same time the [council] staff brings in its technical information. Don't forget that life is more than a model. Before the discussion in the committee there is a discussion in the organization where they have a committee set up along the same lines. There is a difference in opinion and tactics between the employer and the trade unions."[41]

"The natural task of these crown members," NVV President Kloos has said, "is to find compromise. . . . Supposedly these experts have a high degree of objectivity and resourcefulness and also a special sense for diagnosing social undercurrents as well as the scientific integrity needed

37. William Fellner et al., The Problem of Rising Prices (Paris: OEEC, 1961), p. 365.

38. Pels, "Organized Industry and Planning," p. 7.

39. Interview with P. S. Pels, Foundation of Labor and the Social and Economic Council, The Hague, August 6, 1968.

40. Windmuller, Labor Relations in the Netherlands, p. 290.

41. Interview with Pels.

for deflating over-coloured or misshapen arguments of the interest groups."[42]

The members of the council from the public side view their role variously; some see it as mediative, others as a kind of "third force" against latent collusion by the social partners. Windmuller concludes that the public members have been closer to employers on economic policy, closer to the unions on social policy, and have straddled on the issue of wage policy.[43] There is no obligation on the government's part to follow the council's advice, but there is, in the words of a former secretary, a "predisposition" to do so. "Too frequent departures from the advice would imperil the Council's valuable contribution in shaping policy."[44]

The Board of Mediators was established in 1945 and, subject to the "general instructions of the Minister of Social Affairs and Public Health, has the authority to:

"*a*. [Give] force of law to wages and other conditions of employment, either at the request of organisations of employers and employees or ex officio;

"*b*. Approv[e] labour agreements;

"*c*. Mak[e] provisions of collective labour agreements generally binding or non-binding on an entire branch of industry;

"*d*. Dra[w] up directives with regard to the regulation of wages and other conditions of employment;"

e. On request, to grant exceptions from a binding agreement.[45]

The Central Planning Bureau became involved in the later stages of incomes policy administration and prepared annual estimates from which the Social and Economic Council was to set the permissable limits of wage increases.

VI

Dutch wage policy began after World War II by subjecting every increase to control. The controls were exercised by the Board of Mediators and the Foundation of Labor who were mandated "to keep wages at the lowest politically acceptable minimum."[46] This first period of "severe restraint" was characterized not so much by negotiation among con-

42. Kloos, *Het Achterste Van De Tong*, p. 93.

43. Windmuller, *Labor Relations in the Netherlands*, p. 297.

44. G. J. Balkenstein, "The Netherlands Industrial Organization Act of 1950," *University of Pennsylvania Law Review*, quoted in Murray Edelman and R. W. Fleming, *The Politics of Wage-Price Decisions* (Urbana: University of Illinois Press, 1965), p. 228.

45. Netherlands Government Information Service, *Digest of the Kingdom of the Netherlands—Social Aspects* (The Hague, 1964), p. 42.

46. Windmuller, *Labor Relations in the Netherlands*, p. 339.

tending interests as by an effort in problem-solving with "top labor and business representatives . . . of one mind about economic priorities."[47] When the Korean War created serious balance-of-payment problems, the unions consented to what was, in effect, a reduction in real wages.

In the 1954–59 period of "rising real wages," controls were relaxed to permit wage rises, but the wage share of the national income was still intentionally permitted to lag. "The lag in the wage level," the unions said, "was accepted by design so that industry could earn profits which would pay for expansion and modernization of the productive apparatus. From a social point of view, this policy was deemed necessary to create employment for a rapidly growing labor force."[48] But it is also in this period that rumbles from below begin to be heard on the labor side and differences within the union groups emerge. The NVV argued for a "centrally determined wage policy" and blamed the employers for the cracks in the wage front. The other federations, "less ideologically committed to a centrally guided wage policy," urged greater differentiation among industries and enterprises.[49]

In 1957 rising imports and domestic consumption created balance-of-payments stringencies. Again the unions in the Social and Economic Council accepted a government recommendation to permit prices to move ahead of wages.

At the end of the third stage, 1959–63, the composition of the government changed to exclude the Labor Party for the first time since 1945. This period was also marked by a shift of power to the negotiating parties. Division developed within the Social and Economic Council; the confessional federations and their opposite number employer groups on one side favored decentralization of controls and greater differentiation and on the other side the more "equalitarian" NVV opposed it. The former won out "not least . . . because the parties constituting the government depended heavily on the support of the confessional interest groups" with the government establishing productivity as a standard for wage differentiation.[50] Wage bargaining in this period, with its discussions of "output and input figures" took on, in the words of J. Pen, a leading Dutch economist, "surrealistic proportions." In his judgment, "the discovery that, even in statistics, many knots had to be cut deprived the wage policy of its objective basis."[51] During this time jurisdictional "confusion" broke out over the respective boundaries of "cabinet, Board, Foundation and labor and management," which resulted in widespread evasion of controls. Improve-

47. *Ibid.*, p. 347.
48. *Ibid.*, p. 351.
49. *Ibid.*, p. 352.
50. *Ibid.*, p. 355.
51. J. Pen, quoted in *ibid.*, p. 357.

ment in hours, rising labor shortages, wage drift, and "black wages" increased labor costs and inevitably worsened the export position.

In 1963 there was a period of extensive liberalization and a negotiated 10 percent wage increase which ultimately turned out to be closer to 15 percent, despite a 4 percent safety limit set by the Central Planning Bureau. "There is no doubt that the unprecedently generous agreement saved the system, though it is quite another question whether the system was worth saving."[52] But the OECD *Economic Survey* noted that "the Dutch economy absorbed the wage explosion with astonishing resilience."[53]

"What led to the change in climate" after 1963, one government official observed later, "was the loss of authority of the leaders of the labor movement because year-in and year-out they had to argue with their people that the government *had* to advocate wage restraint and that there were so many clouds on the horizon. Every year these appeared too pessimistic. . . . The minimum became the starting point for bargaining rather than the end point. . . . [The] loss of authority was shown by the outbreak of unofficial strikes in 1964."[54]

By 1966 the control system had been shattered and existed only in theory. The federations and the employers associations were at an impasse in the federation. Major contracts were being negotiated in open contravention of standards. In mid-1965 "the Planning Bureau's restrained forecast had once again fallen considerably short of actual economic performance."[55] The Labor Party rejoined the government coalition, which lasted for eighteen months. The control scheme was saved by the 1966–67 recession which provided the leverage for establishing more moderate wage increases.

In 1966 the government reinstituted wage controls when the expected wage moderation failed to materialize. Failing to reach agreement with the foundation, the government ordered a brief wage stop and gave the Board of Mediators authority "to approve, delay, suspend and free wage agreements."[56] The 1966–67 recession resulted in the moderation of wage demands. By December 1967 the method "of prior approval of collective agreement by the Foundation" came to an end. The draft bill submitted to parliament in late 1968 gave the Minister of Social Affairs and Public Health the authority to veto agreements "on grounds of general social and economic requirements after consulting the Committee of Independent

52. *Ibid.*, p. 368.
53. OECD, *Economic Surveys–Netherlands*, Paris, April 1967, p. 39.
54. Interview with members of the Social and Economic Council secretariat, The Hague, August 8, 1968.
55. Windmuller, *Labor Relations in the Netherlands*, p. 375.
56. OECD, *Economic Surveys–Netherlands*, 1967, pp. 39–40.

Experts," and to extend existing agreements for six months also after consultation, if necessary to institute prior approval of agreements with the concurrence of parliament.[57]

Union experience with the liberalization of wage controls, the NVV reported, turned out to be not always "a pleasant one." In particular, the "panic reaction" of the Minister of Social Affairs and Public Health in postponing approval of a Building Workers contract brought about a demonstration by 25,000 Building Workers members in both the NVV and NKV. (The CNV had disassociated itself because it feared "troubles and riots.") The effort by the government to extend all existing contracts "to prolong the terms of collective agreements by six months, which boils down to a decrease in wages of 3%," brought about another demonstration, this time by a "unified labour movement of some 20,000 union members in Utrecht." As NVV reports it, "This determined action by the trade union movement resulted in the political parties (the opposition as well as the Government parties) opposing the Government on this issue," whereafter the government "changed its standpoint and decided to withdraw the . . . measure."[58]

Since 1966 it has clearly not been possible, despite much tinkering, to put together a durable wage control scheme acceptable to the unions. The fundamental blocks seem to be the inability of the government to define wage policy except in terms of repression and the union reassessment of past wage control experience as a disaster.

Beyond wage control, collective bargaining is also subject to statutory restraints originally enacted after the war as emergency measures. "With each passing year," however, these measures which began "as a temporary necessity" have established their "legitimacy more firmly."[59] Included in the nonwage controls are restrictions on voluntary or involuntary employee separation with government approval and prohibition against reducing the work week below forty-eight hours, amended to forty-five hours in 1961.

Union opposition to a law which makes permanent the government's regulation of collective bargaining has caused a deep rupture in the whole Netherlands system of tripartite relationships to the point that the NVV and the NKV are boycotting the wage sessions of the Foundation of Labor and the Social and Economic Council. From the NVV viewpoint, union support of the law "would for the trade unions be tantamount to resigning all influence over the evolution of wages. This is clearly unacceptable."[60]

57. OECD, *Economic Surveys—Netherlands*, Paris, May 1969, pp. 36-37.
58. NVV, "Towards a System of Free Wage Policy," *Informationbulletin*, no. 96, July 1968, pp. 5-6 *passim*.
59. Windmuller, *Labor Relations in the Netherlands*, p. 269.
60. J. Raven, "Industrial Relations Crisis in the Netherlands," *Free Labour World*, March 1970, p. 15; see also "Minister of the Economy Forced to Resign

VII

The Dutch wage control experience indicates several implications for trade union involvement:

1. The unions moved through three stages in their support of wage control. Against the background of the end of World War II and reconstruction, "the labor unions cooperated so closely with the government that they practically identified themselves with the general interest."[61] Both in 1951 and 1956 the unions acquiesced to cuts in real wages "in order to avoid cost pressures on the price level which would have endangered the balance of payments position."[62] In the second stage, with the improvement of the economic situation and the consequent relaxation of controls, the unions still managed to live with government intervention but strains and tensions began to set in. In the third and current stage, the control system slowly deteriorates and is ultimately all but dismantled as the unions, no longer able to withstand the pressure from below, openly resist government intervention.

2. In the earlier stages, adversity exerted a sufficiently strong pull on the parties so that their common purpose in reconstructing the Dutch economy completely overshadowed their special interests. As the situation improved, the parties moved toward more conventional power bargaining but always within the fairly severe constraints imposed by the Dutch position in the international economy.

3. The "centrally-guided wage system" demonstrated extraordinary durability due in considerable part to the setting of terms by negotiation among the crucial parties at interest and the willingness of the parties to carry on the negotiations through highly structured mechanisms and procedures and to expose themselves to analytical processes. "The Government has not simply been able to fix wages as and how it wished," an OEEC commission of experts reported in 1961. "On the contrary its freedom of action has been severely limited" by economic and by social and political forces "finding their expression in central negotiations." While the effects of the negotiations on the economy are inconclusive, it is important that "the bargaining partners had to face up fully to the implications of their actions for the economy as a whole. . . . The two sides were arguing about percentage points of national income rather than cents per hour. . . . [C]learly . . . they had become accustomed to think in terms of real incomes instead of money incomes, and to concentrate attention on longer run trends rather than the immediate past."[63]

because of Metalworkers' Collective Agreement," *Bulletin of the International Metalworkers' Federation*, April 1970, pp. 29-32.

61. Interview with members of the Social and Economic secretariat, The Hague, August 25, 1969.

62. Fellner *et al.*, *Problem of Rising Prices*, p. 387.

63. *Ibid.*, p. 389.

4. The wage control system worked most effectively under relatively simpler guides and controls. As the pressure for differentiations to suit special needs intensified, the "authorities could not design any satisfactory method of keeping the movements of wages in different industries and trades in some reasonable relationship to one another. For several years they seemed to be intent on treating the labour market as if it were a national parade ground on which everyone was supposed to march steadily in step."[64] At various times, either singly or in combination, the standards of differentiation included intricate job evaluation and productivity formulas; the social minimum budget; zonal, cost-of-living, and broad skill differentials. Talking about the 1963 amendments, Windmuller notes the "extraordinary complex[ity] , . . . compromise . . . on top of compromise, . . . a wondrous amalgam of paradoxes, subtleties, escape mechanisms and standby provisions—a bargaining procedure without parallel anywhere in the world."[65]

5. The root cause of the scheme's disintegration was, it is generally agreed, "the very high levels of demand [which] placed excessive strain on the cooperation of the parties, who were increasingly subjected to conflicts of interest between their acceptance of 'the national interest and requirements' and their own sectional or company interests, which appeared to be jeopardized."[66] These very high levels of demand subjected the unions to increasing pressure from their rank-and-file constituencies who could not understand as the emergency seemed to wane why they should be constrained from accepting wage increases "in the face of the demonstrated willingness on the part of the employers" to grant the increases.[67]

6. When "bargaining about wages [became] bargaining about output and input figures," J. Pen observed, "the parties approached the Central Bureau of Statistics for help and so this usually serene government office was implicated in social conflict."[68] The Central Planning Bureau found itself in a similar situation in the later stages of control when its estimates could be used "to affec[t] . . . even determin[e] the results."[69] Technically there seems to have been, as Erik Lundberg and others have

64. Shonfeld, *Modern Capitalism*, p. 215.
65. Windmuller, *Labor Relations in the Netherlands*, p. 302.
66. Derek Robinson, "National Wage and Incomes Policies and Trade Unions," in *International Labor*, ed. Solomon R. Barkin (New York: Harper and Row, 1967), p. 235.
67. Martin P. Oettinger, "Incomes Policy in the Netherlands since 1945" in *Proceedings of the Industrial Relations Research Association* (Madison, 1966), p. 154.
68. J. Pen, "The Strange Adventures of Dutch Wage Policy," *British Journal of Industrial Relations* (London), October 1963, p. 324.
69. Windmuller, *Labor Relations in the Netherlands*, p. 305.

observed, a "systematic tendency toward underestimation" of the economy's prospects.[70]

7. Trade union disillusionment with wage control has produced an anti-collaboration reaction of trade union separatism, direct action, and a class theory of the state. "The decision of the labour movement to give up her autonomy in the field of wage determination" has been viewed by Kloos as "understandable under the circumstances" but "an enormous tactical blunder in retrospect." The appropriateness of government intervention is still conceded, but "the government automatically turns into the employer's ally. The government whatever her political structure is always inclined to take a guarded position [which] usually coincides with the employer's self-interest." Wage control converts the union into "an extension of The Hague" and undermines "the members' faith in the labour movement." Wage determination for the union is "in the long run a matter of 'to be or not to be.' " But more than impairing union autonomy, wage control also "disturbs the balance of power." Since the nonwage incomes, like prices, are not touched by the government, "an autonomous labour movement—with wage demands—is the only effective counterweight to employers who are only too often prepared to pass on price increases."[71]

Disenchantment with methods of collaboration has given a new emphasis to union ideas about direct action. "Demonstrations, a rather old-fashioned means of pressure, ... are again with the labour movement and seem to be effective. The threatening atmosphere of a mass meeting can have an extraordinary useful effect on the progress of consultations especially after long years of quarreling at the round table without any results." The labor movement has been "very reluctant to use" its "last resort." It "used to be the only means workers had to demonstrate resistance against ... capitalistic oppression." But democracy and collective bargaining "have opened different, less spectacular and less revolutionary avenues." The strike must, however, "remain the last means of power to which the workers must be able to resort." The "jurisdictional twist" which "has caused the strike to become ... almost illegal ..." must be repealed. This does not mean that "waves of strikes [will] sweep over the Netherlands." Even "a day's strike by one large group can easily cost a small fortune." There are circumstances when even the political strike is justified: "whenever democracy is threatened from within or without.... [and] when a government or parliament fails morally and remains passive ... [or] when the very freedom of the trade union movement is at stake." The current preoccupation with the strike is especially

70. Lundberg, *Instability and Economic Growth*, p. 299.
71. Kloos, *Het Achterste Van De Tong*, pp. 88–102 *passim*.

significant because on the whole the unions have pursued an "anti-strike policy" in the postwar period.[72]

VIII

The OECD examining team concluded that there is in general "a very favourable disposition . . . towards advisory groups" for manpower as essential "to the attainment of understanding and stability in a country characterised by religious and economic segmentation."[73] The Central Advisory Committee and Assistance Board is concerned with the General Directorate for Manpower in the Ministry of Social Affairs and Public Health. It is appointed by the Minister and includes, but is not limited to, representatives of the employer and worker organizations. "The Director-General informs the Board of all important developments and problems and, as the members receive copies of all instructions to employment offices throughout the country (often before distribution) they are able to form opinions and discuss them freely during the monthly meetings."[74]

Initiative comes mainly from the Director-General. The Central Advisory Committee is regarded as a sounding board for reactions to proposed industrial policies and programs and does not take "many initiatives in reviewing the total labour market and its problems." One government official reported: "The Committee is most useful because on the basis of information presented to it and backed by opinions prevailing in the organizations represented in the Committee, developments and problems are thoroughly discussed. The results of these discussions are fed back into the policymaking machinery of the Directorate-General for Manpower on the one hand and on the other are forwarded by the members of the Committee to the organizations involved."[75]

The central committee has two "branch" committees: one for new employment, the other for general employment and labor market questions—with subcommittees for some of the principal problem areas, for example, vocational training, foreign manpower, agricultural manpower, etc. The committee functions are seen in terms of public relations—"to maintain better relations with the communities and support from all groups."[76] In March 1969 a Labor Market Council was established within the Social and Economic Council on "the initiative of the trade union movement."[77]

72. Windmuller, *Labor Relations in the Netherlands*, p. 397.
73. OECD, *Manpower and Social Policy*, p. 160.
74. *Ibid.*, p. 51.
75. Interview with T. J. v.d. Peijl, Director-General for Employment, Netherlands Ministry of Social Affairs and Public Health, The Hague, August 5, 1968.
76. OECD, *Manpower and Social Policy*, p. 160.
77. NVV, "Labour Market Council," p. 6.

The OECD examiners noted the absence of an advisory council at the level of the ministry to "concern itself with broad issues rather than with the administration of any one segment of the manpower programme."[78] A tripartite committee "could play an effective role in developing guides for personnel and industrial relations policies affecting manpower."[79] One government official pointed out, however, that a general advisory council at the level of the ministry could hardly be effective because the ministry is responsible for a variety of matters (for example, public health, social insurance, manpower, labor safety), each with its own specialized advisory committees.

Regional, that is, local, advisory boards advise the regional employment offices. The regional boards are constituted on the same basis as the Central Advisory Board. In addition, there is a local advisory committee which advises the director on all dismissal and resignation cases.[80] Under law "both employer and job holder are forbidden to terminate relations without the permission of the director of the Regional Employment Office, unless there is mutual consent between the parties or for 'urgent reasons.' "[81]

The OECD examiners directed attention to the inadequate coordination between public and enterprise manpower policies. They recommended an independent tripartite advisory committee, supported by a staff, to consider "enterprise programmes and practices for adjustment to technical and economic change, the aids which public agencies might provide for the effectiveness of such programmes, redundancy provisions, dismissal notices, internal training."[82]

Previously the Social and Economic Council had been relatively inactive in the field of labor market policy. In 1969, responding to a four-year-old request of the government, it issued a lengthy labor market "Advies."

Labor market policy is described in the report as a set of measures to realize optimal economic growth in such a way that the various sectors of the labor market will be in an equilibrium situation. More specifically, the following policy objectives are selected: (1) optimal allocation of manpower; (2) improving the structure of the labor market; (3) guarding against unemployment caused by structural changes in the labor market; and (4) guarding against unemployment caused by a shortage of demand.[83]

78. OECD, *Manpower and Social Policy*, p. 266.
79. *Ibid.*, p. 135.
80. *Ibid.*, p. 61.
81. *Ibid.*, p. 53.
82. *Ibid.*, pp. 264–66 *passim*.
83. Social Economische Raad, *Advies Over Het Arbeitsmarktbelied* (The Hague, 1969). I am indebted to Mr. M. Fase for a summary from which this has been adapted.

The joint consultative body, speaking for all three labor centers, has urged an "energetic and integrated labour market policy" which must be related to national and regional planning and in particular to regional structural unemployment. The vehicle for labor market administration should be a tripartite committee. The content of the "active labour market" policy should include labor market forecasting, public works planning, expansion of retraining, supplementary training, and rehabilitation facilities, and financial aid to redundant workers. Finally, the policy on foreign worker recruitment conforming to EEC treaty obligations must be related to the labor market situation and to available housing facilities.[84]

The unions favor a coordinated labor market policy and mechanism "because labour market policy is divided among 6-7 ministries. Cooperation takes place only in the Council of Ministers [that is, the Cabinet]. Outside of the Council ... there is very little coordination. ..." The unions favor centralization of labor market policy "incidentally to increase union influence. It is not enough to have only the Minister of Social Affairs, there is the building minister, etc. The unions' support of a tripartite council, they recognise, is not acceptable politically."[85]

The Vocational Education Committee of the Social and Economic Council was instrumental in reorganizing the apprenticeship education system. Quasi-public foundations in the form of industry organizations with union and employer representation were established to (1) draft uniform training programs, (2) advise employers and training staff, (3) investigate compliance with the apprenticeship agreement, and (4) prepare and conduct examinations. The entire program is then subject to the approval and financial support of the Ministry of Education.

Lady Williams concludes that "the system is extremely flexible," adjusting quickly to fluctuation in demand, enhanced by "the harmonious relationship between employers and unions."[86] There have been no jurisdictional problems. The only exception to this general flexibility is in the printing trades apprenticeship scheme which adheres strictly to the classic model of craft unionism with a restriction of entry, closed shop, and rigid jurisdiction. The trade unions favor broadening the supporting technical school but employers are opposed, and there is indication that workers prefer to take advantage of employment opportunities without any delay.[87]

84. Consultative Body, *Programme of Action*, pp. 12-13.
85. TUAC, *The Trade Union's Role in the Promotion of Innovation*, pp. 1-2.
86. Gertrude R. Williams, *Apprenticeship in Europe* (London: Chapman and Hall, 1963), p. 73.
87. *Ibid.*, p. 76.

IX

The Netherlands experience in the accommodation between trade unionism and national economic policy has centered almost exclusively on national wage policy, with manpower policy as a significant field of interest emerging only recently. The trade union movement has been one of the principal negotiators of economic policy in a highly structured multilateral negotiation system. The structured quality of the system consists of the ordered places occupied by the institutionalized interest groupings and the effort to integrate analytical processes in the form of economic forecasts and econometric models in the negotiations.

If the test of an economic policy commitment is the willingness to incur risks in its behalf, then the Dutch trade unions have exercised greater forbearance than probably any other labor movement. Perhaps no other labor movement has had as powerful an incentive to exercise forbearance. The "exploiting, plundering and in the end destr[uction of] key sectors of the economy" by the German "occupation created a set of conditions which, after liberation, required the continuation of strict controls in the labour market and over wage determination."[88] Later the major constraining influence on union policy was the imperative need to reestablish the international competitiveness of the Dutch economy. With the improvement in the economic situation and the deterioration of the control system, the temper of forbearance has been to a large degree displaced by a rising spirit of militancy and confrontation.

The context in which economic policy unionism operated is summarized as follows:

1. The sense of urgency which permeated the population
2. The trade union movement as a principal in the negotiation of national economic policy
3. The relatively small scale of the Netherlands economy which made the negotiation of economy-wide policies manageable
4. The open economy where "the consequences of getting out of step with the rest of the world have been so apparent that they could not be ignored by either party to the negotiations"[89]
5. The decline of ideology most notably within the socialist-oriented NVV which paved the way intellectually for trade union collaboration within the trade union movement and with the employers and other non-working-class elements
6. The integrative features of the industrial relations environment, specifically (a) centralized bargaining, (b) coordinated action within the

88. *Ibid.*, p. 90.
89. Fellner *et al.*, *Problem of Rising Prices*, p. 388.

segmented trade union movement, (c) the strong form of federation structure with powerful influence on collective bargaining by affiliates most
marked in the period of high intervention, (d) industrial unionism, (e) the
quasi-"merit system" for the selection of union officers, (f) the institutionalized forms of conciliation, such as the Foundation of Labor and the
Social and Economic Council, (g) the habit of thinking in terms of
"national income, rather than cents per-hour" and of "real incomes
instead of money incomes,"[90] and (h) the effectiveness of the "general
interest" system, especially in the early postwar system, that "considerably facilitated the task of maintaining a high rate of investment and
growth without serious balance-of-payments difficulties."[91]

These integrative influences have been counteracted by the disjoining
effects associated with the too heavy reliance on the policy of wage
repression: (1) the overextension and over-rationalization of controls that
endangered the union hold on the rank and file, and (2) the "politicali-
zation" of economics which was coopted invariably on the side of wage
restraint. There is also the disadvantage of the open economy that "very
sharp changes in the direction of economic policy have been required in
order to maintain growth and employment levels in the face of changes in
the international economic climate."[92]

For the longer run, the lack of legitimacy for the union presence at the
enterprise level and for the union's right to strike creates insecurities which
the union has to overcome before feeling safe enough to take on the
additional risk of subordinating sectional interests. Moreover, denying the
union legitimate access to the shop floor makes it less effective in influencing the shop floor in accord with economic policy objectives. The
unions' lack of strong interlocking relationships with the parties, together
with the shifting coalitions which form the government, discourages the
unions from taking risks which could weaken their political flanks. In light
of these conditions, it is perhaps understandable that separatist influences
seem to be growing stronger in the trade unions—trade unions whose
public posture is increasingly marked by the rhetoric of militancy and
confrontation.

90. *Ibid.*, p. 398.
91. *Ibid.*, p. 359.
92. *Ibid.*, pp. 388–89.

CHAPTER FIVE

Germany: The Road to Integration

The economic and ideological elements of the postwar German economy against which the trade union response was fashioned were (1) the "social market economy" phasing into Keynesian aggregate demand management and post-full employment price pressures, (2) the "social policy" principle, and (3) the labor market situation and administration.

In 1965 Andrew Shonfeld observed that Germany "appear[s] to be out of the mainstream of modern capitalism" in its antipathy to a government-organized pattern of economic behavior. This was due to Germany's traumatic exposure to national socialism—what Ludwig Erhard called the "special circumstances of our history." "More perhaps than any other economy," according to Erhard, "the German one has had to experience the economic and supra-economic consequences of an economic and trading policy subjected to the extremes of nationalism, autarchy and government control. We have learnt the lesson."[1]

This counter-planning ideology known as the "social market economy" relied on "a free market economy with social goals and opportunities. . . . [But] it is wrong to regard the Social Market Economy as merely a variety of neo-Liberalism. . . . Whereas neo-Liberalism regards the machinery of competition as the sole principle of organization," the social market economy represents "a coordination of form . . . between the sphere of life represented by the market, the State and the social groups." It takes into account the social system of values which exists " 'beyond supply and demand.' " The social market economy may be conceptualized in terms of a "magic triangle . . . whose corners represent the objectives of personal freedom, economic and social security and growth."[2]

1. Andrew Shonfeld, *Modern Capitalism* (London: Oxford University Press, 1965), pp. 239–40; *ibid*. for Erhard quote.
2. Alfred Müller-Armach, "The Principles of the Social Market Economy," *German Economic Review*, vol. 3, no. 2 (1965), pp. 90– 93 *passim*.

The social market economy was commonly credited with having produced the "miracle" of German economic recovery. The miracle, however, had strong secular support from the following: the replacement of the old reichsmark with the deutsche mark, the decontrol of prices, Marshall Plan aid, the expansion generated by the Korean War which accelerated Germany's reentry into the world market, the replacement of destroyed and dismantled industry by efficient new plants and equipment, the repletion of manpower resources by massive emigration out of East Germany and later by the planned migration of workers from southern Europe, the remembrance of two catastrophic inflations—1920 and 1948, union strike and wage restraint, and, of course, the extraordinary adaptability of German employers and the well-trained German labor force.

The social market economy did not preclude the entrenchment of non-government mechanisms of control. "The Germans are equipped with both the business habits and institutions which would allow them to make an easy transition to a planned economy of the modern capitalist type." These include a "highly organized [and] hierarchical system of industrial associations" which "traditionally see themselves as performing an important public role as guardians of the long term interests of the nation's industry," a banking system which is "perhaps the most powerful force making for the centralisation of economic decisions," and the systematic planning bent of modern German industry. In addition, there emerged a public policy and practice endowed with the discriminatory equipment that is necessary for modern, long-term planning. The discriminatory equipment consists of "subsidies, cheap loans provided by the state, and above all, discriminating tax allowances which support favored activities."[3]

The attempt in mid-1966 to dampen inflationary pressures edged the economy into a recession because of, in the OECD view, a failure "to arrive at a suitable policy mix. During most of the period, monetary policy had to carry the whole burden of demand restraint and, to this end, was applied with a severity that led to a substantial fall in investment." In addition, the timing of policy was miscalculated. "Fiscal policy became restrictive at a time when monetary policy had already led to pronounced recessionary tendencies, and the general restriction of demand was reversed too late."[4]

The reversal of the 1966–67 economic decline is associated with the ascendancy of the Grand Coalition between the CDU and the SPD, and more particularly with the SPD Economics Minister, Karl Schiller who initiated a Keynesian type of counter-cyclical fiscal policy via public

3. Shonfeld, *Modern Capitalism*, pp. 245–97 *passim*.
4. OECD, *Economic Surveys—Germany*, Paris, April 1968, p. 5.

spending. Schiller stated: "We are now in the process of developing the partial and ad hoc cyclical and growth policy of the past, which often enough was regrettably not a policy at all, into a system of global control in the sense of a fairly long-run, but simultaneously cyclically flexible 'integral economic and financial policy' " or "a meaningful synthesis between the Freiburg imperative of competition and the Keynesian demand for control of effective aggregate demand."[5] *Business Week* commented, "Germany may go down in economic history as the last major country to be seized abruptly by the basic idea of John Maynard Keynes."[6]

There has been no incomes policy in the formal sense: the price pressure did not justify it and central controls would have encountered strong resistance by unions and employers. A kind of informational incomes policy emerged with the establishment of a Council of Economic Experts which sought influence "only through its reports and their impact on public opinion."[7] Schiller initiated a policy of "concerted action" consisting of "social consultations with the autonomous organisations of employers and labour to establish macro-economic orientation data." Schiller saw concerted action as serving the purpose of orientation, and of maintaining lines of communication with "economic and financial bodies and autonomous groups (the employers and employed in other words) to help them in their own decisions." To him it meant "exchange of information and joint establishment of guideposts."[8] One result of this policy, as a commentary observed, might be that "a gentle compulsion will be felt, originating possibly in public opinion and directed at those who are tempted to step out of line...."[9] The Council of Economic Experts coined the phrase "the magic triangle of economic objectives: price stability, full employment and foreign exchange equilibrium" to describe its policy goals; a commentator has added "growth" as a fourth objective. Full employment is set at 0.8 percent unemployment. Price stability is set at 1 percent difference in prices and growth at 4 percent increase in real GNP.[10]

Social policy comprises social insurance, housing, health care, and education. These benefits are available not only to the poor but to almost

5. Karl Schiller, "Stability and Growth as Objectives of Economic Policy," *German Economic Review*, vol. 5, no. 3 (1967), p. 184.

6. "A New Bounce for German Business," *Business Week*, May 18, 1968, p. 76.

7. H. Giersch, "Discussion," in *The Labour Market and Inflation*, ed. Anthony D. Smith (New York: St. Martin's Press, 1968), p. 184.

8. Schiller, "Stability and Growth," p. 187.

9. "Schiller's Prognostications for 1969," *Deutsches Allgemeines Sontagsblat*, February 2, 1969, in *The German Tribune* (Hamburg), February 25, 1969, p. 10.

10. Horst Albach, "New Trends in the Economic Policy of the Federal Republic of Germany," *German Economic Review*, vol. 7, no. 2 (1969), pp. 118–19.

the entire population.[11] The enactment of old age insurance legislation in 1957 and the further development of social security reform generally may have put Germany in the forefront of social policy in Western Europe.

II

"In scarcely any other country . . . has the labour market changed so radically as in the Federal Republic of Germany."[12] From a condition of mass unemployment caused by the destruction of the German economy and the mass influx of expellees, refugees, and prisoners of war, the German economy moved to less than 1 percent unemployment in the early 1960s. The induced unemployment which brought on the 1966–67 recession reached 2.8 percent at its peak, but by mid-1967 the recession was arrested and unemployment receded to 1.6 percent by early 1968.

Problems of structural adjustment have been created by (a) the continuing contraction of employment in coal, steel, textiles, railroads, and residential construction and (b) the continuing shifts from manual to white collar types of employment and from agriculture to industry, characteristic of advanced economies. Disproportionate unemployment in the heavy industry heartland of the Ruhr and the Saar is a major aspect of these structural shifts, as is regional unemployment in the areas bordering on East Germany caused by the tensions of East-West relationships. Employment for the elderly and the unskilled is still another face of structural adjustment.

The major instrument for labor market administration is the Federal Institute of Labor. The name was changed recently from the Federal Institute for Placement and Unemployment Insurance (Bundesanstalt fur Arbeitsvermittlung und Arbeitsloseversicherung). The Institute traces its formal origins back to 1927, but its postwar history begins with a 1952 law.

The Institute's importance for this study is the "participation of the social partners and the representatives of the public corporations in self management" of a wide range of labor market activities.[13] Unemployment benefit programs administered by the Institute cover temporary unemployment, bad weather, short work weeks, and the "indigent" unemployed. Special costs connected with the search for new employment or with retraining to maintain one's current employment are financed

11. Gaston V. Rimlinger, "Social Change and Social Security in Germany," *Journal of Human Resources*, vol. 3, no. 4 (Fall 1968), p. 419.
12. Hans Klabunde and Karl Joseph Myer, *The Labour Market in the Federal Republic of Germany*, Social Policy in Germany Monograph No. 2, Federal Ministry of Labour (Bonn, 1965), p. 3.
13. *The Federal Institute for Placement and Unemployment Insurance, Organisation and Functions* (Nuremberg: The Institute, 1966), p. 1.

through grants for travel, work clothes, relocation, training, and miscellaneous expenses incurred prior to the receipt of wages; in addition, grants to the employer are available to induce the hiring of low-productivity and long-term unemployed workers. To create employment opportunities, the Institute utilizes unemployment insurance reserves to encourage economic expansion in problem regions and loans and subsidies to construction employers to finance the extra costs of winter construction and experimentation with new construction methods.

The Institute administers the placement office system, as well as specialized placement services for white collar, technical, agricultural, women, and handicapped employees. Provisions are made for inter-district and international recruitment and placement; the latter is most conspicuously demonstrated in the massive ingestion of foreign workers into the labor force. The main training responsibility of the Institute is adult training through training centers operated by technical and vocational schools, unions, employers, and trade associations. The Institute encourages housing construction for special groups—miners, steelworkers, apprentices, nurses, and foreign workers—through grants and low-interest loans. Finally, a vocational guidance program aimed initially at youth and school drop-outs is increasingly concerned with adults and such special groups as the handicapped, "rehabilitands, refugees, persons hard-to-control, ex-convicts," and apprentices.[14]

An Institute for Employment Research was established under the Federal Institute to investigate systematically the current labor market situation and to make it possible for the Federal Institute to consider future developments in the labor market. The research institute's projected fields of research activity include "[1] global and sectoral analyses relating to manpower developments in economic growth, [2] investigations into changes in occupational employment structure . . . by economic sector, [3] business cycle research with particular regard to the labour market, [4] observation of technical developments and their effects on the labour market."[15]

The Institute of Labor is undergoing a fundamental transformation in outlook reflecting the shift in social policy emphasis from the "economically weak" toward a "system" of protection for virtually the entire population. The earlier preoccupation with unemployment is being transformed into an "active employment policy to contribute substantially to a high level of employment and to help promote the general economic growth. . . ." In terms of the Institute's mandate it means that "employees will be assisted by the Federal Institute . . during the whole of their pro-

14. *Ibid.*, p. 31.
15. Federal Institute for Placement and Unemployment Insurance, *Institute for Employment Research* (Erlangen: The Institute, 1968), pp. 1–2 *passim*.

fessional [i.e. occupational] lives. The Institute will advise them in the choice of a trade or profession, look after them during their professional career and assist them in any eventual change of profession so as to enable the individual to keep pace with . . . technological developments and to find a post appropriate to his knowledge and skills."[16] This evolving Institute emphasis has to all intents and purposes been codified in the Manpower Development Law passed in 1969 which, as one Institute executive said, "confirmed the practice we took in the past."

The notable feature of the Institute is "self-administration" which means that the Institute is an autonomous corporation composed of labor, employer, and government representatives subject to "legal supervision by the Ministry of Labour and Social Affairs but only as far as the consideration of law and statute is concerned."[17] The governing bodies are an executive board which deals with broad legal questions, budget, and "rationalisation and organisation," and an administrative council which deals with the labor market policy questions. Each body has thirteen members. Under the central organization, there are 9 regional offices administered by tripartite administrative committees, 146 labor offices, and 558 branch offices. The tripartite principle prevails throughout the Institute structure except for the branch offices and constitutes a vast representational network at all levels.

III

For all practical purposes the trade union movement is the DGB—the German Federation of Labor. In 1964 the sixteen industrial unions affiliated to DGB had about 6.5 million members or about 82 percent of all organized employees. The other unionists are accounted for by the DAG, the salaried employees' union, with about 480,000 members; the DBB, the federation of civil servants, with about 660,000 members; and the CGB, the Christian Trade Union Federation, with a membership of 193,000.

DGB membership has not kept pace with increases in the labor force but the relative decline of the labor force from 38 to 30 percent between 1950 and 1966 is less than the relative decline of manual workers in the labor force from 70 to 59 percent in the same period. There was an absolute decline in union membership (166,000 or 2.6 percent) during 1966 and 1967 which was probably reversed by the subsequent economic upturn. The largest and most influential DGB affiliate is IGM with almost 2 million members or 30 percent of the total DGB membership, followed by the Public Service Transport and Communications Workers with 972,000 or 15 percent, the Chemical, Paper, and Ceramics Workers, with

16. *Labour Market and Labour Management*, Federal Republic of Germany Press and Information Office (Bonn, 1969), p. 12.
17. Federal Institute, *Organisation and Functions*, p. 12.

527,834 or 8.2 percent, and the Construction Workers, with 509,000 or 7.9 percent. The four most populated unions have more than 60 percent of the federation's membership.[18]

The supreme body in DGB is the triennial Congress which elects the president, two vice-presidents, and the members of the managing board who are the heads of DGB departments. The departments are Economic Policy, Finances, Vocational Training, Women, Education, Wage Policy, Social Policy, Organization, Youth, Salaried Employees, Civil Servants, and Information and Publicity. The DGB's executive council consists of the members of the managing board and the heads of each of the sixteen affiliated unions. The DGB is also divided into nine regions which are organized, in turn, into district and local councils.

The DGB has no effective authority over collective bargaining, which is the main responsibility of the affiliated industrial unions, but the fact that each industrial union head is a member of the DGB's executive leads to a DGB role as a clearing house and spokesman. The federation's main influence is as trade unionism's advocate in government, parliament, and public opinion.

The important place occupied by broad social and economic policy in the DGB organization is witnessed by the departmental staff structure, for example, economic policy, vocational training, social policy, etc., and by the establishment of a corporately separate Economic Research Institute with a professional staff of twenty.[19] The Institute stresses basic research which includes periodic reports on economic, labor market, and wage developments. The Institute has become increasingly concerned with the methods and goals of governmental forecasts and global controls. Codetermination has involved the Institute in "providing a scientific foundation for the trade union demand for [its] extension." The Institute has also exerted "very great efforts . . . to supplying the bases of the political considerations underlying the reforms" of the social security system and the implications of structural change for labor market reform. With respect to the latter, the Institute is studying the effect of technological change on occupational requirements. Beyond "pure research," the Institute renders technical assistance on trade union questions. The scientific members of the staff are standing members of the consultative and executive committees of the DGB, such as Wages Policy, Economic Policy, and Social Policy committees.

The Institute stresses the importance of its role in imparting an "objective, even scientific" character to trade union policies. "Under strict observance of the universally valid laws of scientific integrity and objec-

18. U.S. Department of Labor, "Trade Union Membership Development Lags," *Labor Developments Abroad*, August 1968, pp. 4–6.

19. Heinz Markmann, "The Economic Research Institute of the Trade Unions (WWI)," *DGB Report* (Dusseldorf), no. 9 (1968), p. 106.

tivity, but by no means dwelling in the 'ivory tower' of unworldly science for science' sake, the Institute places itself at the service of DGB policy and bases itself on the recognition of the fact that, in an increasingly complicated world, policy decisions call for the most analytical and diagnostic preparations."[20]

One observer has suggested that what DGB wanted was "the pride of founding a research institute. . . . But they just didn't know what to do with it." There are indications, however, that the Institute is becoming increasingly oriented to more immediate union needs.

The German Productivity Center known by its German initials, RKW, has no organic connection with the DGB or the trade union movement but is, nevertheless, strongly influenced by trade union views and activity. RKW is a research, training, and consulting organization which encourages productivity improvement, or "rationalisation" (to use the term popularized in the Weimar era by Dr. Walter Rathenau, the intellectual progenitor of the center).

RKW is now an autonomous agency financed by the government. Yet union involvement does exist. A vice-president and board member is a labor member of the board of one of the "codetermined" enterprises, and one of the three "general management" members of RKW who run the center is the former technical head of the DGB Economic Policy Department. The trade unions are further involved in the work of RKW by using it "to obtain scientifically based data in which they are interested." The employers agree to this arrangement "to keep social peace" and to use RKW as an instrument of dealing "with controversial issues in order not to have them develop into strife."[21] The work in labor economics has as its mainspring the balancing of the "diverging interests of industry—aiming at maximisation of profit, and labour—striving for a larger share of the national product." The aspects which the labor economics unit deals with are listed as (1) technical and social change (automation), (2) efficiency of the business organization, (3) labor and the social sciences, (4) labor market, structure of the labor force, and labor potential, and (5) training and supplementary training—as determined by the need existing at the level of the workplace, firm, and economy.[22] The methods which RKW utilizes to achieve these aims are "to stimulate research by giving money . . ., to teach courses to develop methods in plant management and . . . personnel, i.e. to give management certain hints to develop better personnel relations."[23]

The unions influence RKW in the choice of research themes. For example, the pressure for the study of automation's impact and for

20. *Ibid.*, pp. 105–8 *passim.*
21. Interview with Hans Buttner, Manager, RKW, Frankfurt, June 28, 1968.
22. RKW, *Review of Major Activities, 1965–66* (Frankfurt), p. 4.
23. Interview with Buttner.

remedial efforts to offset its effects has come largely from the labor movement. Little has been done in this area, for this kind of research is generally not undertaken by continental universities because they fear that it threatens their academic status. In addition, it usually cannot be pursued by unions, since their professional staff deals mainly with legislation. Only IGM has a department for automation and is thus a major influence in the selection of RKW projects. For most of the other unions the task is to get them "to recognize the problem exists."[24]

IV

The style, the rhetoric, and the long-range goals of the DGB are cast in the socialist mold. DGB's Basic Programme (1963) rings out with "the solidarity of the working classes" and "the social struggle."[25] Ludwig Rosenberg, the former DGB president, sees trade unionism as going beyond "those tasks which are generally considered to be the traditional tasks." Trade unionism must "regard itself as a part of that great liberation movement of all mankind."[26]

But Rosenberg's socialism has been qualified by the grim realities of Germany's recent history. Rosa Luxemburg is cited with approval because "she knew that tactics and revolutionary gestures were no substitute for a clear conception of what was necessary. . . . The ancient formulas have lost their magic. . . . Neither the old type of Liberalism in the economy and in society, nor the old formulas of Marxism, whether of the Moscow or Peking school, can evade the impact of a rapidly changing world."[27] The middle position between American market unionism and French class-warfare unionism is taken by Heinz Vetter, the DGB's new president. "The trade unions . . . consider themselves as an 'integrating constituent' and as a guarantor of the system which, however, will need to be so developed as to ensure a more equitable distribution of wealth and the participation of the workers on the basis of equality on all decisions affecting them."[28]

Georg Leber, formerly president of I.G. Bau and now in the SPD government, was among the most explicit modern "revisionists" of trade unionism's socialist tradition. Nationalization is opposed because the employee gains nothing by "an alteration . . . in the ownership structure of the undertaking in which he is employed." The trade union's job, Leber said, is "to actively look after the interests of labour without looking to

24. *Ibid.*
25. DGB, *Basic Programme of the Trade Union Federation* (Dusseldorf, 1963), p.3.
26. Ludwig Rosenberg, "The Great Uneasiness," pt. 1, *DGB Report*, no. 6/7 (1968), p. 73.
27. *Ibid.*, pt. 2, *DGB Report*, no. 8 (1968), p. 91.
28. Heinz Vetter, "Trade Union Self-Examination," *DGB Report*, no. 3/4 (1970), p. 27.

the left or right. . . . [We must] not permit ourselves to be maneuvered into any pseudo-radical and pseudo-political policy consisting of demonstrations."[29]

Representative of a more leftward pull in DGB is Otto Brenner, the head of IGM, the largest union. Observers are referring to Brenner when they note that some trade unions "are more radical and dogmatic than the party," (for example, the SPD).[30] Yet the paradox is that, as Brenner himself says, the IGM has been the "pacemaker" union in "successful trade union activity."[31] A historian of the German labor movement has written that Brenner "tried to carry out a meaningful union policy which would avoid the extremes of unlimited accommodation on the one hand and impotent resignation on the other while at all times raising the workers' demands to the very limits of what was feasible."[32]

What has emerged has been an economic policy which, despite its socialist style and except for the emphasis on codetermination, is mostly welfare statism—that is, full employment, just distribution of incomes and wealth, stability of the currency, prevention of the abuse of economic power, and international economic cooperation within a framework of "both planning and free competition." But the planning must be limited to "detailed overall national economic reports . . . which will lay down the targets" binding only on the "organs of governmental economic policy. . . . The individual sectors and branches of the economy" need only to give "due consideration" to these targets in reaching their "free and independent decisions." Otherwise the "methods of economic policy" are fiscal policy, controlled investments, "publicly owned and cooperative undertaking as a controlling and corrective medium in the economy," and the control of economic power to prevent abuse. [33]

The right of "free and independent" decision has special application to workers and unions in the DGB program. Workers must have "a free and unfettered choice of employment, of occupation and of . . . apprenticeship" and "the right to join a trade union. . . . The trade union's right to strike is inviolable," and "any and every attempt by the state to intervene in the process of free collective bargaining is impermissable," as is "every form of compulsory arbitration."[34]

29. Georg Leber, *Our Objectives* (Frankfurt: Industriegewerkschaft Bau Steine-Erden, 1965), pp. 25, 33.

30. David Childs, *From Schumacher to Brandt* (London: Pergammon Press, 1966), p. 69.

31. Otto Brenner, "Organisation, Aims and Objects of the Metal Workers' Union," *DGB Report*, no. 10 (1968), p. 126.

32. Helga Grebing, *The History of the German Labour Movement* (London: Wolff, 1969), p. 178.

33. DGB, *Basic Programme*, pp. 11–12.

34. *Ibid.*, p. 16.

Codetermination partakes of socialism in that it seeks to give "equality for the representatives of the workers in the controlling organs of the great undertakings,"[35] but falls short of socialism in that "the German trade unions have quite deliberately refrained from demanding in principle the abolition of private enterprise: their endeavor has been, rather, to improve the existing order of society from within."[36] Moreover, codetermination falls short of classic socialist doctrine in not seeking "the imposition of a crude and rigid form of democracy," a device to replace "one control group by another." Codetermination is intended to take account "not only of the workers alone, but of the whole community."[37]

The DGB advances three reasons for promoting codetermination: (1) "to restrict existing positions of power and to subject them to effective control," (2) to humanize "the whole of our social and economic life," that is, the workshop as not only "a place of production" but also "a place of human associations," and (3) to put "formal democracy" into practice "in a decisively important sphere of life."[38] It is likely, a DGB statement asserted in 1950, that "the political upheaval of 1933 would not have occurred if political democracy had been bolstered by genuine economic democracy."[39]

The end of ideology for the trade union movement, or at least its deemphasis, has its analogue in union-party relationships. Historically, Germany represented the ideal type of socialist party tutelage over the unions. The postwar transformation of the unions into autonomous organizations represents the lessons drawn from the pre-war experience regarding the fragmenting effects of unions tied too closely to political ideologies. The transformation consists of the depoliticization of both the unions and the SPD. The depoliticization of the unions has meant severing trade unionism's formal ties with the SPD, and the SPD's depoliticization has converted an ostensible working class party into an essentially classless party appealing to all sections of the society.

The Social Democratic trade unionists who by every count are the preponderant political group "have been prepared to exchange trade union unity for formal political neutrality."[40] In return, the traditional denominational unions gave up their separate institutional existence to move into the DGB although "the socialists and Catholics still retain their separate

35. "DGB May Manifesto," *DGB Report*, no. 2 (1969), p. 14.
36. DGB, *Codetermination Rights of the Workers in Germany* (Dusseldorf, 1967), p. 80.
37. Wilhelm Haferkampf, *Codetermination in the Basic Programme of the German Trade Unions* (Dusseldorf: DGB, 1964), pp. 18-19.
38. *Ibid.*, pp. 20-22 *passim*.
39. Cited in Adolf Sturmthal, *Unity and Diversity in European Labor* (Glencoe, Ill.: Free Press, 1953), p. 186.
40. Childs, *From Schumacher to Brandt*, p. 68.

identities in the DGB."[41] Depoliticization has meant most concretely the end of the substantial financial support which the union movements gave to their parties. It has not meant the end of the dominant role of the socialists in the DGB and in the affiliated unions. Nor has it meant neutrality on political issues.

It is now even possible for the union to conceptualize the diversity of interest between union and party. "In the degree to which the workers' parties develop into governmental and all-embracing people's parties," Ludwig Rosenberg has said, "to a similar degree differences arise in the appraisal of many questions—even though agreement on basic principles remains. The job of the trade unions, which is to represent primarily and in particular the interests of the workers, and the problems facing a comprehensive popular party, namely to weigh various claims against each other, can and do certainly give rise to differences of opinion without prejudice to the common aim."[42]

Depoliticization has, then, converted the SPD from a Marxist party into a welfare state party which has openly abandoned the class struggle and nationalization as major doctrines. Karl Schiller, the SPD's leading economic authority, has lauded "the dynamics of [a] market economy as an inalienable part of a libertarian economic order."[43] The doctrinal gap between the SPD and the other parties to the right has been narrowing: according to Willy Brandt, "in a sound and developing democracy," it is "the norm rather than the exception, that the parties put forward similar, even identical demands in a number of fields." He says that the parties are divided not so much by substance as by priorities, "accents," and methods.[44] "Nowadays no one is in doubt that the SPD can carry on an economic policy which conforms to market trends and that the party wants to do this."[45]

The method and style of the SPD is also in marked contrast with its past. SPD no longer sees the day of socialism as an overriding vision. "We need aims and objects: We must plan for the future." But, Brandt has said, "there is no purpose in simply offering Utopias. The people whose confidence we are striving to get expect a policy of practical reason, not revolutionary acrobatics."[46]

41. Sturmthal, *Unity and Diversity*, p. 209.
42. Ludwig Rosenberg, "Trade Unions and the Political Parties," *DGB Report*, no. 10 (1968), p. 116.
43. Quoted in Otto Kirchheimer, "Germany—The Vanishing Opposition," in *Political Oppositions in Western Democracies*, ed. R. A. Dahl (New Haven: Yale University Press, 1966), p. 245.
44. *Ibid.*, pp. 246–47.
45. "SPD Economics Causes No Fear," *Handelsblatt*, October 16, 1969, in *The German Tribune*, November 4, 1969, p. 10.
46. Willy Brandt, "Political Guidelines for the '70's," *DGB Report*, no. 5 (1970), p. 14.

Differences between the SPD and the DGB developed over the pro-market economics and wage guideline tendencies of Minister Schiller and the weakened support of the SPD for codetermination. Schiller's association with Germany's economic advance after the 1966–67 recession and an appreciation of the compromises necessary to produce an SPD government have so far muted both criticisms. Earlier strains in DGB-SPD relationships were caused by doubts in many union circles as to whether the Grand Coalition partner, the CDU, was a reliable democratic ally. In this period Brandt castigated the DGB left "more than any other [SPD] party leader before him for its obstructive intransigence in many fields."[47]

Despite formal neutrality and differences between party and trade union interests, there is an underlying spirit of accord between SPD and DGB. A large proportion of the 40 percent or so trade unionist members of the Bundestag belong to the SPD and, in fact, act as parliamentary spokesmen for trade union interests. In the first year of the SPD-led government the relationship between the government and the unions has been regarded as excellent by both sides. The easy access to the Chancellor, the Chancellor's willingness to listen, the presence of trade unionists in important cabinet posts, and the labor movement's strong identification with the Federal government have been major influences cementing union-party-government relationships and, in general, making the movement more responsive to national economic policy than if there had been a hostile government in power.

V

The DGB regards itself as the prime mover for both the concept and implementation of an active manpower policy. Mid-1966 is marked as the watershed year of manpower policy. The downturn which began in this period dramatized the imperfections in labor market policy and organization. Prior to SPD participation in the Grand Coalition there was in the DGB view a "complete lack of any active manpower policy."[48] In 1964 DGB had suggested that the RKW do research "on qualitative and quantitative labor force projections." The proposal was rejected by the Economics Minister at that time on the ground that "a policy of prognosis and projection would be incompatible with the free undertakings and free economy in this country." Failing in this period to gain government acceptance of a labor market policy, the DGB "tried to do something on the international level with the OECD, ILO and the Common Market."[49]

47. "The Umbrellas of Nuremberg," *The Economist* (London), March 23, 1968, p. 37.
48. W. Henklemann, "Germany," in *International Trade Union Seminar on Active Manpower Policy, Supplement to the Final Report* (Paris: OECD, 1963), p. 138.
49. Interview with W. Henklemann, DGB, Expert on manpower policy, Dusseldorf, August 11, 1969.

The "active labor market" policy is described as "one big concept" which integrates "economic policies together with labor market policies. . . . A policy instrument must be developed that in the event there is imbalance in the economy measures can be taken or foreseen to level off the depths and heights."[50] DGB claims much of the credit for the reorientation of labor market policy as evidenced in the new Labor Promotion Act. The reorientation is "from the principle of repairing damage once done . . . [to] the principle of preventing damage before it occurs." This approach, DGB adds, "creates, in fact, the conditions necessary for influencing the labour market in a positive and preventive manner."[51]

There are two caveats which the trade union view asserts with respect to manpower policy: (1) "Parliament is responsible for economic and manpower policy." The trade unions "cannot relieve the politicians of this responsibility, nor do we wish to do so."[52] (2) The question of centralized government authority under an active manpower policy "gives rise to a number of special problems" in the light of German experience between 1933 and 1949. There must be no "infringement on the rights of the workers. There is a further danger . . . of the working man being regarded as an 'economic factor' or a 'potential' and 'regimented' or 'administered' by a government department."[53] Even if policy formulation belongs to parliament, the government policy implementation may properly be subject to self-administration. "The administrative rights of the state are . . . conferred on those chiefly concerned."[54]

In the DGB view, "the Federal Institute has proved to be an excellent instrument" for the administration of manpower policy. It is "fully autonomous" and is "empowered to make actual decisions."[55] The participation of the union representatives in the "self-administration" of the Federal Institute is by all accounts real and effective. For example, "DGB sometimes has more ideas than the Federal Institute administration can digest."[56] It was on DGB's initiative "after the Federal government had not taken up the problem that the research institute was set up."[57]

Even though there are "natural differences" between the employer and union representatives, there is not, an employer representative observed,

50. *Ibid.*
51. Wilhelm Musa, "The Labour Promotion Law (AFG) of 1969 as the Basis of an Active Labour Market Policy," *DGB Report*, no. 5 (1970), p. 38.
52. Henklemann, "Germany," p. 137.
53. *Ibid.*, p. 137.
54. Hermann Beermann, "The Trade Union Attitude toward an Active Manpower Policy," in *International Trade Union Seminar on Active Manpower Policy, Final Report*, (Paris: OECD, 1964), pp. 156–57.
55. Henklemann, "Germany," pp. 138–43 *passim*.
56. Interview with W. Henklemann, DGB, Expert on manpower policy, Dusseldorf, June 26, 1968.
57. Interview with Henklemann (1969).

"a collective bargaining atmosphere" on the Executive Board. Much of the discussion is on an "objective basis."[58] The union and employers are able to unite against the government on the continuing issue of how labor market activities should be financed. A DGB spokesman takes the position that "labor market policy is a matter for the entire population not only the workers. If that is the case it must be financed by the community—by tax funds. We have had bad experience with these [unemployment] funds when they were confiscated by the Nazi regime."[59]

A case in point on the social partners vs. the government was the "bitter tug of war . . . behind the scenes" over the Manpower Development Law. The difficulties were "not so much in the bill itself as in the familiar matter of who is going to raise the necessary cash." Hans Katzer, the Labor Minister, was thinking of the Institute which "was not exactly overjoyed . . . and suggested in turn that the expense involved should be covered by the Federal budget or by contributions from industry." One of the Katzer proposals would have built up special reserves "from surplus revenue which in time of crisis, as in 1966–67, would help bridge dangerous gaps [in] the labour market." The Institute's fear was that these reserves would "encroach upon the Institute's management of its own affairs, causing its working capital to be soon exhausted. For its part the legislature was probably thinking of the memorable 'Sable tower' [Anton Sable was president of the Institute] of over 6 billion marks in reserves."[60]

Educational policy is an important social policy objective despite some public criticism that it lies outside of the normal bounds of trade unionism. From the DGB standpoint, educational policy is critically relevant to the strengthening of the democratic structure. The prevailing focus "of all forms of education . . . [on] university entrance . . . is based on traditional conceptions of social advance." DGB counters this traditional educational philosophy with proposals for a "fundamental reform of the system." The key to "fundamental reform" is the comprehensive school "which will provide all pupils with a type of education corresponding to their talents and interests."[61] "Full integration" of adult education in the system is important in the "education of men of democratic ideas and needs."[62] The long-standing collective bargaining demand for paid educational leave is trade unionism's attempt to implement this principle in part.

In vocational education (a topic important enough to be included in the DGB's 1969 May Day Manifesto), the great emphasis is on updating and

58. Interview with Rolf Weber, BDA, Cologne, June 24, 1968.
59. Interview with Henklemann (1968).
60. "Hans Katzer's labour bill gains wider acceptance," *Deutsches Allgemeines Sontagsblatt*, April 20, 1969, in *The German Tribune*, May 6, 1969, p. 5.
61. Wolfgang Schleicher, "Special Paid Leave for Educational Purposes, and Educational Policy," *DGB Report*, no. 5/6 (1967), p. 47.
62. *Ibid.*, p. 49.

reforming traditional concepts. Labor market forecasts should provide the basis for rational vocational guidance for both young people and adults. In addition, modernization requires restructuring of vocational education. The DGB and IGM have presented an alternative to traditional methods in the form of "phased training". Phase one will provide a foundation in vocational education which will be the same for all young people; phase two will provide training in five broad craft groups to advance the ultimate goal of training a craftsman; and phase three will undertake to turn out "a fully qualified craftsman." In-plant training is "in many instances completely unsatisfactory." Regulations are needed to "ensure the suitability of the place of training" in the enterprise and "an adequate system of control to enforce compliance" with proper training standards. Existing standards require eight hours of instruction in schools away from the plant, but six hours is the actual amount spent, "at a time when theoretical training to say nothing of personal and social education are acquiring ever increasing importance." Beyond this "a system of adult vocational training is necessary."[63]

A DGB spokesman on vocational education pointed with pride to the enactment in 1969 of a comprehensive vocational training law bringing together in one integrated system training, supplementary training, and retraining. Of special importance to the trade unions is the provision for "scientific research into vocational training . . . to adapt the system . . . to changes in technology, the economy and society."[64] Also important are the provisions for union representation on vocational education committees at the federal, Länder, and regional levels and for a Federal Institute for Research on Vocational Education. The new law is still regarded as inadequate in the degree of codetermination and in central administration by the labor ministry.

The labor movement is severely critical of apprenticeship as a backward "Hans Sachs" type of apprenticeship system, as one DGB spokesman put it. It is too rigid in its structure, and does not adjust flexibly to modern technological change. Apprenticeship in the handicraft and artisan employment has little training value and is a thinly disguised cover for substandard wages. The combination of early school leaving and virtual universality of apprenticeship has the effect of perpetuating closed class patterns. Apprenticeship has traditionally been regarded as a teacher/learner relationship "so that the apprentice receives a grant rather than a wage." The unions argue that apprenticeship is really "an employer/worker relationship" calling for the payment of a wage or salary

63. Maria Weber, "On the Future of Vocational Training," *DGB Report*, no. 1 (1969), p. 15.
64. Trante Pütz, "The Vocational Training Law," *DGB Report*, no. 9/10 (1969), p. 74.

to be laid down in collective agreements.[65] The absence of effective union participation subjects apprenticeship to the authoritarian control of the employer classes. A DGB draft law opposed by employers would transfer direction of apprenticeship from the employer chambers to vocational education boards at the Länd and local level with worker, employer, youth, and teacher representation.

The German labor movement is itself a significant producer of vocational training. The DGB operates 100 vocational training schools. Other affiliated unions involved include the Construction Workers which operates residence schools and correspondence courses in construction skills; Postal Workers and Railroad Workers; and the unaffiliated Salaried Workers' which offers a major program in the "automation" subjects—electronics and data processing—and in the commercial subjects. The DGB centers also have important programs in these fields as well. Most of these programs receive federal aid to cover approximately one-third of the total expenditures.

The problem of seasonality in the construction industry has become the special interest of the I.G. Bau "which supplied the essential ideas and . . . the decisive impulse" for the enactment of legislation to permit utilization of unemployment insurance funds to promote winter construction.[66] The financial problems of "the additional costs caused by winter work and . . . the loss of wages on days when climatic conditions actually rendered work impossible" were met by "financial support to owners, contractors and building workers and compensation for wages lost owing to inclement weather." The union also proceeded to implement the year-round work objective through collective bargaining, propaganda, and education—that is, technical instructions and advice. The program seems to have resulted in "great reduction in seasonal unemployment. . . . Seasonal dismissals have been virtually abolished in medium-sized and large firms." In addition, a "rapid increase in the number of applications . . . has greatly contributed to a new attitude to winter building."[67]

In general, the trade union specialists in labor market problems see "strict limitations . . . on geographical mobility" measures "since frequent changes of residence have adverse human and psychological effects on the worker and even on his family." They favor putting greater emphasis on the "mobility of the job." With respect to foreign worker importation, "no real integration . . . actually takes place" and there is, it is argued, no real net advantage to using immigrant workers.[68] Nevertheless, the Insti-

65. DGB, *Basic Programme*, p. 35.
66. Leber, *Our Objectives*, p. 34.
67. Jan Wittrock, *Reducing Seasonal Unemployment in the Construction Industry* (Paris: OECD, 1967), pp. 137–44 *passim*.
68. Beermann, "Trade Union Attitude," pp. 147–48.

tute, which was the key agency in organizing the importation of foreign workers, seems to have had the support of the trade union members. On the local level, the trade union representatives "made a very valuable contribution," according to a regional director of the Institute, "in making it clear to the public that we needed the foreign labor."[69] To strengthen the representation of Yugoslav "guest workers," the DGB has arranged a plan with Yugoslav unions to provide "trained Yugoslav trade union functionaries" to Germany. The Yugoslav workers "will be encouraged to join competent German DGB unions with equal rights and duties as German members."[70]

VI

Collective bargaining as the term is commonly used in Germany is carried on between an industrial union and a regional industry federation of employers. The employer's association is part of a vast, highly organized network of employers' associations capped by the Confederation of German Employers Association or BDA. The parties negotiate a master contract (*manteltarif*) covering working conditions and a wage agreement (*lohntarif*). A second level of agreement (*betriebsabkommen*) is negotiated between the individual company and the works council.

German industrial relations law is the most comprehensive in Western Europe.[71] Labor law protects the freedom of association of each side in interest to conclude collective agreements which under specified conditions may be extended to nonunion workers in an industry. Employment terms regulated by law include an elaborate social security system (old age, invalidism, death, sickness, maternity, work injury, unemployment, and family allowance), dismissals as to notice and proper cause, paid holidays, and health and safety. Law also regulates the organization of works councils and codetermination, as well as extension of collective agreements to all employees in a given industry.

"The characteristics that essentially give an organization its bargaining capability have not been prescribed by statute, but have been developed in theoretical discussion and judicial practice." In effect these characteristics—that is, exclusion of employers and employees from the same organization, freedom from control by political parties and religious organizations, acceptance of the strike and lockout, and joint regulation of working conditions—constitute the terms under which legitimate conflict between employees and employers may proceed.[72]

69. Interview with O. G. Schlatte, Vice-President, Landesarbeitsamt, Dusseldorf, June 26, 1968.

70. U.S. Embassy, Bonn, February 6, 1970 Airgram A134, *Annual Labor Report*, p. 20.

71. OEEC, *Human Relations in Industry* (Paris, 1956), p. 11.

72. Heinz Markmann, "Incomes Policy in Germany—A Trade Union View," *British Journal of Industrial Relations* (London), November 1964, p. 323.

Judicial regulation of industrial relations in Germany constitutes not only "a general frame of reference for negotiations but also a guide for daily routine decisions and this has created strictly separated areas of autonomous and law bound behavior."[73] Heinz Vetter, the new DGB president, views collective bargaining as being "cribbed, cabined and confined by the judicature."[74]

Employers, on the whole, are viewed by trade union leadership as lacking a "positive outlook" and as "merely tolerating" the unions. Leber urged that "the employers . . . abandon their fight against the trade unions as part of the democratic order, . . . a struggle which is being fought more or less zealously and more or less openly in all branches of industry." The union objective must not be to "change the opposing positions of the employers and workers determined by their different situations." What must be changed "is the enmity itself, the mutual rejection now prevalent, the pushing away or keeping out—that is struggle as a goal by itself."[75] The employers are taxed with resisting collective bargaining at the plant level so that they may preserve their prerogatives.

A writer in the *Frankfurter Allgemeine Zeitung* charges the employers' associations with a "lack of understanding of their functions in the liberal social order." Employer associations "regard their main task as maintaining established structures and guarding against progress. . . . Above all, they have given far too little thought to the question of how employers and unions could help to shape this country's free society and economy. . . . They wait tensely from day to day to see what demands their opponents will come up with, so that they can then react to these demands."[76]

The principle of collective bargaining for social justice—"equal participation . . . of all social groups in the national product provided there is no reduction in the efficiency of the economy and that no one feels that one group has suffered compared with another"—is embodied in union proposals for worker participation in capital formation.[77] The pioneer thinker in this area is Dr. Bruno Gleitze, former director of the DGB's Economic Research Institute, who has argued that wage policy has only limited effectiveness for income redistribution. Accordingly, Gleitze has evolved a plan "to increase capital asset formation in behalf of the workers and

73. Friedrich Fürstenberg, "Workers' Participation in the Federal Republic of Germany," *International Institute for Labour Studies Bulletin* (Geneva), June 1969, pp. 96–97.

74. Heinz O. Vetter, "The DGB on the New Federal Government," *DGB Report*, no. 7/8 (1969), p. 63.

75. Georg Leber, "German Unionism's First Century: The Balance Sheet," *AFL-CIO Free Trade Union News* (Washington, D.C.), August 1963, pp. 3–7.

76. Ernst Günter Vetter, "Unions and Employers Must Look to the Future," *Frankfurter Allgemeine Zeitung*, July 29, 1968, in *The German Tribune*, August 10, 1968, p. 4.

77. Markmann, "Incomes Policy in Germany," p. 329.

thereby increase their share of the national product."[78] As urged by DGB, the plan aims to (1) "prevent the accumulation of wealth in a few hands," (2) "redistribute wealth and income," and (3) "provide investment funds for industry."[79]

The Leber Plan entails the negotiated allocation of wage increases into an investment fund for additional capital formation in the construction industry with individual workers having shares in the fund's assets subject to withdrawal when they retire or if they become disabled. A major breakthrough on worker savings was achieved in 1969 and 1970 when several important unions, including IGM, negotiated plans ultimately affecting several million blue- and white-collar workers.

The trade union support for worker savings is not, it is emphasized, a substitute for codetermination. Some union leaders are opposed to worker savings schemes in principle because it is a "capitalist subterfuge [of] no use to the employee and . . . suited to cement old structures."[80] On practical grounds, these unions "are not keen to see the workers supplied with a piece of paper which may well bring interest or dividends but which is not ready cash and cannot be used to buy a washing machine."[81]

VII

Germany probably represents for the early postwar years the most conspicuous case of wage restraint by a trade union movement. The factors behind the wage restraint were both institutional and economic. On the economic side, mass unemployment and later immigration of foreign workers, together with high productivity, combined to hold wages down. On the institutional side, the DGB leadership understood very early that Germany's high unemployment rate was due to structural, not cyclical, causes and that the fundamental remedy lay with qualitative changes in patterns of investment.

The DGB leadership in the period of Hans Böchler, its first president, "was prepared to restrain the unions' demands for higher pay."[82] The union leadership in those years was "mainly preoccupied with reorganisation and the improvement of labour's position through political action" to

78. "A Trade Union Plan for Promoting Asset Formation for Workers," *ICF Bulletin* (International Federation of Chemical and General Workers' Unions, Geneva), July–August 1970, p. 28.

79. OECD, Manpower and Social Affairs Directorate, *Non-Wage Incomes and Prices Policy* (Paris, 1966), p. 127.

80. Antonius John, "Walter Arendt, The New Minister of Labour," *Christ und Welt*, November 7, 1969, in *The German Tribune*, December 2, 1969, p. 5.

81. "Give the Workingman a Fair Deal," *Die Zeit*, December 5, 1969, in *The German Tribune*, December 23, 1969.

82. Geoffrey Denton *et al.*, *Economic Planning and Policies in Britain, France and Germany* (London: Allen and Unwin, 1968), p. 279.

exert maximum pressure through collective bargaining.[83] In addition, the traditionally well-organized and disciplined employers' associations had by the early 1950s recaptured the initiative. By all accounts employers' associations were more than a match for the trade union movement which was relatively strong on paper but weak in the underlying support of a rank and file more concerned with protection against unemployment and inflation than with large wage increases.

As the 1960s began, the OECD experts committee reported that "the German trade union movement resembled its counterparts in the United States and the United Kingdom much more closely than it did in 1953." Led by the Metal Workers, collective bargaining concentrated on increasing labor's shares. The unions were no "longer prepared to accept uncritically the argument that wage increases must be kept in line with productivity."[84] Nevertheless, the German unions continued to acknowledge that full employment shifts "the balance of power in the labour market in favour of the unions" and that under such circumstances "the trade unions' wage policy can have particularly important repercussions." Understanding this, the union "executives have managed to demonstrate the limits of trade union power to the officials and members, thereby protecting the economy from damage."[85]

The DGB participation in "concerted action" has represented a guarded acceptance of a legitimate government interest in union wages policy, made easier by Minister Schiller's SPD connection. In principle, DGB has rejected wage guidelines as "endanger[ing] the traditional freedom of bargaining."[86] But the union leadership seems to be "quite satisfied with the practical results of the 'concerted action program.'" The reason is that "for the first time in post-war history, union leaders have gained the impression that they are being treated as equal 'partners' and . . . their arguments are being taken seriously."[87] The 1969 DGB Congress reaffirmed its participation in concerted action but warned that this was not to be interpreted as deterring its freedom of action which it "will defend . . . to the last extremity."[88]

83. William Fellner et al., The Problem of Rising Prices (Paris: OEEC, 1961), pp. 354–55.

84. Ibid., p. 355.

85. Heinz Markmann, "Employers' and Workers' Wage Policies and their Effect on Inflation," in The Labour Market and Inflation, ed. Anthony D. Smith (New York: St. Martin's Press, 1968), pp. 94–95.

86. Heinz Beykirch, "Wages Policy Achievements in the Federal Republic of Germany in 1967," DGB Report, no. 7/8 (1967), p. 51.

87. U.S. Embassy, Bonn, February 10, 1969, Airgram A129, Annual Labor Report, p. 11.

88. Richard Becker, "Balance Sheet of the Munich Federation Congress," DGB Report, no. 3 (1969), p. 26.

Concerted action has been interpreted as "much less an instrument of economic policy with a binding effect than [as] an organisation dealing with social policy whose purpose is first and foremost to bring conflicts of interest to the surface so that they can be dealt with. The success of concerted action rests upon the way it makes pluralism of interests within the economy lose a lot of its aggression."[89]

Beyond concerted action, the DGB insists on the principle of "social symmetry," a phrase coined by Schiller without clear definition, which suggests the need for balance among the classes in the distribution of the national product. Social symmetry has not been achieved. "We have already been kept waiting too long for social symmetry," Heinz Vetter, the new DGB president, told the 1969 DGB Congress, "and we must have it, if only to retain the confidence of our members."[90]

The newest DGB approach is to come to the "concerted action" round table with its own forecasts and a "medium term program" for the period 1969-74 in which it projects a 60.9 percent total increase in salaries and wages.[91] The DGB is now careful to point out that it will not permit concerted action to evolve imperceptibly into a social and economic council. In addition to "social symmetry" the DGB wage policy is not receding from its commitment to investment wages. Schiller's concerted action has diminished in importance somewhat, since under the SPD-FDP government the unions can deal directly with the SPD chancellor. The DGB headquarters has also achieved more direct access to the Ministries of Economics and Finance, which indicates that concerted action is assuming a different form.

In the fall of 1969 an unprecedented wave of wage militancy erupted, marked by a "large number of 'wild' [sic] strikes" and "spontaneous downing of tools."[92] A national DGB spokesman interpreted the situation: "During 1968 in order to make the contribution expected of them towards the revival of the economy the trade unions had pursued a restrained terms and conditions policy." For 1969 the pursuit of a much more energetic "terms and conditions policy" was required.[93] The DGB position has been that a "wage arrears" had developed. In 1969 and 1970 there was a "profits explosion and the accompanying distortion of incomes." Making good these arrears "is compatible with a great deal more price stability than [Germany] has had in the past."[94]

89. "SPD Economics Causes No Fear," p. 12.

90. Heinz O. Vetter, "8th Ordinary Federal Congress of the German Federation of Trade Unions," *DGB Report*, no. 3 (1969), p. 10.

91. U.S. Embassy, *Annual Labor Report* (1969), p. 12.

92. Heinz Beykirch, "Spontaneous Downing of Tools," *DGB Report*, no. 9/10 (1969), pp. 77-78.

93. Bernhard Tacke, "Terms and Conditions Policy 1969—In Retrospect," *DGB Report*, no. 1 (1970), p. 6.

94. Rudolf Henschel, "The Tasks of Economic Policy in the 1970's," *DGB Report*, no. 9 (1970), pp. 74-75 *passim*.

From the rank and file worker's viewpoint, the " 'spontaneous strikes' are a clear and unmistakable indication that the much-vaunted discipline of German workers (often incomprehensible to our colleagues abroad) . . . has its limits" which have been "much more quickly reached than had commonly been supposed." The strikes are a warning against "technocratic interference."[95]

VIII

The union which has been most prominently identified with a collective bargaining approach to the displacement effects of technological change is the Metal Workers. Its president, Otto Brenner, and its director of automation, Günter Friedrichs, operate with a flair very much like that of the leaders of the American UAW. "The German trade unions have repeatedly made it clear," Friedrichs has said, "that they are not against technical progress but in favor of it. In doing so they have recognised the necessity, and indeed the inevitability, of reducing manpower."[96] But there need to be some "indemnities" to "workers who lose their jobs through no fault of their own." The indemnities are not "merely . . . compensation for the hardship suffered by workers" but "first and foremost, a penalty for bad management and an incentive to plan ahead."[97] There is nothing new in "the demand for the formulation of long-term manpower programmes. . . . The basic guidelines for such programmes can be found in most handbooks and primers for modern management techniques. It is rather odd, however, that it is the trade unions which, by introducing contractual penalties, should have to compel employers to take the steps management experts have been advocating for quite some time."[98]

IGM techniques consist of popularizing the issue, developing a general policy, and then seeking to implement the policy in collective agreements. In 1968 IGM called an international conference on the "Computer and the White Collar Worker" and later published the papers presented at the conference. In 1965 the conference topic was "Automation: Risk and Opportunity." Friedrich's office is probably one of the best informed sources on automation in Europe.

IGM stresses the displacement consequences of technological change. Brenner attributed the 1967 recession, "the biggest economic recession of the post-war period," in large part to "rationalisation and labour saving methods." The union calls for "basic sociological research into the impact of modern technology" along the lines of the National Commission on

95. "The Facts about Unofficial Strikes: II Germany," *Free Labour World* (ICFTU, Brussels), April 1970, p. 14.

96. Günter Friedrichs, "Planning Social Adjustment to Technological Change at the Level of the Undertaking," *International Labour Review* (ILO, Geneva), August 1965, p. 5.

97. *Ibid.*, p. 7.

98. *Ibid.*, p. 15.

Technology, Automation and Economic Progress in the United States. But "over and above this, the two sides in industry should solve matters arising in connection with technical problems at plant level."[99]

A model rationalization agreement, drawn up by IGM, establishes a jointly administered "adjustment fund" financed by an employer contribution of 1.5 percent of the monthly payroll. The adjustment fund will finance a specified commitment that "in the event of rationalisation and operational changes the social standards of the workers (manual and non-manual) shall at least be maintained."[100] Rationalization was defined as "changes in the former production processes, techniques of work, organisation of the plant and the work, as well as of manpower needs."[101] The commitment requires the establishment of a joint Committee for Personnel Planning composed of management and works council representatives, supplemented as may be required by "experts." The employer will be required to make quarterly estimates of his manpower situation from which the committee will decide on measures "to provide social safeguards for the workers." If agreement cannot be reached by the committee, the disputed issues will be taken successively to the employer and to the full works committee, and, if no consensus is reached, to a tripartite conciliation authority established under the agreement whose "decision shall be binding." Until the issues are resolved, "the employer cannot effect any changes in personnel within the meaning of the present agreement."

The ameliorative measures in the model agreement aim at minimizing the displacement impact on the existing work force through elimination of overtime, a ban on new hiring, and "even [ing] out temporary fluctuations in labour requirements within the firm" through a Personnel Adjustment Department. Where transfers are made, the transferees, "as far as possible [must] be given equivalent and reasonable work [as defined] carrying at least the same earnings for an equal performance." If transfer is not possible, then the displaced employee must have first claim, respectively, on new jobs in his department, in other departments, and finally in other sections of the enterprise. The employee is entitled to appropriate training within or outside of the firm to maintain his previous earnings opportunity for his new job.

If there are no transfer opportunities at equivalent work and pay, the model contract establishes income protection for the displaced worker

99. Otto Brenner, "Automation and Technological Change in the Federal Republic of Germany," *Computers and Non-Manual Workers*, International Conference, IGM (Frankfurt, 1968), pp. 1–3.

100. IGM, "Draft of a Protective Agreement for Use in the Case of Rationalisation," *Computers and Non-Manual Workers*, International Conference, IGM (Frankfurt, 1968), p. 1.

101. Hans Mayr, "Important Agreements in the Metalworking and Steel Industries Won by the I.G. Metall," *Bulletin of the International Metalworkers' Federation* (Geneva), October 1968, p. 35.

which takes into consideration whether he has been transferred at less than equivalent work, permanently separated with severance pay, or is undergoing training. Its purpose is to compensate the worker during a specified period for the losses that he suffered as a result of change due to "rationalisation."[102]

IGM began to negotiate on these principles with the overall metal employers' association, Gesamtmetall, in February 1968—"the lengthiest negotiations ever to have been conducted in the Federal Republic since 1945."[103] It withdrew demands for a personnel planning committee, a conciliation agency, and an adjustment fund (it felt each employer should "meet the costs himself"). Dismissals due to "economic policy or structural reasons" were excluded from the application of the agreement. Rationalization was defined in the 1968 agreement as "changes in production processes, by the use of equipment and machinery with greater technical efficiency, brought about by the employer, due also to an obligation to follow instructions. This means changes in working techniques through the use of manufacturing installations with greater technical efficiency and considerable reshaping of organisation in the plant intended to save costs, insofar as the immediate effects of these measures are displacements, transfers or regrouping, retraining or dismissals."[104]

Major principles of the model have also been incorporated in an agreement between IGM and the Bavarian Confederation of Metal Employers Association, the Principal Federation of Paper and Cardboard Manufacturers, and the Printing and Paper Workers Union, which deals with advance notice and consultation, job transfers, retraining with maintenance of earnings opportunities, and, in the event of loss of employment, some form of income protection. On the recommendation of the conciliation agency, the agreement included a provision for educational leave of two weeks limited to one percent of the work force in any year.

IX

Below the industry level where workers are represented through union collective bargaining, worker involvement functions at the levels of the enterprise and plant. The key instrumentality for worker involvement at the plant level is the works council, a legal entity in its own right and formally "independent of both management and trade unions." In reality, however, most works council members are union members "and to some extent the trade unions control the activities of the works councils."[105]

102. IGM, "Draft of a Protective Agreement," p. 2.
103. "Review of Wages and Collective Agreements, 1968, in the Federal Republic of Germany," *Economic and Social Bulletin*, (ICFTU, Brussels), January–February, 1969, p. 21.
104. Mayr, "Important Agreements," p. 37.
105. Fürstenberg, "Workers' Participation," pp. 116–17.

The works council exercises co-decisionmaking with management; that is, it effectively engages in the negotiation of such terms as "daily hours of work and breaks, . . . work rules, . . . piece work rates," and also vocational training, plant welfare, and the administration of the collective agreement. In many respects, it acts as the enforcement arm of both the industrywide agreement and the statutory labor standards. With respect to "personnel and managerial matters," the works council has the right only to information and, in rare instances, the right to protest and appeal to the labor court. The works council must be heard by the employer before mass recruitment and dismissals are put into effect, and disagreements may be appealed to the labor court. "Codetermination at [the] establishment level . . . has the full approval . . . of all social groups including the employers."

Worker involvement at the level of the enterprise functions through representatives from "the top-level trade union organisation" on the Board of Supervision and a labor director from the trade unions on the Board of Management.[106] This degree of worker involvement is to be found only in the mining and iron and steel industries, and its extension to all large-scale enterprise is the key and almost overriding demand of the trade union movement.

The social plan is a program negotiated between the management and union and/or works council to ameliorate the effects of any major change. An especially comprehensive social plan has been negotiated on the government-owned railroads which includes a study of the characteristics of the employees affected by change and the opportunity to examine each displacement case separately in terms of reemployment and protection of earnings opportunities.[107] Protective clauses against displacement have been negotiated in printing (emphasizing guarantee against job loss due to technological change) and in textiles (emphasizing the protection of older workers).

Worker involvement at the level of the enterprise has probably made for greater participation in the daily personnel and manpower actions, especially those associated with short-run technological change and other forms of rationalization. The "best" social plans, for example, have been developed in the codetermined industries of iron, steel, and coal mining.[108] Very likely "every employee has gained certain fundamental rights ensuring the protection of his vital interests."[109]

106. F. Farthmann, "The Various Forms of Codetermination in Germany," *DGB Report*, no. 3 (1969), p. 35.

107. Jack Stieber, *Manpower Adjustments to Automation and Technological Change in Western Europe* (E. Lansing: Michigan State University, School of Labor and Industrial Relations, 1966), p. 91.

108. *Ibid.*, p. 93.

109. Fürstenberg, "Workers' Participation," p. 147.

But on the whole, worker representation at the shop floor level has lacked the power to be more than a peripheral or marginal influence on enterprise policies. The limiting influences are bureaucratization, cooptation by management, and the ambivalent relationship of the shop floor to the unions. With respect to the more extensive form of codetermination in iron, steel, and mining, "the trade unions have made rather limited use of the power given to them by law. . . . Those who are obliged to manage adopt management ways of thought."[110] Overall, the major influence of the various forms of worker and union participation at the level of the enterprise has been rather more formal than operational. This is not to discount it unduly; even the formal effects have been important in giving the workers and the unions a sense of importance after one of being outsiders.

X

The broad context for trade union involvement in general interest issues has been formed by the recoil from National Socialism, the agonizing process of reconstruction, the achievement of the German "miracle," and the ascendancy of SPD to governmental power. Management of the labor market through the Federal Institute of Labor represents the most systematic form of trade union involvement. Although the point is frequently made that the Institute is only an instrument of administration, not policy, which is made by the Bundestag and the government, the Institute has, in fact, hewn out policies on its own initiative which, as in the instance of the most recent Manpower Development Law of 1969, are then confirmed by parliamentary enactments. The direction of policy has been toward the transformation of the Institute from an unemployment office into a broad instrument of manpower policy; this is symbolized in the change of name from the Federal Institute for Placement and Unemployment Insurance to the Federal Institute of Labor. The principal initiating force in the transformation has been the trade union movement.

Collective bargaining has become an instrument of manpower policy to cope with the displacement effects of technological change and other forms of rationalization. Here the role of IGM as the leading and largest industrial union has been central. IGM strategy is not simply to negotiate individual adjustments but to initiate and gain public acceptance of wholesale approaches to the rational administration of change. Collective bargaining became an instrument of wage policy as manifested in the self-imposed strike and wage restraint practiced by the unions during the reconstruction and recovery period. "The unions were conscious of the necessity to avoid wage increases which might diminish the number of jobs

110. *Ibid*.

available and were satisfied to accept a slowly increasing level of real income."[111] Capital savings by way of collective bargaining becomes an instrument for income redistribution.

In order to travel the road to "integration" in the democratic society—to involvement in national economic policy—German trade unionism has muted ideological socialism and anticapitalist rhetoric. This is partly the price paid for a unified trade union center but also an open recognition by the unions and the SPD of the diminished relevance of classical socialism to the modern economy. Socialist doctrine has not, of course, been abandoned; but it has, under great tension, been made compatible with incremental change, including the emphasis on collective bargaining as a major vehicle of change. Socialism as the umbrella answer to the economic problem has given way to an attempt—again under tension—to master the economics of the micro-situations in their own special contexts, for example, the labor market, technological change, or incomes policy; and to offer incremental constructive programs, for example, investment wages, winter building, and model rationalization agreements. In effect this means that in policy and program, if not always in explicit doctrine, the trade union movement has come to terms with reformist Keynesianism and its heir, the economics of full employment inflation. The abandonment of orthodox Marxism has enabled the labor movement to grapple with problems of the modern economy more realistically and to find common ground with the nonsocialist elements.

The tension between trade unionism's socialist tradition and its incrementalism has yet to be completely resolved. The tensions imposed by the attempt at resolution create many difficult problems which are manifested in the codetermination question. Codetermination's object of democratizing economic power is, in the light of German history, not exclusively a socialist demand, but there can be little doubt that the high and continuing priority which the issue has enjoyed in the postwar period stems in large part from the commitment to socialism as a creed. This need not have been a serious problem if codetermination could be satisfactorily identified with improved efficiency and morale. Even the strongest supporters, however, do not argue this with conviction. The effect of codetermination, then, is to interpose an extra ideological block to full acceptance of the trade unions as partners by the powerful nonsocialist elements among the employers and the political parties for purposes which do not seem to be strongly related with real union or working class power. In the case of the employers, codetermination reinforces a traditional resistance, also chiefly ideological, to an effective union presence on the shop floor.

The features of the German industrial relations structure which enhance the trade union capability to act cohesively in national economic policy

111. Fellner *et al.*, *Problem of Rising Prices*, p. 336.

are industrial unionism, freedom from rival unionism, and industrywide bargaining. The presence of a sympathetic political party in power encourages trade union forbearance up to a point, achieves a measure of coordination between union and public policy, and reduces the union fear of political vulnerability. The first year of the SPD-led government is also associated with positive benefits for the trade unions in the form of high wage gains in collective bargaining and improved social security benefits. Internally the unions are developing the research resources essential to support their participation in complex issues of economic and social policy and educational resources to keep their constituents informed.

There are features of the industrial relations structure which seem to impede the trade union involvement in the making of national economic policy. The most important of these is the lack of union penetration on the shop floor which has come about from a variety of influences: (1) "the lack of a coherent idea on which to base their shop-floor activities,"[112] or as put by a recent investigation, "German trade unions . . . have always aimed not so much at having a decisive influence upon the actual work situation within a specific plant as at trying vigorously to influence large-scale social and economic policy";[113] (2) "the considered opinion of German businessmen that trade unions as such should have no direct responsibilities at the plant or company level";[114] and (3) "the bureaucratisation" of shop floor industrial relations, with "negotiations . . . mostly carried out in a strictly juridical manner."[115]

The ability of the unions to influence economic policy is additionally weakened by the large area of employment policy subject to legal regulation rather than to collective bargaining. This need not have a negative effect if the union can call the options between collective bargaining and legislative enactment, as in Sweden; but it is not clear in the German situtation that the trade union movement is in this strategic position. Finally there is the impeding influence exerted by the relatively narrow base of union membership which has been stagnating at somewhere around one-third of the labor force. At this time, though, it is still too early to tell whether the integrative process will be weakened by the sustained inflationary pressure which is affecting most of Europe and, consequently, by rank and file disaffection which usually accompanies prolonged inflation.

On balance, the integrative position of the German trade union movement has been strengthened in the postwar period. The capstone of the integrative process may have been the rise of the SPD to government

112. Grebing, *German Labour Movement*, p. 182.
113. Fürstenberg, "Workers' Participation," p. 97.
114. Siegfried Balke, *Expansion of Codetermination in the Federal Republic of Germany* (Cologne: BDA, 1966), p. 6.
115. Fürstenberg, "Workers' Participation," p. 115.

power. Previously the unions felt like "a force apart in the political life of the country";[116] now, in a significant sense *their* party is in power. The president of the German Railway Workers' Union captured the essence of the change in his setting. "The representatives of a once-persecuted and despised organisation are now members of the controlling body of the German federal railways. . . . Ten members of our organisation are members of the Federal Parliament."[117]

Supplementary References

Dahrendorf, Rolf. *Society and Democracy in Germany*. New York: Doubleday and Co., Anchor Books, 1969, pp. 156–87.

De Schweinitz, Dorothea. *Labor-Management Consultation in the Factory*. Honolulu: University of Hawaii, Industrial Relations Center, 1966, pp. 23–36.

DGB. *The Educational Activities within the German Federation of Labour*. Bonn, 1964.

Edelman, Murray, and Fleming, R. W. *The Politics of Wage-Price Decisions*. Urbana: University of Illinois Press, 1965, pp. 82–143.

ILO. *Labour and Automation: Manpower Adjustment Programmes*. Vol. 1, *France, Federal Republic of Germany, United Kingdom*. Geneva, 1967, pp. 81–130.

Kerr, Clark. "Collective Bargaining in Postwar Germany." In *Contemporary Collective Bargaining*, edited by Adolf Sturmthal. Ithaca: New York State School of Industrial and Labor Relations, Cornell University, 1957.

Selekman, Benjamin, *et al. Problems in Labor Relations*. New York: McGraw-Hill, 1964, pp. 713–20.

Sturmthal, Adolf. *Workers Councils*. Cambridge: Harvard University Press, 1964, pp. 53–85.

Tilford, R. B., and Preece, R. J. C. *Federal Germany: Political and Social Order*. London: Wolff, 1969, pp. 84–105.

Williams, Lady Gertrude. *Apprenticeship in Europe*. London: Chapman and Hall, 1963, pp. 17–47.

116. Jean Daniel Reynaud, "The Role of Trade Unions in National Political Economies–Developed Countries of Europe," in S. Barkin *et al., International Labor* (New York: Harper and Row, 1967), p. 47.

117. Philipp Seiberg, "The German Railway Workers of Europe," *DGB Report*, no. 2 (1968), p. 21.

CHAPTER SIX

United Kingdom: In Transition

The economic situation in Great Britain, characterized by full and nearly full employment most of the time, has been dominated by the search for a workable policy to counteract the persistent inflation, recurring international payments crises, and sluggish economic growth. Policy has been directed toward increases in productivity and the control of growth in domestic demand. Major impediments to productivity improvement have been commonly identified as the uneconomic practices of unions and the arrested development of management technique. The inadequacies of the economic performance, in OECD words, "have to do with the supply, deployment and use of manpower—persistent shortages of skills, uneven distribution of job opportunities between regions and frequently too an attitude of reluctance to come to terms with industrial and technological change, leading to wasteful use of manpower and retard[ed] productivity."[1]

This chapter is organized around five major policy areas in which the unions have been involved, namely: economic planning at the levels of the economy and of industry, training, incomes policy, and industrial relations. In addition, the Labour Party-government-trade union interaction is examined as part of the process of union involvement in policy.

II

Economic planning in the postwar period began with the efforts of the Labour government's Sir Stafford Cripps to promote industrial modernization through tripartite development councils. A change in government in 1951 and lack of management support ended this experiment. In 1962 the Conservative government, influenced by the apparent success of French "indicative" planning and prodded by a balance-of-payments crisis, under-

---

1. OECD, Manpower and Social Affairs Committee, "Manpower Policy in the United Kingdom: Report by the United Kingdom Authorities," mimeographed (Paris, 1968), p. 1.

took to establish a tripartite National Economic Development Council as "effective machinery for the coordination of plans and forecasts for the main sectors of our economy."[2] It was to be "under 'the aegis of but not in' the Government."[3] As distinguished from typical advisory committees, NEDC "was established deliberately to act as a new pressure group."[4] The mandate given to the council was:

> (a) To examine the economic performance of the nation with particular concerns for plans for the future in both the private and public sectors of industry.
> (b) To consider together what are the obstacles to quicker growth, what can be done to improve efficiency and whether the best use is being made of our resources.
> (c) To seek agreement upon ways of improving economic performance, competitive power and efficiency; in other words, to increase the sound rate of growth.[5]

The new Labour government established the Department of Economic Affairs (DEA) to take over the planning function. NEDC was now to serve "as an outside body in which representatives of industry and commerce can discuss the Government's economic plans at the various stages of their formulation and can discuss more generally policies directed to securing economic growth, particularly those dependent on the understanding and cooperation of industry, and finally, a body to provide a proper channel of communication with various industries for the purpose of securing that the implications of the National Plan are understood in each industry. . . ."[6] A reorganization in the fall of 1969 abolished DEA and many of its functions were transferred to the Board of Trade.

As an avowed socialist movement, "trade unionists play a positive role in planning, a role which they have sought for many years."[7] Moreover, their ideology does not preclude planning under "capitalism." Trade union economic theory, as we piece it together, is willing to accept the common economic analysis of the situation which Britain finds itself in, but with somewhat different policy emphases. The TUC acknowledges that the full employment era "is a whole new environment within which trade unions

2. Selwyn Lloyd, quoted in Richard Bailey, *Managing the Economy* (London: Hutchinson, 1968), p. 19.

3. Geoffrey Denton *et al.*, *Economic Planning and Policies in Britain, France and Germany* (London: Allen and Unwin, 1968), p. 117.

4. *Ibid.*, p. 113.

5. Lloyd, quoted in Bailey, p. 19.

6. *Ibid.*, p. 26.

7. TUC, *Trade Unionism* (London, 1966), p. 9.

now operate and that almost every problem . . . [bears] some relation to the characteristics of an economy operat[ing] permanently at a very high level of demand. . . . It is still only a relatively short time ago, and within the working lifetime of the majority of trade unionists that full employment became a permanent feature of industrial life."[8] TUC recognizes further that "sustaining full employment, restraining inflation, balancing overseas payments, preserving the value of sterling" and "at the same time sustaining the rate of economic growth" are often in "apparent conflict" and difficult to reconcile.[9]

It is additionally conceded that "if we are to be in planning we have to give as well as take. . . . If we believe in having a planned system of society, it does not mean freedom with licence. It means freedom under control, and everybody, every member of any trade union, has got to acknowledge the difficulties and responsibilities of his fellow trade unionists. We must be able to work out a plan in which we all play a part, not just those people who have the greatest economic strength. . . . People who have got the strength will assist people who have not got the strength."[10]

It is possible, however, that "rapid economic growth can, past a certain point, be too costly." The union is after all a "protective" institution and is unwilling "to pay *any* price for possible benefits. It is not the agent of *any* programme which discounts the present in favor of the future. . . . Trade unions by their actions reflect the extent to which working people prefer jam today to more jam tomorrow."[11]

Trade union theory departs from the government's in rejecting "the proposition that if Britain runs into economic difficulties the only thing that gives way is the level of employment." In 1968 the TUC, unlike the government, found that the level of unemployment was "intolerable, apart from being a waste of the resource of manpower that we have so often been told is in short supply." The essential condition for getting workers to cooperate for higher productivity is "full employment"; otherwise, workers "know that they will simply be working themselves out of jobs."[12]

In defense, the TUC has constructed an economic analysis which seeks to broaden the focus of economic policy away from the excessive preoccupation with the balance of payments. The balance of payments must not continue to override all other goals,[13] which include, in the TUC view,

8. *Ibid.*, p. 51.
9. *Ibid.*, p. 7.
10. S. F. Greene, in TUC, *1968 Report*, London, pp. 502–4 *passim.*
11. TUC, *Trade Unionism*, p. 76.
12. Greene, in TUC, *1968 Report*, p. 503.
13. TUC, *1969 Report*, London, p. 347.

regional development, investment allocation, updating of the capital stock, new technologies, improved marketing techniques, and more efficient utilization of transport and distribution facilities.[14]

TUC consequently advocates two kinds of corrections: a broadening of the policy options which planning must take into account and a broadening and perhaps deepening of the planning process. Broadened policy options are designed initially to correct the excessively short-term bias of the planners. "It may be that the National Economic Development Council spends too much time on problems which have only short-term effects on the economy rather than on matters with long-term prospects." Or phrased differently, "If . . . the real short-term question at present is that of correcting the balance of payments problem, short-term remedial action and its likely effectiveness has to be distinguished from long-term policies which will inevitably be judged to be a failure by a short-term yardstick." There is also an overcautiousness in projecting the economy's growth potential; "the General Council have repeatedly said that a rate of growth of three percent is just not good enough."[15] It is emphasized that "the possibilities for economic expansion are much greater than has hitherto been assumed in Britain."[16] The TUC estimates that a 6 percent growth rate is possible, but the government believes that 6 percent is a "strain, is taking risks . . . and that we ought to seek to limit the expansion . . . to something like 4 per cent."[17] What the government means "by productive potential is not a measure of the economy's capacity for growth but a measure of the average rate of growth over the last few years."[18] Targets can more appropriately be fixed on the basis of the *real* productive capacity.[19] The government, TUC appreciates, is likely to take a more cautious view because it is "mainly concerned about the possible effects on the balance of payments and the danger of an increase in inflationary pressures if the existing spare capacity was used up too quickly or if the level of unemployment fell too fast."[20]

The planning process needs restructuring with respect to the locus of power. Planning, in the TUC view, consists of negotiation among the three parties at interest. In the discussions leading to the establishment of the NEDC, TUC insisted on and gained as the price for its participation (1) tripartite negotiation—"the potential value of N.E.D.C. lies in the fact

14. TUC, *Economic Review, 1968* (London, 1968), p. 7.
15. Greene, in TUC, *1968 Report*, pp. 502–3.
16. TUC, *Economic Review, 1968*, p. 82.
17. *Ibid.*, p. 99.
18. TUC, *1967 Report*, London, p. 337.
19. *Ibid.*, p. 340.
20. Greene, in TUC, *1968 Report*, p. 503.

that it provides a forum in which agreements can be reached between the government and the two sides of industry"; (2) a relatively small council; (3) an independent technical staff responsible to the council—"not open to the suspicion—as a government department would be—that its work is influenced by pre-determined Government policies";[21] (4) an unlimited agenda; (5) the right of the parties to initiate proposals and state their views publicly even if they are critical of government policy; and (6) no *a priori* commitment to the principle that "the solution to Britain's economic difficulties is to be found in wage restraint."[22]

The planning role of the technical elite, it follows, must be subordinate to the bargaining partners and the government.[23] The shift of planning authority from the interest-representative NEDC to the DEA was interpreted as a shift of influence from the partners to "an administrative elite." "The views of major Departments add up to the consensus of opinions of the administrative elite, one which is to a greater or lesser extent shared by those of similar status working in business, the law, the City, universities, and the 'quality' press. They can in a quite special sense, because of their common educational background, be objectively described as the Establishment. Theirs is a very different perspective from that of the working people of Britain, and basic social attitudes are likewise different."[24]

By 1968 TUC evaluated NEDC as no longer "fulfilling its original function," useful more as "a sounding board for Government policies" than as an agency dedicated to creating "an agreed development programme on the basis of tripartite discussion and commitment."[25] General Secretary George Woodcock characterized NEDC as a "mere talking shop."[26]

Deepening of the planning process entails, according to TUC, forecasts, targets, and "action programmes to ensure that these targets are met." Planning is credible only if something is done to implement the plans. TUC seems to be suggesting that government planning fails to penetrate actively and directly into the productive enterprises. "There are more progressive ways of dealing with Britain's problems" than simply to attack the level of employment; they can be better solved "by direct action on both the capital and current accounts of the balance of payments and by direct action to improve the structure and performance of industry."[27]

21. Murray Edelman and R. W. Fleming, *The Politics of Wage-Price Decisions* (Urbana: University of Illinois Press, 1965), p. 216.
22. Bailey, *Managing the Economy*, p. 17.
23. TUC, *1967 Report*, p. 384.
24. *Ibid.*, p. 382.
25. TUC, *1968 Report*, p. 374.
26. George Woodcock in *The Times* (London), August 19, 1968, p. 1.
27. Greene, in TUC, *1968 Report*, p. 503.

III

The TUC's objective for a more penetrating planning process may come closer to realization in the activities of the Economic Development Committees or the "little Neddies" as they are better known. The EDC's are tripartite bodies for twenty-four industry groupings. Conceived at first as analogous to the vertical modernization commission in the French plan, the EDC's were intended to "examine the economic performance, prospects and plans of the industry, and assess from time to time the industries' progress in relation to the national growth objectives, and provide information forecasts to the Council on these matters." The idea was that the EDC's would provide the micro-estimates on the basis of which the NEDC would project its macro-economic targets, disseminate national growth projections, and identify any obstacles to achieving those projections.[28]

With the shift in planning function to DEA, the EDC's emphasize "ways of improving the industries' economic performance, competitive power and efficiency and formulate reports and recommendations on these matters. . . ."[29] The major problem areas in which the committees function are exports and imports, industry structure, and manpower.

EDC "findings are not mandatory but they are intended to create an atmosphere, a climate of thought and to generate thought, discussion and reappraisals on the part of decision makers on both sides of industry."[30] Essentially the EDC's are information agencies for the dissemination of comparative data on industry performance and good management practices.

Although "Government has a predominant say in proposing the industries for which committees should be established and the order in which this should be attempted the process remains one of bringing the three contracting parties together to establish by consent and on a mutually agreed basis."[31] Besides the representatives of the partisan interests, the EDC's utilize industrial advisors, commonly "seconded" from industry, and staff representatives from the NEDC office to service the committees with technical assistance; the criticism is that there is an insufficient number to render full service. The members of the committees organize themselves into working parties and subcommittees to study and report on

28. Richard Caves *et al.*, *Britain's Economic Prospects* (Washington, D.C.: Brookings Institution, 1968), p. 318.

29. National Economic Development Office, *Activity Report*, no. 3, London, March 1967, p. 1.

30. T. C. Fraser, "Economic Development Committee—A New Dimension in the Relations between Government and Industry," Lecture given at the London School of Economics and Political Science, February 10, 1966, mimeographed, p. 13.

31. *Ibid.*, p. 4.

special issues. The committee output consists of conferences, reports, and statistical surveys.

Most active is the Distributive Trades EDC, composed of eighteen members who include on the union side the general secretary of the Union of Shop, Distributive and Allied Workers, the assistant secretary of the Clerical and Administrative Workers Union, the secretary of the General Workers trade group of the Transport and General Workers Union, the general woman officer of the General and Municipal Workers Union, with a research officer of the first-named union and a representative of TUC as "attending members." The management representatives include high officials of large trade enterprises and associations. Special subcommittees have been organized to deal with training, staff training, management training, wholesale trade, labor utilization, shopping capacity, and statistics. The committee publishes pamphlets—for example, "Grow Your Own Sales Staff," "Trouble Getting Sales Staff," "Investment and Productivity in Retailing"—on recruitment, selection, and training in the small shop. An accounting guide for small retailers will also be published. In addition, the EDC runs conferences, such as the conference on computers in distribution, and conducts surveys, such as consulting services provided by trade associations.[32]

"The trade union members of EDC's," according to the TUC's research director, "armed with much more extensive and detailed information than has ever before been available, will be able to check and comment directly on the achievements of their industries."[33] The TUC reviews the operations of the EDC in some detail in the reports to the annual congresses. In addition, the TUC brings together the union members of the EDC's for discussion and evaluation. Some of the problems of participation noted by TUC are (1) the irregular attendance by the union participants; (2) the growing technicality and specificity of the topics covered by the EDC's; (3) "the many documents and technical papers which had to be assimilated by trade union representatives added to the specialist nature of much of their work [and] meant they needed the full support of research departments in their own unions in addition to the TUC services";[34] (4) the "fragmented" character of communications between the EDC and individual firm which is now inadequately served through trade associations; and (5) the inadequate communication between the EDC's union representatives and the shop floor.

32. NEDC, *Economic Development Committee for Distributive Trades*, Newsletter No. 6, London, June 1968.

33. Lionel Murray, "Economic Planning and Incomes Policy in Great Britain," *Free Labour World* (ICFTU, Brussels), February 1966, p. 6.

34. TUC, *1966 Report*, London, p. 334.

In general the TUC holds with the consensus that "the return on the EDC's work [has] been well worthwhile in relation to the small scale of the resources involved, that active support for the EDC's by the participants was an essential condition of success, that their aim must not be confined to analysis and reporting but must be to ensure that action followed, and that there was considerable scope for further useful activity."[35] As to the EDC interest in manpower, "the difficulty is to find things which the trade unions can be involved in without duplicating the role of the negotiators. They are most effective when they deal with things on the business side rather than the manpower side which may involve the problem of negotiations." The EDC's appear to have more for the employers than for the unions. It is the union reservations, however, which limit the work of the "little Neddies." In the engineering field, for example, "the unions are very sensitive about any encroachment on collective bargaining." On balance, the major manpower effect of the EDC's "is drawing attention to the problems and leading the people who have the responsibility to carry them out."[36] According to National Economic Development Office Activity Reports (March 1967, Autumn 1967, and Summer 1968), some of the manpower "problems" and issues that have been brought to attention and discussed have included:

Agriculture: manpower trends in relation to future needs
Building: forecasting, decasualization, obstacles to manpower efficiency; anomalies in main union-management agreements in wages and working conditions; vocabulary of management functions to encourage standardization of terminology, absenteeism, wage incentives, nonproductive time, recruiting and training
Chemical: field investigation to compare UK and US manning schedules
Civil Engineering: work in adverse weather conditions; welfare facilities code; absenteeism; wage incentives, subcontracting; protective weather and safety clothing; decasualization
Clothing: labor turnover; management development
Distributive Trades: management training; training in small shops; pilot study of labor turnover, vocational guidance
Electrical Engineering: comparative study of productivity in British and US refrigerator manufacturing; inter-firm comparisons
Electronics: "future manpower requirements in final stages"; "increasing productivity by improving company information and communications, target setting"
Food Processing: high labor turnover
Hosiery and Knitwear: improved use of manpower; employment of married women; labor turnover; manpower planning

35. TUC, *1968 Report*, p. 376.
36. Interview with K. Dallas, National Economic Development Office, London, August 19, 1968.

Hotel and Catering: labor turnover; labor cost content of personal services in hotels; inter-firm comparison of labor productivity; manpower survey

Machine Tool: forecasts of 1970 manpower situation

Motor Vehicle Distribution and Repair: sources of increased productivity, that is, greater specialization; "less frequent need for servicing; more petrol pump self-service; training"

Newspaper Printing and Publishing: establishment of industry training board

Paper and Board: questionnaire on productivity

Post Office: employment of female and part-time labor

Rubber: manpower utilization; obstacles to increasing productivity; productivity agreements; application of industrial engineering techniques; recording and costs of labor turnover

Wool Textiles: shortage of manpower

IV

The Industrial Training Act of 1964 represents a significant departure from traditional practice. As Lady Gertrude Williams, Britain's outstanding authority on training, put it in 1963 on the occasion of the issuance of the White Paper which introduced the Industrial Training Act: "The belief that industrial training is the sole responsibility of industry itself, of employers and employed, has for a long time been one of the sacred cows, and if there has ever been any suggestion that anybody should intervene, advise, have a right to be consulted or to criticise, or in any way lay a finger on it, both sides of the industry have immediately said, 'Hands off.' "[37] The enactment of the legislation was made possible "through the large degree of support provided by employers and trade unions based on a widespread feeling that something had to be done."[38]

The act authorizes the Minister of Labour to appoint industry training boards. The industry boards, of which there are now twenty-six,[39] are composed of "an equal number of employer and trade union members (appointed after consultation with appropriate organisations) and a number of educational members. Representatives of the Ministry of Labour,

37. Lady Gertrude Williams, quoted in BACIE, *Industrial Training, Whose Responsibility* (London, 1963), p. 11; see also p. 30.

38. OECD, Manpower and Social Affairs Committee, "Manpower Problems and Policies in the United Kingdom, Report by the Examiners," mimeographed (Paris, 1968), pt. iv, p. 1.

39. The TUC *1969 Report* lists the following industry boards: Agriculture, Horticulture and Forestry; Carpet; Ceramics, Glass and Mineral Products; Chemical and Allied Products; Civil Air Transport; Construction; Cotton and Allied Textiles; Distribution; Electricity Supply; Engineering; Food, Drink and Tobacco; Footwear, Leather and Fur Skin; Furniture and Timber; Gas; Hotel and Catering; Iron and Steel; Knitting, Lace and Net; Man-Made Fibres Producing; Paper and Paper Products; Petroleum; Printing and Publishing; Road Transport; Rubber and Plastics Processing; Shipbuilding; Water Supply; and Wool, Jute and Flax (p. 108).

the Department of Education and Science and the Scottish Education Department attend meetings of boards but have no vote."[40]

The act empowers each board to impose a levy on each employer within its industrial jurisdiction. In return the board provides training facilities, establishes standards, and pays grants "to firms whose standards of training are in line with [its] recommendations." The employer is not compelled to adhere to the standards but "there will be a considerable incentive for him to do so."[41]

In addition, a Central Training Council is established to advise the Minister of Labour, especially on the establishment of new industry training boards, and to review and provide broad policy guidance to the boards ("e.g. training methods, training of training officers and instructors, training of clerical and commercial staff and the use of proficiency tests").[42] The council consists of six employer and six trade union members, two members from the nationalized industries, six educationists, not more than six chairmen of training boards, and six other members "who have a special interest in industrial training."[43] Almost all boards are divided into "subject committees." In engineering, the board covering the largest number of employees in its jurisdiction, the subject committees include finance, staffing, grants, research, and "training policy committees" for operators, craftsmen, technologists, commercial and clerical employees, management supervisory and first-year craftsmen, and technicians.[44] All boards are regionalized with training officers attached to each region.

The board training recommendations provide "detailed guidance" on syllabi and training methods. For example, some of the boards have urged that the first year of apprentice training "must be provided in special centres or schools in technical colleges, away from production pressures and under fully competent instructors."[45] A more general type of recommendation deals with "the steps a firm should take to establish training schemes"—for example, induction training, written job analysis, trainee supervision, release for external courses, and trainee evaluation.[46]

One of the most innovative training ideas has been the concept of the "module" developed by the Engineering Board. The module is a "training package" which is an integrated unit of skill and for each module the

40. Ministry of Labour, *Industrial Training Act—General Guide* (London: HMSO, 1966), p. 7.

41. *Ibid.*, p. 11.

•42. Gary B. Hansen, *Britain's Industrial Training Act*, National Manpower Policy Task Force, Washington, D.C., 1967, p. 37.

43. Ministry of Labour, *Industrial Training Act*, p. 15.

44. BACIE, *Industrial Training Boards*, Progress Report No. 2 (London, 1967).

45. Central Training Council, *Second Report to the Minister* (London: HMSO, 1967), p. 11.

46. *Ibid.*, p. 12.

board provides: "(i) a skill specification. . . . (ii) a training specification. . . . (iii) an instruction manual. . . . (iv) a set of sample performance tests. (v) a recommendation for further education. (vi) a log book in which the trainee records the training received."[47] The modules are used after the trainee's "first year of basic training in a wide range of skills carried out in a training workshop under the guidance of full time instructors and teachers" and in turn are followed by "experience in using the skills learned in an industrial environment."[48]

The construction industry apprenticeship of four to five years has been reduced to one and one-half to two years of basic training, that combines training centers instruction and on-the-job training. For those seeking additional skill in their craft, advanced training modules are available. Paving the way for this change was a study which showed, for example, "that bricklayers with 6 months training at a government training center could serve between 6 and 18 months as improvers or trainees and do the same range of work as those whose practical training had consisted of 5 years' site experience."[49]

In general, traditional apprenticeship is being altered at several critical points. If the flexible module system is used, "the total period of training of the craftsman will not be the same in all trades regardless of the skills required." There is no reason "why a recognised craftsman should not undergo further modules to develop or modify his initial training later on in his career."[50] The apprentice terms are being modified further (1) to permit workers to acquire a craft skill at any age and not only as a youth, (2) to enhance the formal training component, and (3) to adjust training to the aptitudes and needs of the trainee so that the acquisition of skilled worker status depends on skill, not on time. "Decisions regarding training are being made on the basis of what needs to be learned and the best method of acquiring skills and knowledge without regard to the once sacred five-year apprenticeship."[51]

The union's main influence is in the ordering of training board priorities. The initiative, however, seems to come from the permanent staff. The lack of an independent staff in the Central Training Council weakens the council's independence, in the view of TUC, and accordingly the "papers considered . . . tend to reflect" Department of Employment and Productivity "thinking rather than its own."[52]

47. Engineering Industry Training Board, *Training for Engineering Craftsmen—The Module System* (London, 1968), p. 7.

48. *Ibid.*, p. 3.

49. Herbert A. Perry, "New Training Plan in Britain's Construction Industry," *Monthly Labor Review* (Washington, D.C.), February 1970, p. 27.

50. Central Training Council, *Second Report*, p. 11.

51. Hansen, *Britain's Industrial Training Act*, p. 51.

52. TUC, *1969 Report*, p. 106.

In regard to training, the TUC indicates that the following are still. needed: (1) "more information to enable decisions about training to be better related to economic needs and technological developments"; (2) greater awareness "of the interests of young persons . . . for whom systematic training has hitherto not been provided"; (3) "a stronger Central Training Council, with its own staff" and funds so that it will not be "merely an advisory body to the Minister of Labour" but will "give strength and direction to the work" of the various boards; (4) expansion of the training program for training officers; (5) day release for continued part-time education; (6) increase of opportunities in the government training centers "for adult men and women to gain skills or qualifications to fit them for occupations or for advancement in their present employment . . . [or] for those workers who find themselves displaced through industrial change"; and (7) vocational guidance through the employment service for "all who seek it" and "training and financial assistance on a much larger scale."[53]

The training boards have been responsible for a quickening of "the pace of change,"[54] first because they are endowed with the authority, finances, and technical staff to formulate and carry out policy. Second, employers and trade unionists view the boards as the training arms of their own industries and not as interlopers. Third, there is a dispersion of participation through an extensive subcommittee system. Finally, the trade union members who sit on the industry training boards have no collective bargaining responsibilities in their capacities as training board members and hence are able "to take a more objective view of training needs."[55]

V

"There has hardly been a year since the Second World War in which it could be said that there was no incomes policy at all in the United Kingdom."[56] In the immediate postwar period the labor movement followed "with remarkable fidelity" the appeals of the Labour government plea for wage restraint.[57] Revolt by the rank and file responding under pressure of cost-of-living increases and the "disturbance of customary relativities" caused the breakdown of the wage restraint policy and provided an early signal of the risks which union leadership takes on when it consents to a

53. TUC, *1967 Report*, pp. 165–69 *passim*.

54. "Manpower Policies and Problems in the United Kingdom," *OECD Observer* (Paris), August 1969, p. 15.

55. Interview with D. P. Buckley, Training Division, Department of Employment and Productivity, London, August 19, 1968.

56. Denton *et al.*, *Economic Planning and Policies*, p. 254.

57. E. H. Phelps Brown, "Guidelines for Growth and for Incomes in the United Kingdom, Some Probable Lessons for the United States," in *Guidelines, Informal Controls, and the Market Place*, ed. George P. Shultz and Robert Z. Aliber (Chicago: University of Chicago Press, 1966), p. 154.

wage restraint policy. "Throughout the whole experience there was a progressive weakening of TUC authority over affiliated unions which culminated in the defeat of the General Council's proposals for a renewal of wage restraint."[58]

In the later 1950s the Conservative government's independent Council of Prices, Productivity and Income—composed of a judge, an accountant, and an economist—shifted to "incomes" rather than "wages policy." The trade unionists resented particularly a council statement in 1958 that "in our opinion it is impossible that a free and flexible economic system can work efficiently without a perceptible (though emphatically not a catastrophic) margin of unemployment. . . ."[59] The year 1961 was marked by a Conservative attempt at a voluntary wage restraint policy guided by an impartial National Incomes Commission. The policy consisted of "pay pauses" (1961) and "guiding lights" (1962). In 1964 the new Labour government continued for a time the voluntary restraint strategy via a tripartite Declaration of Intent setting out wage-price-policy guidelines, the establishment of a National Board for Prices and Incomes (1965), and an "early warning system" to review increases before they take effect. Unlike the National Incomes Commission, the NBPI did "not sit to pass judgment but entered into discussion with the parties whose agreement it endeavored to influence but not to supersede."[60]

According to the 1964 Declaration of Intent signed by all three parties, the government's part is (1) to "implement a general plan of economic development through the N.E.D.C.," (2) to aid increases in productivity, and (3) to contain "excessive growth in aggregate profits as compared with the growth of total wages and salaries." In return, the unions and employers "therefore undertake, on behalf of our members: to encourage and lead a sustained attack on the obstacles to efficiency whether on the part of management or of workers, and to strive for the adoption of more rigorous standards of performance at all levels; to cooperate with the Government in endeavoring, in the face of practical problems, to give effective shape to the machinery that the Government intend to establish," for reviewing "the general movement of prices and money incomes," and to investigate the behavior of prices and wages in particular cases for their implications for the "national interest."[61]

The emergence of statutory restraint characterized by a "standstill" on incomes and prices, "severe restraint" (1967), and wage increase criteria tied to productivity, equity, and substandard wages was evident in 1966.

58. John Corina, quoted in John Sheehan, *The Wage-Price Guideposts* (Washington, D.C.: Brookings Institution, 1967), p. 106.
59. Brown, "Guidelines for Growth," p. 155.
60. *Ibid.*, p. 158.
61. OECD, Manpower and Social Directorate, *Non-Wage Incomes and Prices Policy* (Paris, 1966), p. 163.

Although the legislation gave the government "quite draconian powers," the incomes policy "was largely based on voluntary understandings among organized labor, employers and the government."[62]

The 1969 budget message of the Labour government announced that a situation had been reached where the government could contemplate moving to a policy which would offer a long-term solution to the problem of moderating the growth of prices and incomes "without resorting to stringent compulsory powers."[63] Or as one commentator said in February 1970, "Incomes policy . . . is dead."[64] Major reliance is now placed on early warnings and postponement of increases pending consideration by the Prices and Incomes Board.

The labor movement shared with the Labour government a common economic theory that an incomes policy is essential to Britain's economic prosperity; it recognized "that real income cannot for more than a short time rise faster than overall productivity and that the balance of payments position would be assisted if money incomes and national productivity were both to rise in step."[65] TUC also understands the political pressures for an incomes policy. "One of the Government's purposes was to be able to say to foreign Governments and to foreign bankers who provide us with short term financial assistance, 'Here is a Labour Government getting rough with the unions, keeping those people in their place. You can depend on us; we are following good orthodox policies. Your money is safe with us.' "[66]

In Woodcock's view, an incomes policy is not a necessary evil. It has a constructive place in union objectives. Incomes policy is really about "a better-ordered and more methodical and more sensible and more just system of collective bargaining and wage settlement." To him, a "better-ordered" collective bargaining system meant "one with a much wider purpose than simply strengthening little groups to do what they like and to hell with the rest of us."[67]

Woodcock shared with the Labour government the view that the labor movement, together with employers and government, must have an influential voice in the determination of policy. The Conservative incomes policy administered through the National Incomes Commission and earlier

62. Derek Robinson, "Implementing an Incomes Policy," *Industrial Relations* (Berkeley), October 1968, p. 74.

63. "Britain Raises Corporate Taxes, but Aged and Low Wage Earners Benefit by New Budget," *The Wall Street Journal*, April 16, 1969, p. 8.

64. Geoffrey Goodman, "Incomes Policy—Lessons of a Failure," *Socialist Commentary* (London), February 1970, p. 3.

65. TUC, *Trade Unionism*, p. 78.

66. Lionel Murray, "Lionel Murray on Incomes Policy," *TUAC Bulletin* (Paris), December 1969, annex 2, p. 5.

67. TUC, *1968 Report*, p. 551.

efforts were defective precisely because they sought to displace the interested parties in management and labor and "appl[y] a policy from the
top."[68] By contrast, the NBPI is cited as a proper example of participation
by the parties at interest. Its "broad philosophy and standards of judgment
were not left to the Board alone to decide but were laid down by the
Government after consultation with both sides of industry." Still acceptable to all is the condition that the incomes policy cannot simply be a
wage restraint policy but must represent "a coherent and agreed policy for
productivity, prices and incomes,"[69] and "the claims of social need and
justice."[70]

The divergence between trade unions and the Labour government begins on the question of how the incomes policy is to be implemented.
When the Labour government finally demanded legislative compulsion,
TUC took the contrary view that "a policy of partnership with the trade
union Movement could never be successful on the basis of legislative control." Incomes policy has "to rest on persuasion and dealing with the
parties involved in bargaining."[71] Paraphrasing Hobbes, Woodcock, in the
course of the 1968 TUC debate, said that "a statutory incomes policy is of
its nature 'nasty, brutish and short.' "[72] In fact, "it was the intervention of
the law into incomes policy which brought the strands of [TUC] opposition together into a united opposition to the policy."[73]

Although it rejected a statutory policy, TUC nonetheless recognized the
gravity of the situation and proposed its own "voluntary incomes policy."
TUC admits that it "cannot exist entirely on a negative—you cannot make
anything of Congress if all we do is to repeat and reiterate the things that
we do not like. We have to have a constructive purpose." The TUC policy
has been essentially an attempt "to set out a figure or a norm or a standard
or an average of increase in incomes that could be sustained without any
bad or side effects."[74]

The norms were presented in the *Economic Review*, an annual publica-
tion that Woodcock characterized as "probably the most important document that the Trades Union Congress ever produced."[75] The *Economic
Review* has been offered as a "new basis for consulting and influencing
government." Although it accepted the principle of an incomes policy, the
TUC, in the *Economic Review*, nevertheless thought it necessary "to recast

68. George Woodcock, quoted in Robinson, "Implementing an Incomes Policy,"
p. 80.
69. TUC, *Trade Unionism* p. 81.
70. Woodcock, quoted in Robinson, "Implementing an Incomes Policy," p. 76.
71. TUC, *1968 Report*, pp. 358–59.
72. *Ibid.*, p. 550.
73. Murray, "Lionel Murray on Incomes Policy," p. 1.
74. TUC, *1968 Report*, pp. 549–50.
75. George Woodcock, in TUC, *Economic Review, 1968*, p. 95.

incomes policy on the basis of their own assessment," especially when the government's wage freeze brought out "the growing divergence between the General Council's view of economic policy as a whole and that of the Government." The *Economic Review* "creates a more constructive framework within which the trade union Movement could discuss the whole issue of collective bargaining developments in relationship to the growth of incomes." In subsequent editions, TUC plans to "concentrate somewhat less on detailed technical points on the economic growth rate, and more on such issues as the development of active manpower policies designed to combat growing problems of structural unemployment, and on the impact of industrial rationalisation on employment policies."[76]

The basic pressure which the 1968 *Economic Review* sought to document was that "Britain's potential for economic growth may once again be underestimated" and that hence "the possibilities for economic expansion are much greater than has hitherto been assumed."[77] Accordingly, the wage policy advocated by the *Economic Review* was that "for the period mid-1968 to mid-1969, the economy should be allowed to grow at the rate of more than 6 per cent. On this assumption and the linked assumption that productivity will rise by more than 5 per cent an increase of weekly pay of 5% (out of which about 1½ per cent would have to be allowed for increases arising from local bargaining) would be compatible with stable labour costs across the economy as a whole for the period." Limits on general increases should not preclude preferential treatment to "the lower paid, to those who make significant contributions to productivity, and where there is a clear need to recruit labour."[78] It is possible that TUC has given up on incomes policy "as a method of promoting social equity" in favor of "taxation, social insurance benefits or perhaps through a national minimum wage."[79]

In "bargaining" with affiliates to support the need for a trade union incomes policy, Woodcock argued that if those in government do "not get any easement and retain their apprehensions and their fears about what is happening or likely to happen on the incomes side, . . . [and] find themselves forced to fiscal measures, some of those who do not like wages policy or incomes policy will like even less the fiscal measures that may have to be taken as a substitute or alternative to an incomes policy."[80] In short, it is either TUC incomes policy or statutory and/or unemployment-creating deflationary fiscal policy which represent the real alternatives for trade unionists.

76. TUC, *1969 Report*, pp. 341–43 *passim*.
77. TUC, *Economic Review, 1968*, p. 106.
78. *Ibid.*, pp. 89–90.
79. Murray, "Lionel Murray on Incomes Policy," p. 5.
80. TUC, *1968 Report*, p. 551.

TUC's review of affiliates' wage claims—the so-called "vetting"—began in 1965. For the period July 1967–May 1968, "the General Council were notified of 376 claims covering 9,500,000 workers, an average of 34 claims each month." Ten percent of the claims accounting for about 4 percent of the workers were regarded as inadmissable under TUC's incomes policy. No objection was raised to about one-fourth of the claims covering about 13 percent of the workers. In the rest of the cases, "considerations of incomes policy did not themselves preclude the unions from proceeding with negotiations but in some instances they asked the unions to reduce the size of the claim, to phase it over a period of years, or to delay its implementation."[81] When claims by affilates exceeded TUC wage norms, a justifying case had to be made. Vetting was abandoned in January 1970 and replaced by a collective bargaining committee advising unions on "how much should be claimed in the light of TUC's own assessments of the economy."[82]

It is difficult to say how representative the views stated above are of the labor movement as a whole. The TUC's 1968 Congress barely approved the TUC's own incomes policy but rejected overwhelmingly the Labour government's incomes policy.[83] The grounds on which trade unionists criticize the incomes policy approach may be characterized as pragmatic, sectional, and doctrinal. The pragmatic criticism holds that the policy, however desirable in the abstract, is not working. It has not stabilized prices, and unemployment is still a fact of life. Some go beyond this to assert that incomes policy is irrelevant; according to Clive Jenkins, a gadfly of the TUC "establishment," from the Scientific, Technical and Managerial Staff Employees, it is "as irrelevant as a blush on a dead man's cheek. . . . Was the agony of this Movement worth a restraint of one percent? . . . The bankers may believe that incomes policy is central to our economic problems, it is not."[84]

The sectional view holds that the trade unions have to get theirs like everybody else. In Hugh Scanlon's (AEFU) words—Scanlon is a prominent left-wing spokesman—"All directors seek maximum profits for their shareholders, all manufacturers seek maximum prices for their goods. So long as this continues all trade unionists are compelled to seek maximum wage increases for the members they represent."[85]

The doctrinal criticism takes several forms. From the standpoint of trade unionism doctrine, incomes policy restraint "means turning our backs on the fundamental fighting purpose of the Movement and making it

81. *Ibid.*, p. 354.
82. American Embassy, London, *TUC's New Wage Claim*, January 21, 1970.
83. TUC, *1968 Report*, pp. 571–72.
84. *Ibid.*, p. 507.
85. TUC, *Economic Review, 1968*, p. 117.

a minion of the Government's will and purpose." Rejected also on trade union grounds "is sacrificing our bargaining rights to the TUC and this we will not support."[86] From another critic (Scanlon) in the same vein, prices and incomes policy "undermines the self-government which trade unions and employers have established after many years of conflict. It erodes the basis of our system of industrial relations because it ignores the element of consent upon which it depends."[87] Further along the doctrinal spectrum is the view that wage and incomes restraint represents a surrender to Tory and elite group economics—"a policy on the old traditional Tory lines, committed and perpetrated with the full approval of the Treasury, a Department much less concerned with expansion than the protection of the pound in the world's markets."[88]

It is also Scanlon who articulates the most fundamental doctrinal criticism: a wage restraint policy will not yield results (1) "whilst we are spending the fantastic sum of 2,300 million a year on the most efficient ways of destroying mankind" and (2) "because in the type of society in which we live it is virtually impossible to control those other aspects of the economy, profits and prices."[89] Or the doctrinal argument in its classic "anti-capitalist" form is: "The measures now imposed and inflicted upon us have the same object, to defend capitalism, and the whole operation is dictated by international bankers to preserve the rights of private profit, or unearned income, of massive takeovers, and to support the sacred cow, the pound sterling, which in turn, sustains the God Almighty dollar."[90]

VI

The shortcomings of the industrial relations system have been extensively probed. The most systematic reassessment of industrial relations has come from the Royal Commission on Trade Unions and Employers' Associations 1965-68, better known as the Donovan Commission—named after its chairman. The coexistence of formal and informal systems "at odds" with each other was diagnosed as the fundamental defect impeding orderly and effective collective bargaining compatible with the economic needs of the society.[91]

The formal system is based on "the industry-wide collective agreement in which are supposed to be settled pay, hours of work and other conditions of employment. The problem is, however, that "actual earnings have

86. *Ibid.*, p. 111.
87. TUC, *1968 Report*, p. 551.
88. *Ibid.*, p. 557.
89. TUC, *Economic Review, 1968*, p. 117.
90. TUC, *1968 Report*, p. 556.
91. Royal Commission on Trade Unions and Employers' Associations, *1965-68 Report* (Cmnd. 3623) (London: HMSO, 1968), p. 261.

moved far apart from the rates laid down in industry-wide agreements . . . and that the bargaining which takes place in factories," which is
the informal system, "is largely outside of the control of employers' associations and trade unions."[92] Instead it is controlled by shop stewards and
company and plant management, and is "largely informal, largely fragmented and largely autonomous."[93] "Extreme decentralisation and self-
government" have deteriorated "into indecision and anarchy" and have
bred "inefficiency and the reluctance to change."[94] It is the informal
system which controls "incentive schemes, the regulation of hours actually
worked, the use of job evaluation, work practices and the linking of
changes in pay to changes in performance, the facilities for shop stewards
and disciplinary rules and appeals."[95] The word "system," however, is a
misnomer, since there are no integrating principles, and hence no orderly
regulation exists.[96] This lack of any orderly regulation is accentuated
when wages must be brought into line with a national policy.

The structural sources of disorder are the multiplicity of unions, the
craft system, and the steward system. At the end of 1966 there were 574
trade unions with a membership of 10,111,000, of which 170 unions with
9 million members were affiliated with TUC. By way of comparison, the
German DGB consists of 16 industrial unions; the AFL-CIO consists of
128 national unions. Union membership has increased absolutely but declined relatively from 45 percent to 42 percent of the total labor force.
The multiplicity of unions as a fragmenting influence is reinforced by craft
unionism "which is deeply rooted in much of British industry."[97]

Craft unionism, however, does not totally describe multi-unionism. Excluding white collar workers, "about four out of every five trade unionists
in Britain work in a multi-union establishment, and perhaps one in six of
them belongs to a grade of workers in which two or more unions are
competing for members."[98] The most prevalent type of multi-unionism is
craft multi-unionism where each craft union in a plant is the exclusive
representative for its craft. The second type is noncraft multi-unionism
where competing unions vie for the loyalty of the same unit of workers.

Multi-unionism is, in turn, part of the causation chain which strengthens the steward system at the expense of the trade union, and the shop
floor understanding at the expense of the industrywide agreement. The

92. *Ibid.*
93. *Ibid.*, p. 18.
94. *Ibid.*, p. 262.
95. *Ibid.*, p. 40.
96. Alan Fox and Allan Flanders, "The Reform of Collective Bargaining–From
Donovan to Durkheim," *British Journal of Industrial Relations* (London), July 1969,
p. 163.
97. Royal Commission, *1965–68 Report*, p. 87.
98. *Ibid.*, p. 29.

steward is the union member's spokesman in a given section of the plant. His tasks include membership recruitment, enforcing the informal "closed shop," collecting union dues, and negotiation with plant level management.

The steward system derives its power from the inability of the industry-wide bargain to comprehend more than minimum wage rates. The effect is to transfer to the shop floor and hence to the multi-union steward system the responsibility for negotiating wage and work rules. Bargaining at the workplace level is largely independent of the control of the unions and employer associations and "conducted in such a way that different groups in the works get different concessions at different times."[99]

The decentralization of collective bargaining power to the shop floor began with full employment which increased the employer's ability to pay and generally enhanced union power. Moreover, mass production as a production technique generates "conditions of tensions and pressure" and strengthens "the strategic role that particular shop floor work groups play." Given these decentralizing influences, management is willing "to reach agreement quickly with a union representative who has intimate knowledge of local circumstances."[100]

The fragmenting influences of multi-unionism, craft unionism, and steward autonomy produce inefficiencies in the labor process in the form of restrictive practices, irrational wage structures, and "unofficial" strikes. Common restrictive practices include:

1. *Craftsmen's mates.* Characteristically underemployed, these helpers "represent one of the most serious and widespread examples of wasted manpower in British industry."[101]

2. *Overmanning.* These rules consist of specifying manning of machines and equipment in excess of technical requirements.

3. *Restriction of output.* This means "the pegging of output on various machines well below the reasonable potential."[102]

4. *Excessive overtime.* "Management is often obliged to grant 'custom and practice,' 'policy,' 'guaranteed' or 'artificial' overtime even if under-utilized employees are already on the payroll."[103]

5. *"Welting"* and *"spelling"* on the docks. "This is the practice whereby only half a gang is working at any given time."[104] In addition, it

99. *Ibid.*, p. 18.
100. R. F. Banks, "The Patterns of Collective Bargaining," in *Industrial Relations*, ed. B. C. Roberts (London: Methuen, 1968), pp. 106–7 *passim*.
101. Royal Commission on Trade Unions and Employers' Associations, *Productivity Bargaining*, Research Papers no. 4 (London: HMSO, 1967), p. 49.
102. *Ibid.*
103. Lloyd Ulman, "Collective Bargaining and Industrial Efficiency," in Caves *et al.*, *Britain's Economic Prospects*, p. 356.
104. Royal Commission, *Productivity Bargaining*, p. 62.

is estimated that late starts, early quitting, and extended tea breaks cost one hour's work a day.

6. *Apprenticeship*. This is used as a method of restricting entry to the trade and regulating the content of the craft. "Training plays only a secondary part in an apprenticeship" and "provides less training than a properly instructed course lasting a few weeks."[105]

7. *Rigidity of jurisdictional or demarcation lines between unions*. Most often found in the craft unions but not unknown among the more inclusive unions, this rigidity impedes the flexible assignment of manpower. It is not the initial acquisition of jurisdiction but its perpetuation in the face of changing technology which is the source of industrial inefficiency.

The wage structure, according to the chairman of NBPI, is a "basic rate on which there is piled a super-structure of supplements making up an earnings packet that is probably on average around twice the basic rate, though it can be more." This wage structure resists incentives for more efficient work. "A relatively low basic rate plus variable supplements leaves the worker with a source of insecurity, even in an age of full employment, and makes him resistant to any change which appears to place the supplement in jeopardy."[106] Hugh Scanlon, president of the AEFU, in demanding a more rational wage structure, commented on "the craziness that goes to make our present wage structure of basic rates, national bonuses, consolidated time rates, cash prices, piece rates, merit rates."[107]

The major problem for Britain is not the authorized strike, which ranks very low when compared to other countries, but the brief "unofficial" strike which is aimed at "issues arising at plant level which are not dealt with at all in agreements negotiated by union leaders, such as rates of pay or piece rates settled at workplace level, dismissals, or working arrangements."[108] "A given number of man-days lost is probably more costly to the employer in the form of a series of isolated quickie strikes than in the form of one protracted companywide strike."[109] The unofficial strikes are more likely to have a productivity-retarding effect because they are more unexpected, and are more likely to arise out of immediate efficiency questions like discipline, wage structure, and work practices.[110]

To remedy the "central defect" of the informal system—"the disorder in factory and workshop relations and pay structures promoted by the

105. Royal Commission, *1965–68 Report*, p. 87.
106. OECD, *Report by the Examiners*, p. 14.
107. Hugh Scanlon, "New Three Year Agreement in the Engineering Industry," *Bulletin of the International Metalworkers' Federation* (Geneva), March 1969, p. 45.
108. Royal Commission, *1965–68 Report*, p. 108.
109. Ulman, "Collective Bargaining," p. 354.
110. See H. A. Turner, *Is Britain Really Strike Prone* (Cambridge: Cambridge University Press, 1969); W. E. J. McCarthy, "The Nature of Britain's Strike Problems," *British Journal of Industrial Relations*, July 1970, pp. 224–36.

conflict between the formal and informal systems"—the Donovan Commission proposes factory bargaining "to advance effective and orderly collective bargaining over wage terms and work rules."[111] The factory agreement can, if its negotiators desire it, not only specify very general minimum conditions—the inherent limitation of the industrywide agreement—but also *regulate* in detail wage rates and the method of measurement, work rules, and terms of employment.

Productivity bargaining represents a special form of factory (or companywide) agreement and "is fundamental to the improved use of manpower."[112] A productivity agreement is "one in which workers agree to make a change, or a number of changes, in working practice that will lead in itself—leaving out any compensating pay increase—to more economical working; and in return the employer agrees to a higher level of pay or other benefits."[113]

The initial impetus to productivity bargaining came from the case study by Allan Flanders at Esso's Fawley refinery, and the NBPI policy of allowing wage increases which could be offset by concrete productivity gains. The changes in restrictive working practices advanced by productivity agreements are (1) the reduction of overtime as a regular arrangement, (2) flexibility in the allocation of manpower, that is, a freer interchange of tasks between different groups of workers, especially in respect to craftsmen, (3) work pace restrictions, (4) reduction in manning, and (5) simplification of labor grades.[114]

The employers have been prompted to initiate productivity bargaining "by labour shortages and rising labour costs."[115] Some unions, such as the Transport and General Workers, have promoted productivity bargaining as a matter of policy. "On the basis of scattered returns, productivity bargaining shows considerable promise. Estimated net reductions in the neighborhood of 10 to 15 percent of the wage bill do not appear to be uncommon. . . . Specific productivity increases can be very high."[116] Productivity bargaining can encourage capital investment and increased productivity by minimizing restrictive practices—"hence its broad appeal as a 'growth policy.' "[117] Noninflationary objectives are achieved at reduced levels of unemployment. Furthermore, productivity bargaining enhances the steward's importance by bringing him into the formal wage determination process. The national union's role is also enhanced, because productivity

111. Royal Commission, *1965–68 Report*, p. 40.
112. *Ibid.*, p. 265.
113. NBPI, *Productivity Agreement* (London: HMSO, 1967), p. 1.
114. *Ibid.*, pp. 3–10.
115. Royal Commission, *1965–68 Report*, p. 5.
116. Ulman, "Collective Bargaining," pp. 364–65.
117. *Ibid.*, p. 366.

bargaining underscores the need for technical competence on the union side.[118]

For Allan Flanders, productivity bargaining "is the most revolutionary thing that has happened in collective bargaining thus far because of what it implies in the change of attitude. . . ." Although he concedes that it has many shortcomings, he says that "the real thing about it is the comprehensive agreement where productivity bargaining really reforms industrial relations in that establishment. It is there clearing up a backlog of neglected problems due to the fact that we had no formal plant bargaining."[119] More skeptical is Ben Roberts who views productivity bargaining as "a temporary thing. It has the seeds of conflict because it rewards the higher productivity sector. Once you have bought out the restrictive practices the productivity bargaining ends."[120] TUC is favorably disposed to productivity bargaining but believes that the workers' share should be related to the total cost benefit accruing to an employer. "The workers' participation in the enterprise, not merely his direct physical contribution measured in productivity terms, is essential to its prosperity and his share in the rising prosperity ought not to be limited to assessments in savings in labour costs." In addition, the productivity guidelines, oriented as they are to manufacturing industries, do not fairly reflect productivity problems in nonmanual employment.[121]

Reform of the bargaining system, in the Donovan view, has strong implications for trade union structure and government. Industrial unionism as a remedy for multi-unionism is good in theory but not workable in practice. "It is necessary therefore to seek the benefits claimed for industrial unionism in other ways," specifically (1) mergers and joint union agreements on "rights of representation"; (2) TUC establishment of the principle of "one union for one grade of work within one factory"; (3) "constitutionally recognised committees to perform many of the functions now carried out by unofficial shop stewards' 'combine' committees"; and (4) more full time union officials.[122]

The Labour government's attempt to implement parts of the Donovan recommendations supplemented by its own measures in the White Paper, *In Place of Strife*, brought about an almost shattering confrontation with the trade unions. The government's proposals in the latter contained both constructive and punitive measures. On the constructive side, the newly

118. *Ibid.*, p. 369.
119. Interview with Allan Flanders, Oxford, August 15, 1968.
120. Interview with B. C. Roberts, London, August 20, 1968.
121. Patrick Fisher, "National Trade Union Reports, The United Kingdom," *Trade Union Seminar on New Perspectives in Collective Bargaining*, OECD, Manpower and Social Affairs Directorate (Paris, 1969), p. 5.
122. Royal Commission, *1965-68 Report*, pp. 271-72 *passim*.

established Commission on Industrial Relations would investigate ways "of improving and extending procedural arrangements" to strengthen collective bargaining—for example, how to promote suitable companywide procedures, how to develop acceptable rules governing disciplinary procedures and dismissals, how to encourage effective and fair redundancy procedures, how to bring shop stewards within a proper framework of agreed rules in their firms, and how to ensure that they are provided with the right kind of facilities to do their jobs.[123] A grants-and-loans system was proposed to help meet the costs of: (a) trade union mergers, (b) training of union officials and shop stewards, (c) trade union research, and (d) improvement of union administration. The objective was to improve union efficiency.[124] Other recommendations dealt with the right of unions to information, the right of employees to union membership, and the employer's obligation to negotiate with unions.

The most controversial proposal and the one on which TUC government focused—the constructive proposals were dismissed by TUC as "sops"[125]—would have subjected "unconstitutional strikers," that is, wildcatters, to fines. As reported by the TUC General Council, the government's position was that three years had been consumed in the Donovan investigation and report. Now "the public were looking for action against unofficial strikers who brought about industrial anarchy."[126] The government said it would withdraw its proposals only if an alternate plan could be proposed by the TUC that was "equally as urgent and equally as effective."[127]

The TUC countered that it had already began a constructive review of Donovan in *Action on Donovan* and had come to some common terms with the Confederation of British Industry "that action is possible and necessary" in defining "the respective scope of industry-wide agreements on the one hand and company and factory agreements on the other, and the proper relationships between them." In other respects, however, the Donovan recommendations may have been "too sweeping."[128]

Pressed further, TUC's General Council called a special Congress—the first in fifty years—and secured the approval of *A Programme for Action* which empowered the TUC General Council to take internal action against unconstitutional strikes. Counterproposals were contested by the government as lacking "the missing link": the sanctions which would be applied ultimately "if those concerned refused to resume work."[129] For its part,

123. *In Place of Strife* (Cmnd. 3888) (London: HMSO, 1969), p.13.
124. *Ibid.*, p. 23.
125. TUC, *1969 Report*, p. 133.
126. *Ibid.*, p. 132.
127. *Ibid.*
128. *Ibid.*, p. 125.
129. *Ibid.*, p. 136.

the General Council refused absolutely to consider criminal sanctions established under law.

The contest was finally settled on TUC's terms and the "surrender" of the government. TUC would investigate disputes involving unconstitutional work stoppages by "large bodies of workers" likely to have "serious consequences." TUC could "order an unconditional return to work" or advise the unions concerned on approaches to settlement. In the former, the General Council would "place an obligation" on the concerned unions "to obtain an immediate resumption of work." Refusal to comply with the obligation would be cause for an order to "report to Congress" or for suspension until the next Congress.[130] "Since June 18," the General Council reported to the September 1969 Congress, it has "given advice and assistance on a number of disputes and in all cases unions have readily cooperated in responding to enquiries and suggestions."[131]

VII

The British Labour Party "was the child of the trade union movement."[132] It was an 1899 TUC resolution which helped to create the Labour Representation Committee which was converted into the Labour Party in 1906. There is an organic connection between unions and the Party in that unions may choose to affiliate en bloc and levy a political assessment on its members subject to an individual member's right to "contract out." Although the affiliated unions represent a minority of the unions, they represent a large majority of trade union membership, and in fact represent the dominant bloc of members in the Party Conference as against the local constituency parties. Unions are additionally tied to the Party through the practice of union subvention of Labour M.P.'s. "To the politicians, the trade unions bring money, helpers and votes. . . . To the unions the Party offers the certainty of the satisfaction of their reasonable demands for legislation and rule-making in the fields of economic and social policy when Labour is in office, and their advocacy in Parliament and on other political platforms when Labour is in opposition. It gives them a regular and familiar channel for political action on thousands (literally) of minor matters as well as on many major ones."[133]

Despite the organic ties which make the Party "the political arm of the trade union movement," the TUC says that "trade unions and political parties perform quite distinct functions" and that when the Party is in

130. *Ibid.*, pp. 147, 167.
131. *Ibid.*, p. 147.
132. David Marquand, "Labor's Moment of Truth," *The New Leader* (New York), June 9, 1969, p. 6.
133. William Pickles, "Trade Unions in the Political Climate," in *Industrial Relations*, ed. B. C. Roberts, p. 257.

office they perform *divergent* functions.[134] There are basic differences
between the government's interest in the general welfare and "the free
choice of working people" as reflected by "free trade unions." "Part of a
trade union's job is to be protective. . . . Rapid economic growth can, past
a certain point, be too costly" to working people. Unions, to repeat, "are
not the agents of any programme which discounts the present in favour of
the future. . . . Trade unions by their actions reflect the extent to which
working people prefer jam today to more jam tomorrow."[135]

The divergence between party and government on one side and trade
unions on the other has been accentuated by the economic condition of
full employment, the political condition of Party reliance on middle-class
electoral support, and finally by the trade union commitment to voluntarism in an increasingly regulated economy. Full employment–induced
inflation endangers Britain's position in the international economy and
forces the government to "court . . . exhort . . . cajole . . . threaten . . . and
pillory" the trade unions in the interest of economic stability.[136] When
the unions become unwilling to exercise the forbearance demanded of
them, the image of the unionized working class as an object of exploitation and therefore of special sympathy gets tarnished.

The Labour Party's middle-class support diminishes "the class basis of
party allegiance" reflected in the "increasingly middle class" character of
the candidates and officeholders. "In Britain as in other countries, growing
affluence tended to undermine the idea of politics as a zero-sum game in
which the gains for one class are seen as losses for the other."[137]

The TUC recognizes in principle that the national labor movement
cannot escape its role as "the lads in the middle between your [that is, the
trade unions'] legitimate aspirations, your real needs, your particular circumstances and the requirements of the nation." TUC cannot retreat to a
position of simply advancing "the narrow interest of this or that particular
group of workmen. . . . We are not speaking for particular groups—craftsmen, non-craftsmen, manual, non-manual—we are seeking to assimilate out
of these great diversities and jealousies some kind of a common purpose."[138] "There was a time when we could afford to say to governments,
'Leave us alone: Your knowledge, your interests, your involvements in the
affairs of our people is so limited that we would liefer you stayed aside
and let us do the job ourselves.' " But the role of government in the
welfare of the people is so pervasive that "there is no future in . . . going

134. TUC, *Trade Unionism*, p. 56.
135. *Ibid.*, p. 76.
136. V. L. Allen, *Militant Trade Unionism* (London: Merlin Press, 1966), p. 50.
137. David Butler and Donald Stokes, *Political Change in Britain* (London:
Macmillan, 1969), pp. 115, 116, 119.
138. TUC, *Economic Review, 1968*, pp. 139–40 *passim*.

back to the 19th century, keeping ourselves away from governments."[139] Trade union spokesmen recognized further "the need not to embarrass maliciously a government sympathetic to their interests."[140] The Labour-TUC relationships became more abrasive with the successively heavier doses of pressure which the government felt necessary to apply in behalf of incomes and industrial relations policy, especially when in the union's assessment results were slow in coming. "How can we be expected to convince our members to give up protective practices against the background of these unemployment figures."[141] "Neither responsibility nor faith," *The Economist* observed, "has buttered their parsnips."[142]

In the view of some of the trade unionists, the Labour government had abandoned its socialist principles in favor of "perpetuating the class economics of Toryism based upon the deliberate creation of unemployment and underemployment." The TUC has said that in its one hundredth year "it is tragic . . . that we not only have to fight restrictive employers but have to fight our own protégé."[143] The Party's divergence from the cause of socialism and trade unionism was traced, as noted earlier, to the "administrative elite" of the civil service whose perspective is "different . . . from that of the working people of Britian, and [whose] basic social attitudes are likewise different."[144] Ultimately the trade unions for all practical purposes seemed to have had their way both in the abandonment of wage restraint and the withdrawal of the government's punitive proposals against wildcat strikes. But this has not prevented the unions from feeling "alienated from the party they themselves created."[145]

The TUC relies more on consultation with the Party and government than on politics in influencing national policy. "The predominance of trade union representation in the Labour Party Conference and National Executive Committee did not make consultation with the TUC supererogatory."[146] Consultation increasingly became bargaining. "We have come to treat our relations with the Government as being not a matter for supplication, but of adopting a bargaining attitude—of saying, if you will do certain things for us (e.g. factory legislation or social welfare) then we will do certain things in the field of manpower and incomes policy."[147]

139. TUC, *1968 Report*, p. 550.
140. Hugh Scanlon, in OECD, *Geographic and Occupational Mobility of Workers in the Aircraft and Electronics Industry* (Paris, 1966), p. 70.
141. TUC, *1968 Report*, p. 566.
142. "The Old Grey TUC," *The Economist*, September 7, 1968, p. 20.
143. TUC, *1968 Report*, p. 505.
144. TUC, *1969 Report*, p. 382.
145. Rita Hinden, "No Escape.from Politics," *Socialist Commentary*, November 1969, p. 12.
146. Pickles, "Trade Unions in the Political Climate," p. 281.
147. Murray, "Lionel Murray on Incomes Policy," p. 6.

The TUC has analogized the consultation network to an industrial parliament. "All Governments recognize that it is not possible to run a country through a Parliament. It might be said that Governments treat the TUC as a sort of industrial Parliament; in the first place to obtain the benefit of the views and experience of the trade union movement in framing legislation or developing policies in general, and second to secure the approval or endorsement of TUC for the broad terms of legislation" which affect the trade unions.[148] Consultation takes a variety of forms. Permanent consultation is exemplified in the tripartite NEDC and the National Joint Advisory Council to the Minister of Employment and Productivity which also includes representatives from the nationalized industries. The 1968 NJAC agenda included "redundancies and employment, manpower planning, supply of skilled manpower and the manpower situation in particular industries or areas and arising from the report by the Royal Commission on Trade Unions and Employers Associations."[149]

There is also what the TUC calls "ad-hoc" consultation to discuss particular issues with a minister—for example, regional planning or incomes policy—or "to clarify a particular question."[150] The "In Place of Strife" controversy brought the General Council and the Prime Minister together in eight meetings; a General Council subcommittee and the Prime Minister met in four meetings. The TUC is the first point of reference for the appointment of labor representatives to the "innumerable government committees of one sort or another."[151] The "office level" type of consultation represents a "continuing contact between the TUC and Government Department and is often concerned with the background to policy issues or with the details of policy and administration."[152]

The supporting personnel for this "industrial parliament" comes from two sources: the elected leaders of the TUC and affiliated unions—at the highest level the General Council and the general secretary who man the committees—and the professional staff of the TUC and affiliated unions who provide the technical support. Major TUC committees have been established for economic policy, incomes policy, production, nationalized industries, social insurance, and industrial welfare. The main staff departments are economic, education, international, organization, production, and social insurance.[153]

Regarding the quality of trade union technical services, including economic research, one practitioner holds that "unions have not adapted

148. TUC, *Trade Unionism*, pp. 66–68 *passim*.
149. TUC, *1968 Report*, p. 166.
150. TUC, *Trade Unionism*, p. 67.
151. *Ibid*.
152. TUC, *1967 Report*, p. 381.
153. TUC, *Trade Unionism*, pp. 3–19.

themselves quickly enough from general to specialist functions. Many of the newer aspects of trade union work are severely undernourished because of a lack of hard information in the hands of the right people." This is particularly true of the national unions. "Only very large unions can afford a staff of sufficient size to allow the required range of specialisation."[154]

VIII

TUC's authority over its affiliates is "moral" rather than formal and the prospects are that it will continue this way.[155] Its formal authority extends mainly to inter-union disputes and internal union conduct, and the General Council accordingly may recommend expulsion for violation of TUC rules on these points.

TUC's contribution in arresting fragmentation has been its long-time effort, now renewed, to encourage, if not industrial unionism as such, then more inclusive unionism. TUC has relied on voluntary methods of education and persuasion, and on playing "the part of a marriage broker bringing unions together."[156] It has taken the initiative in recommending amalgamation to sixty unions and holds the view that amalgamation "should be complemented by much more active discussion on rationalisation in eliminating duplication and waste of effort."[157] These efforts resulted in the reduction of affiliations as a result of amalgamation from 182 unions in 1962 to 170. The net reduction has been 19, and 7 new unions joined TUC in this period. The advantages of amalgamation which TUC cites are (1) economies of scale in staff, research, education, and legal service; (2) the effectuation of more comprehensive policies; (3) greater union effectiveness in the EDC's and industry training boards; and (4) the reduction of inter-union competition and jurisdictional disputes.[158] The Bridlington principles regulate the terms of inter-union transfers of membership and rival organizing. On balance, TUC influence has grown in the postwar period "because the increasing participation of the Government in economic affairs has shifted the emphasis from industrial to political action and the representation of the trade union point of view on any proposed legislation or administrative action can best be undertaken by a central body."[159]

154. Colin Beever, "Trade Unions, Please Note," *Socialist Commentary*, February 1968, p. 16.
155. Allan Flanders, *Trade Unions* (London: Hutchinson, 1968), p. 61.
156. TUC, *Trade Unionism*, p. 166.
157. TUC, *Action on Donovan* (London, 1968), p. 38.
158. TUC, *Trade Unionism*, p. 164.
159. Flanders, *Trade Unions*, p. 61.

IX

The case for trade union involvement in national economic policy starts with the theory of a full employment-induced inflation which is powered by excessive wage demands and uneconomic practices of trade unions. The components of national policy which the unions have been coopted into participating in are national economic planning at the economy and industry levels, industry training, incomes policy, and reform of industrial relations.

Economic planning, which was the responsibility of NEDC when the trade unions negotiated their way in, was shifted to the DEA soon after the Labour government came into power, and NEDC was relegated to an advisory role. The trade union movement could accept neither the specific planning assumptions nor the outlook of the "establishment" planners in DEA. By 1968 NEDC became for Woodcock a "talking shop." Under the circumstances, the TUC objective of economic planning by negotiation at this level never materialized.

By contrast, participation by negotiation in the EDC's and the industrial training boards has yielded favorable union outcomes. The reasons may be conjectured as: (1) the decentralization of administration so that the trade union representatives have had something important to do; (2) the usability of the kinds of skills and insights which practical trade unionists are likely to bring; (3) the opportunity for *all* interests in the longer run to improve their respective positions even though in the short run unions gave up some vested advantages—for example, in apprenticeship; and (4) the availability of a relatively broad range of options and hence the opportunity for the exercise of initiative and discretion.

On balance, incomes policy proved not to lend itself to constructive union involvement. The reasons may be summarized as:

1. The lack of efficacy—that is, the inability of incomes policy to stabilize prices and the "intolerable" level of unemployment. Until the latter part of 1969 the charge of inefficacy also applied to the measures utilized to improve the payments balance.

2. The lack of a bargaining structure capable of making a binding commitment and enforcing it on the shop floor

3. The rejection by the trade unions of state intervention in collective bargaining as a matter of principle

4. The threat of mass rank and file disaffection from the union leadership which acquiesced in incomes policy

5. The existence of labor shortages which encouraged employers to bid up wages beyond the agreed terms, that is, the phenomenon of wage drift. "If an employer is standing there after a negotiation with his hand held

out with money in it there is no power on earth which can prevent the workers concerned from accepting the money."[160]

6. The tendency to "scapegoat" the unions as the restricting factor

7. The limited participation of the unions and the constricted range of options in formulating the terms of incomes policy

8. The inability of the incomes policy to comprehend effectively nonlabor incomes

9. The absence of a "clearly perceived threat to the nation's economic health"[161]

On the positive side, the TUC's need to respond with an incomes policy of its own provided an "institutional framework" for TUC to talk with unions on wage policy which it "had never had before." Historically TUC intervention in this area would have "been interpreted as an interference in the union's affairs which it would not accept." With the wage claims as leverage, TUC discussions with the union could also consider "wages structure in the firm or industry, . . . collective bargaining patterns . . . and even industrial disputes."[162]

Incomes policy brought in productivity as a permanent factor in wage increases. Most importantly, incomes policy forced the trade union movement to confront the problem of economic stability and to offer responsive alternatives. To the extent that incomes policy may be regarded as a permanent feature of a full employment economy, the incomes policy debate, as "savaging" as it has been, has sensitized trade unionism to the relevance of its wage policies to national economic goals.

Reform of industrial relations via Donovan and *In Place of Strife* represented an attempt on the part of government to institute "radical changes . . . needed in our system of industrial relations to meet the needs of a period of rapid technical and industrial change."[163] The radical nature of the change, especially marked in *In Place of Strife*, is the principle of government intervention in industrial relations "if it could be shown that certain important economic or social objectives were not sufficiently furthered or were frustrated by collective bargaining."[164]

The Labour government employed two types of intervention strategies. The Donovan report relied mainly on education and persuasion to achieve the desired reforms. In *In Place of Strife*, the cutting edge was the threat of penal sanctions for unauthorized strikes. The sanctions, to be sure, were

160. Murray, "Lionel Murray on Incomes Policy," p. 4.

161. Lloyd Ulman, "Wage-Price Policies Abroad," *Industrial Relations*, May 1969, p. 211.

162. Murray, "Lionel Murray on Incomes Policy," p. 6.

163. *In Place of Strife*, p. 5.

164. *Ibid.*, p. 6.

evaluated in many circles as being more symbol than substance; that is, the sanctions expressed a mood and not an efficacious instrument of reform. For their part the trade unions have not moved from their central position "that the best way of promoting good industrial relations [is through the] medium of voluntary collective bargaining." But in countering government demands, TUC has expanded voluntarism to mean self-regulation of union wages policy and unauthorized strikes; it has, however, been only partially successful in this.

It is a Labour government that has confronted the trade unions most insistently with the issue of short-run protectivism vs. forbearance to maximize longer-run advantage. The trade union movement has recognized the legitimacy of the question in the first place and in practice has exercised forbearance in the interests of specific national policy. At the same time it has also recognized that trade unions cannot be, as we have been emphasizing, "the agents of *any* programme which discounts the present in favor of the future."[165]

There are, however, defects in the industrial relations structure which obstruct a coherent union response to national economic policy: the multiplicity of competing unions, the lack of coordination between industrywide and shop-floor bargaining, craft-conscious unionism, the meagerness of union research and other technical resources, and the encrustation of union custom. Especially marked and highly visible is "the continued spread of workplace bargaining" and the development of "more militant styles of union leadership."[166] Militancy is in any case a labor movement value in its own right with strong roots in British trade union history. But it runs counter to the kind of "responsibility" which economic policy commitments demand.[167]

On balance and within limits, the Labour Party-trade union relationship is a positive factor in union responsiveness to national economic policy. The favorable features are the trade unions' moral and political stake in party effectiveness, trade union willingness to practice some self-denial to maintain that effectiveness, and the network of consultative mechanisms at all levels of policy and government (that is, the "industrial parliament" concept alluded to earlier).

The trade unions approach consultation and other forms of participation in national economic policy as a species of negotiations among the three parties at interest. Planning, in the TUC view, should operate "on the

165. TUC, *Trade Unionism*, p. 76 (emphasis added).
166. H. A. Turner, "Collective Bargaining and the Eclipse of Incomes Policy: Retrospect, Prospect and Possibilities," *British Journal of Industrial Relations*, July 1970, pp. 203–5 *passim*.
167. Allen, *Militant Trade Unionism*, pp. 18–54.

basis of consultation with both sides of industry."[168] The expert does not occupy a favored place in the trade union conception of the policy-making process, evidenced in the TUC characterization of the government's economists as an "administrative elite" whose perspective and "basic social attitudes" are "very different" from "the working people of Britain."[169] Statistical and factual analysis is not highly valued in the British unions. The research departments "often have little importance in the trade union hierarchy."[170]

The trade union commitment to national economic policy goals has entered a new phase with the unexpected accession to power of the Heath Conservative government in 1970. The trade unions seem to have moved from negotiation—albeit hard negotiation—with a Labour government toward confrontation with a Conservative government. Indeed, the common view is that it was precisely the inability of the Labour government to resolve through negotiations the problems of unauthorized strikes and price and wage inflation which caused its loss of power.

Both the Labour and Conservative governments have had the same interest in curbing strikes and inflation with the difference that the latter has also brought to the government-trade union relationship an ideological attitude which clashes fundamentally with trade union beliefs. The Conservative ideology is composed of: (1) a perceived mandate to get tough with the unions; (2) a "classic conservatism [in *The Economist's* words] as it has not been practiced for many decades";[171] and (3) a legislative program to curb "unfair industrial actions" by the unions, modeled it is said, after the American Taft-Hartley law.

The Conservatives' ideological push catches trade unionism at a time when it is involved in the most militant strike activity since the General Strike of 1926. The strikes are not only notable for their large number but for their shop-floor origins, and their penetration into the most important sectors of the economy; such as electric power, sanitation, docks, coal, automobiles, subways, nursing, and newspapers. The strikes are mainly for wage increases and thus reflect the pressures of the inflationary situation.

The militancy is not only anti-Tory; it was already apparent in the later days that the Labour government was "overdrawing on its reserves of union loyalty."[172] But against a Tory government it was possible to

168. TUC, *1967 Report*, p. 384.
169. *Ibid.*, p. 382.
170. Robinson, "Implementing an Incomes Policy," p. 83.
171. "Under Siege," *The Economist*, December 5, 1970, p. 12.
172. Giles Radice, "Trade Unions and the Labour Party," *Socialist Commentary*, November 1970, p. 8.

organize an unofficial one-day strike which brought out 350,000 workers in opposition to the industrial reform bill.

In assessing the quality of the trade union performance in national economic policy, due weight should be given to the obstacles imposed by the sheer size and complexity of the British economy. "During the post-war period, the British economy was faced with particularly complex problems, heavily influenced by changes in the world political situation and the role of Britain in international affairs, and by the weak balance of payments and low reserve position with which the country emerged from the war. . . . Throughout the period, the margin of permissable error has been narrower for the United Kingdom than for any other country here considered" (Belgium, France, Germany, Italy, Sweden, and the United States).[173] It is important to observe, then, that the "narrow band" of options within which British economic policy has had to operate may overstate the structural shortcomings of trade unionism and industrial relations as contributing causes to Britain's difficulties.

173. Walter Heller et al., Fiscal Policy for a Balanced Economy (Paris: OECD, 1968), pp. 62, 63.

CHAPTER SEVEN

France: Polarization

The French case best exemplifies the polarization of interests in the making of national economic policy. The state bureaucracy and the business classes are inside the circle of policy-making, while the trade unions, as part of the left, are for all practical purposes excluded.

This chapter first sketches the economic and trade union background and then briefly examines trade union involvement in four contexts: the French Plan, the 1968 general strike, and union involvements in the undertaking and selected institutions of the labor market. The scope of this inquiry is meant to be indicative rather than exhaustive.

Prior to the 1968 strikes the French economy was just beginning to emerge into a period of "greater buoyancy" after a period of leveling of consumption and production.[1] The 1968 general strike cost about 3 percent of the annual hours worked and the same amount in production. Considered in the larger frame of the postwar period, the performance of the French economy has "turned out to be better than anything France had known for a very long time, if ever."[2]

II

Union membership in France, taking into account only those who have paid their dues and are in good standing, numbers about 3 million or about 20 percent of its potential. This is the lowest ratio of any Western European movement. A crisis confrontation can bring out more workers; approximately 10 million workers participated in the 1968 general strike, but this was something which CGT or the other unions had little to do with. "We simply coordinated a movement that was the result of rising discontent," an influential CGT leader said.[3]

1. OECD, *Economic Surveys–France*, Paris, April 1969, p. 6.
2. John Sheahan, *An Introduction to the French Economy* (Columbus: Merrill, 1969), p. 6.
3. Marc Piliot, quoted in Sanche de Gramont, "The French Worker Wants to Join the Affluent Society," *New York Times Magazine*, June 16, 1968, p. 51.

French unionism is divided into three rival confederations: the communist-controlled CGT with about 1,500,000 members, one-third of whom are estimated to be Communist Party members; the CFDT, formerly the Catholic federation but now disassociated from Church influence, with about 600,000 members; and the CGT-FO, which broke away from the CGT, with rather vague socialist orientation and with a membership of about 500,000.[4] In addition, there is the CGC, a nonpolitical organization with a membership of about 200,000 among engineers, general technicians, and salesmen.

The CGT is weak and incapable of sustaining coordinated action. It is an association of (1) national unions in trades and industries which are, in turn, loose federations of geographic or plant local unions or regional associations of local unions, and (2) "horizontal" associations—city centrals and department federations bringing together locals of all trades in each of the ninety departments into which French political government is divided.

Dues are low—"the French worker wants a low-cost union; he pays dues amounting to one-hour's wages a month," a CGT functionary remarked.[5] Even so, the proceeds of the dues are divided among the national union, the department federation, and the local. The unions are poor, the staff resources are inadequate—CGT has five full-time organizers[6]—and "union research is largely non-existent."[7] The union personnel and finances have to be augmented by external assistance, mostly political.

The hallmark of French trade unionism is its fundamentalist revolutionary anticapitalism. The revolutionary spirit, most unrelenting in the CGT, asserts "hostility to any form of cooperation with the enemies of the working class be they in the form of the employer or the state."[8] FO and CFDT are somewhat more moderate but they do not permit themselves to lag too far behind the revolutionary sentiment of the presumably opinion-leading CGT.

The way French unions use the strike is a sign of "weakness rather than strength."[9] The low dues precludes the accumulation of strike funds, and as a CGT unionist said, "since we don't have a strike fund [strikers] can't

4. Sanche de Gramont, "French Worker Wants to Join the Affluent Society," p. 6.

5. Piliot, quoted in Sanche de Gramont, "French Worker Wants to Join the Affluent Society," p. 56.

6. Michel Crozier, "White Collar Workers—The Case of France," in *White Collar Trade Unions*, ed. Adolf Sturmthal (Urbana: University of Illinois Press, 1966), p. 119.

7. Benjamin M. Selekman *et al.*, *Problems in Labor Relations*, 3d ed. (New York: McGraw-Hill, 1964), p. 692.

8. L. Freyfié de Bellecombe, "Workers' Participation in Management in France: The Basic Problems," *International Institute for Labour Studies Bulletin* (Geneva), June 1969, p. 64.

9. Sheahan, *Introduction to the French Economy*, p. 43.

hold out for long."[10] For this reason especially, the typical strike is a one-day or one-hour affair. The French have coined the phrase "la grève illimitée" to describe the uncharacteristic longer strike.

"French management has until now been able to enforce its philosophy that the factory is an extension of the family and thus must remain non-equalitarian."[11] The dominant management approach to unionism is, therefore, one of containment. The need to negotiate with the unions at the level of the industry and even economy is recognized, but enterprise negotiation is strongly resisted. A "military-type leadership . . . still generally prevails in French businesses," characterized by "autocratic rule of the chairman and managing director," not infrequently the same person, and "promotion according to the caste system."[12]

Collective bargaining is relatively new in France, having been legalized in 1919, experimented with in some degree in 1936, but not accepted as a common practice until the 1950s. Although growing, collective bargaining is distinctly subordinate to state intervention in regulating the terms of employment, and the collective bargaining which does operate is under the tutelage of the government. The excessive reliance on legislation is a sign of weakness in the trade union view. "In France we feel that legislation generally only puts on paper," a CFDT officer has said, "things that exist already. Therefore, we are rather inclined to say in France that we can only really expect progress when there is action, when there is negotiating, and when there are collective agreements."[13]

III

The French Plan has enlisted the most formalized and systematic trade union involvement in national economic policy. "The drafting of the plan is open broadly to representatives of all socio-occupational categories, and the plan's successful implementation," according to the official view, "hinges on the determination of all to reach its targets."[14]

The constitutionally established Economic and Social Council, "made up of representatives from all socio-occupational categories . . . serves as a link" between the plan's committee structure and parliament and as a point of consultation for the final drafts of the plan.[15] Approximately 10 percent of the council's 200 or so members are appointed from lists sub-

10. Piliot, quoted in Sanche de Gramont, "French Worker Wants to Join the Affluent Society," p. 56.
11. Sanche de Gramont, "French Worker Wants to Join the Affluent Society," p. 51.
12. Pierre Drouin, "Death Knell for Imperial System of Company Management in France," *Le Monde Weekly Selections*, July 10, 1968, p. 4.
13. François Rogé, *ICF Bulletin*, (International Federation of Chemical and General Workers' Unions, Geneva), July–August 1970, p. 26.
14. Ambassade de France, Service de Presse et d'Information, *The Fifth Plan, 1966–1970* (Washington, D.C., 1967), p. 31.
15. *Ibid.*, p. 7.

mitted by the four major labor federations. Trade union representatives, among others, sit on the rarely convened Higher Council for the Plan which acts as a consultative arm of the plan's commissioner general.

The main thrust of worker participation in the plan is through the modernization committees carrying out the principle that "the preparation and reappraisal of the plan should be a continuous process. In a concerted economy, as opposed to a bureaucratically directed or corporative economy, this is the only way of ensuring the resolution of problems by a permanent exchange of views between the administration and the country."[16] The "horizontal" modernization commissions deal with problems common to all sectors and include "General Economics and Finance, Manpower, Productivity, Research and Regional Development"; the vertical commissions "represent different sectors of activity."[17] In addition to the worker and employer representatives, the commissions also include technical experts. Exclusive of ex officio members the size of the commissions ranges from twenty (newspaper printing) to about eighty (manufacturing and agriculture). Interest representation on the committees is designed not to get a vote but to provide a hearing for all viewpoints. In theory the partisan members are appointed in their personal capacities; in practice they are selected from lists presented by the various organizations.

The trade union membership on the commissions has fluctuated widely from plan to plan, ranging from about 5 percent (34 out of 604) in the Second Plan to about 15 percent (77 out of 494) in the First Plan and 15 percent (291 out of 1,950) in the Fifth Plan. The trade unionists are always outnumbered by representatives from employer organizations, heads of undertakings, and civil servants, with the last-named consistently the most numerous and generally believed to be the most powerful group. Committee chairmen are more likely to come from the employer group; in addition, because of the technical qualifications that their profession requires, *rapporteurs* are usually government experts.[18]

Although other members of commissions are not paid, the trade unionists receive traveling expenses and compensation equal to twice wages lost. In addition, the government gives financial support to union- and

16. Jean-Jacques Bonnaud, "Participation by Workers and Employers' Organisations in Planning in France," *International Labour Review*, (ILO, Geneva), April 1966, p. 342.

17. Pierre Massé, "The Guiding Ideas Behind French Planning," in *Capitalism, Market Socialism and Central Planning*, ed. Wayne A. Leeman (Boston: Houghton Mifflin Co., 1963), p. 369. These different sectors include: Agriculture; Agriculture and Food Industries; Artisans; Building and Public Works; Chemicals; Culture and Arts; Energy; Fisheries; Housing; Non-Ferrous Mines and Metals; Oil; Overseas Territories; Post Office and Telecommunications; Radio and Television; Sanitary and Social Equipment; School, University, and Sport Equipment; Steel; Trade; Transport; Transportation Industries; Tourism; and Urban Equipment.

18. Bonnaud, "Participation by Workers and Employers' Organisations in Planning," p. 344.

university-sponsored training programs for the education of union representatives and active members in economic and social planning. Prior to
the Fifth Plan, employer and union participation was limited to setting
plan goals and implementation, but did not include a review of the plan in
action. The preparation for the Fifth Plan permitted somewhat more extended involvement in the review process.

The Manpower Commission, similar to others insofar as it is limited to
advice and research, claims a membership of fifty, including the trade
union, employers, and government experts. The commission (1) builds up
vertical committee estimates into an aggregate forecast of economywide
manpower requirements, (2) measures trends in skill requirements against
training programs and facilities, and (3) draws up forecasts of manpower
needs by region in order to correct imbalances. Regional interests are
integrated through consultation with private regional development boards
on which trade unions are represented.

A high-ranking civil servant assessed labor's role as largely "public relations. The real contact is between industry and the State, and these two
effectively exclude the 'third partner' from the serious discussions.
Frankly neither the businessman nor the civil servants want to discuss their
plans with union people (with rare exceptions) because they know
(1) most union people aren't really qualified to participate and (2) most of
them have short-term political interests which tempt them to leak the
results of committee deliberations as one means to advance their interests
with the rank and file. . . . We maintain the facade of a three-way dialogue,
when in fact it is only two-way for the most part."[19]

The government-employer strategy of union containment of the
planning process thus seems to consist of these tactical pieces:

1. "Depoliticalization" or the "third choice" beyond capitalism or
communism: "the technical aspect dominates the tactical" and becomes
" 'as impervious to shifts in the political climate as possible.' "[20] One of
the leading civil service planners characterized this tactic as "opaque
technicity."[21]

2. Involvement of union participants at all levels in the planning process but with calculated organizational restraints on their authority by:
(a) limiting the committees to a "hearing" or advisory function, (b) constituting the commissions as large and unwieldy groups in which the
unions are a small minority in a sea of "representatives from socio-
occupational categories," (c) selecting the key officials of the committees
from the employer groups and the higher civil servant groups.

19. Quoted in John H. McArthur and Bruce R. Scott, *Industrial Planning in
France* (Boston: Harvard Graduate School of Business Administration, 1969), p. 418.
20. John and Ann Marie Hackett, *Economic Planning in France* (Cambridge:
Harvard University Press, 1963), p. 335.
21. François Bloch-Lainé, in Stephen S. Cohen, *Modern Capitalist Planning–The
French Model* (Cambridge: Harvard University Press, 1970), p. 198.

3. Isolation of the trade union representatives within the planning community: "The trade unionist arrives at the Plan and finds himself an isolated man. The businessmen know one another . . . and they pass around statistics prepared by their own well equipped professional staffs. The trade unionist is the only one to feel lost. . . . He will try to pose some questions. He will worry about the source of statistics being used and he will seek aid from the tutelary ministry. . . . The civil servant, however, will rarely be disturbed. He will generally accept the statistics supplied by the business groups without having the inclination—or the technical resources—to check them out. The trade unionist will be presented with a technical report of some 400 pages and asked for his views. He might ask some additional questions but then the businessmen, civil servants and experts will begin to express their disapproval of this man who only criticizes and questions—and that only in general terms—without offering any detailed, constructive alternatives."[22]

For their part, the unions have erected what has thus far proved to be an unbridgeable ideological barrier to full participation in the planning process. In essence the unions view themselves as "a permanent opposition to the economic system."[23] In the words of a representative spokesman of the French left, "If we are in a capitalist regime, in a regime of exploitation, to participate in the realisation of the capitalist plan means, in good French, to participate in the exploitation of the workers."[24] A CFDT spokesman fears the "risks of integrating the leadership of the working class into the system"[25] and an FO secretary sees the plan as "technocratic 'planning' which reduces [the union] to the role of voting and executing instructions from on high, . . . to . . . a mere transmission belt between the state and the workers. . . . The real negotiations have already taken place between the government and the employers' federation before the trade unions are called."[26]

Actual trade union participation in the French Plan is limited, as one official put it, to "an attempt to put their case. . . . They have a very real fear of appearing to underwrite representatives who may find themselves collaborating in a plan the technical demands of which clash with the claims of their members."[27] A recent commentary on French planning characterized the strategy of French trade unions as "contestative participation" which favors "a trade union role in the planning process," but this

22. Phillipe Bauchard, quoted in Cohen, *Modern Capitalist Planning*, p. 197.
23. Bonnaud, "Participation by Workers and Employers' Organisations in Planning," p. 360.
24. André Heursteault, in Cohen, *Modern Capitalist Planning*, p. 209.
25. G. Delclercq, in Cohen, *Modern Capitalist Planning*, p. 200.
26. G. Ventejol, "French Unions and Economic Planning," *Free Labour World* (ICFTU, Brussels), April 1964, pp. 15–16.
27. Bonnaud, "Participation by Workers and Employers' Organisations in Planning," p. 360.

role "should be not merely getting 'scraps from the table' but the step-by-step public exposure of the plan and the political-economy it symbolizes as capitalist and profoundly inimical to the real interests of the French working people." The objective is "to use the planning process as an educative battleground to elevate the political and class consciousness of the workers."[28] In line with this strategy an abortive attempt (as it turned out) was made in 1964 to introduce a "Counter Plan" which would expose the "clearly reactionary" aspects of the Fifth Plan.[29]

Ideological resistance to participation in planning is reinforced by the poverty of union research resources. "The French trade unions simply do not have enough properly trained men to represent them in the subtle and technical deliberations of the planning process."[30]

IV

The general strike of May 1968 pointed up the importance of confrontation as the form of interaction which was apparently necessary to bring the parties—unions, employers, and government—to bargain national economic policy. The strikes themselves had "no equivalent in the economic history of France or indeed other [OECD] Member countries. More than 10 million wage and salary earners out of a total of some 15 million stopped work for about three weeks or longer."[31] The climate for the general strike was generated by the student rebellion but the seeds of worker protest had been planted much earlier and more gradually—so gradually that the sit-ins took the confederations by complete surprise. The first sit-in began at the nationalized Bouguenais Sud-Aviation plant with 2,800 workers. The cause of the sit-in was the reduction of the work week in April from 48 to 46½ hours with another cut announced for July, without adjustment of hourly rates to recompense for the cut.

The workers responded with daily half-hour strikes capped by a half-day strike on April 29. The management responded by telling the workers how well off they were and chiding them that the more they got the more they wanted. "The workers were in an ugly mood. Sensing the mood, a delegate of the CGT . . . shouted, 'Since management will not give in, comrades, let's all go and pay them a visit.' "[32]

As the workers began a march on the management offices, the manager "confronted them in the hall and said dramatically, 'I am your prisoner; do what you want with me.' " The union leaders then decided to occupy

28. Cohen, *Modern Capitalist Planning*, pp. 212–13.
29. *Ibid.*, p. 216.
30. *Ibid.*, p. 195.
31. "Prospects in France after the Strike," *Economic Outlook* (OECD, Paris), July 1968, pp. 55–56.
32. Sanche de Gramont, "French Worker Wants to Join the Affluent Society," p. 9.

the plant because if they did not, they "would be locked out the following day."[33] The nationalized Renault plant near Rouen followed suit on May 16—two days after Bouguenais, and thereafter the sit-in movement spread to hundreds of other plants.

A major grievance, perhaps as important as any in the strike, was the refusal of management to give recognition to the union on the shop floor. "Union dues must be collected clandestinely, union posters and announcements are subject to management censorship and union meetings must be held outside the plant and working hours. Overzealous union delegates are threatened with transfers to other plants."[34] Workers also demanded that the discretionary productivity and Christmas bonuses be approved.

The Bouguenais workers resented the suggestion that their militancy had been ignited by the students. "We've been fighting management for years, so we don't like to hear them lecture us about the revolution. We realize they have their own problems, but we just don't talk the same language. And remember this: We'll get something out of this strike, but what will they get after building barricades and throwing paving stones."[35]

The CGT leaders denied that they were planning an armed insurrection. "We prefer to work things out through the existing electoral process. Conditions are not ripe for an armed uprising. We feel that when the workers' demands have been met, they should go home peacefully. . . . We can't take the responsibility for making each factory into a fortress."[36]

The Grenelle framework agreement—perhaps protocol is the better term—settled the general strike, even though shop protests continued for a period thereafter. The agreement provided for a 35 percent increase in the minimum wage, a 10 percent increase in the general wage in two installments, regular meetings on wages and prices, agreement in principle on hours reductions, and major changes in medical care reimbursement. The government undertook to enact legislation which would protect union rights in the enterprise including union recognition, dues collection, dissemination of union propaganda, monthly union meetings on the plant premises, and the legitimation of the steward's functions. Present at the negotiations were "four members of a united Government in coalition with 10 members of a united management association against 34 members of disunited labor groups." According to a CGT participant, "While management and the Government worked hand in glove, the unions were often at odds. There was no tactical coherence. Each one had different priorities, some wanted to keep up the lock-ins, others did not; some were satisfied with the compromise, others were not."[37]

33. *Ibid.*
34. *Ibid.*, p. 51.
35. *Ibid.*
36. *Ibid.*, p. 56.
37. *Ibid.*

The events of May 1968 and the Grenelle aftermath could have the result of furthering national agreements between the employers and the trade union confederation. There was some precedent prior to 1968 for these agreements: a pension scheme had been negotiated in 1947 and unemployment insurance in 1958. In 1966 identical letters from the CGT and CFDT to the employers' confederation requested negotiations on shorter hours of work, union rights, and compensation for partial unemployment. The proposals were rejected by CNPF on the ground that a discussion of these issues could "only have consequences incompatible with the requirements of economic and social progress" and that "the confederation is not the normal level of discussion."[38]

Reinstatement of the discussions required the initiative of Prime Minister Pompidou who urged joint consideration of income guarantees, joint employment committees, advance notice, reemployment problems of mergers, and compensation for partial unemployment. CNPF's initial reaction was to reject the government's invitation because it called into "question the balance of relationships between the social partners" and would therefore "modify the traditional conditions of free discussion."[39] Subsequently CNPF relented and agreed to discussions which began in January 1968. At first CNPF anticipated a model agreement binding only in the event of formal approval by an industry agreement. Later, in February 1968, an "interindustry agreement was signed," endorsed by all the employer and union parties except CFDT. Compensation for short work weeks and joint employment committees were approved, but by May 1968, agreement could not be reached on the other issues.

Grenelle required reinstatement of discussions on the employment and training items and in February 1969 agreement was reached. Part I establishes joint employment committees at the industry level to study employment conditions, vocational training, and reemployment and retraining in the event of "collective dismissals." Part II brings the works councils into the process of "collective dismissals on economic grounds," requiring information and consultation on the details of dismissals and advance notice. Part III deals with "guarantees in the event of transfers and collective dismissals on economic grounds." This part requires that displacement be achieved insofar as it is possible through natural attrition and transfers, that downgraded workers receive some indemnification, and that displaced workers be entitled to specified reemployment rights.[40]

"The real importance of the agreement," *The Economist's* Paris correspondent noted at the time, "is that it promises to clear the way for direct

38. Yves Delamotte, "New Developments in Collective Bargaining on Productivity and Manpower Adjustment," mimeographed (Paris: OECD, Manpower and Social Affairs Directorate, 1969), pp. 85–86.
39. *Ibid.*, p. 88.
40. Text of agreement in *ibid.*, pp. 126–33.

contact between employers and unions at the local level. This has been one of the main long-term objectives of the Chief of the Patronat, M. Paul Huvelin, whose philosophy has been one of breaking down and decentralising the conflict and distrust between the two sides at the national level."[41]

The general strike of 1968 represented tripartite, economywide negotiation of policies on wages, social security, and union-management relations. The employers and the government were brought to a bargaining posture by disruption of the economy which was triggered not by the union leadership but by the rank and file who, in turn, rode the wave of a student revolt. Despite the revolutionary ideology of the leaders and the anticapitalist impulses of the workers, the confrontation was not utilized to introduce radical change.

In the fall of 1969, confrontation once again, but on a smaller scale, served as the medium through which the government of President Pompidou and Prime Minister Chalban-Delmas and the trade union movement came to terms of a sort. Dissatisfaction with the effects of devaluation, the deflationary bias of the government's stabilization program, and declining real wages triggered a wave of wildcat strikes in transportation and public service. CGT's General Secretary Séguy, also a member of the French Communist Party's Politburo, warned Pompidou that he might be "worn down" by "a combined labor offensive and replaced by a leftist government with Communist participation."[42] In response, Pompidou charged that " 'some people' wished to use the strikes for political purposes" and served notice that the law will be "respected" and "republican order . . . maintained."[43]

The government also responded with an increase in the minimum wage and, by way of long-range reform, with a program to create a " 'new society' that will be more effective in achieving well being, more just toward the underprivileged, more responsible in its own operation, more human in everyday living."[44] More specifically, reforms in the interests of the workers included "the introduction of the monthly remuneration system—50% of the labor force is already covered by agreements concluded— . . . the development of employee participation in profits— involving 45,000 agreements and 2,500,000 workers— . . . new experi-

41. "France: Preparing the Ground for March," *The Economist* (London), February 15, 1969, p. 76.

42. Henry Giniger, "French Debate Economy as Unrest Spreads," *New York Times*, September 16, 1969.

43. Henry Giniger, "Pompidou Answers Red Threat," *New York Times*, September 18, 1969.

44. Statement by Premier Jacques Chalban-Delmas before the French National Assembly on October 15, 1970, Ambassade de France, Service de Presse et d'Information, no. 1488, New York, p. 4.

ments in employee shareholding [and] . . . the more effective exercise of the right of every worker to vocational training."[45]

By the fall of 1970 the Paris correspondent of *The Economist* was commending the restraint of the French unions "to their counterparts in almost every big industrial nation. . . . [Séguy] is working at full steam to group the unions into a coherent left-wing political force, which will negotiate its demands not in the streets but around the conference table."[46] Despite the relative calm at the end of 1970, Séguy saw "the 'aggression and antagonisms' between workers and the 'power interests' leading to new confrontations early in 1971."[47]

V

Worker representation at the level of the plant or undertaking provides some limited opportunities for concern with manpower utilization. Workers' interests can be asserted variously through direct presentation to the management, and also through shop stewards, plant committees, health and safety committees, safety delegates, representation on the board of directors in the nationalized industries, special disciplinary committees, labor courts, and labor inspectors—all regulated by law.

Shop stewards are elected from lists prepared by the "most representative unions," that is, CGT, CGT-FO, CFTD, and the Cadres, under a system of proportional representation. The steward's main job is grievance representation. Grievances may also be mediated or decided by a labor court—the Conseil des Prud-hommes—through Ministry of Labor inspectors, or even through the plant committees.

The plant committee, obligatory in enterprises with fifty employees or more, is composed of employee and employer representatives. It is an advisory mechanism designed to enhance labor-management cooperation but without authority to conclude collective agreements. The scope of the committee's competence includes economic and financial matters relating to the firm—the field in which "the committees have played the smallest part"[48]—improvement of employment conditions, and plant medical and social services and welfare activities—the area in which the plant committee exerts its greatest influence.

Consultation is obligatory on vocational training and retraining, employment of women and young workers, changes in the size and structure

45. Chalban-Delmas, p. 7; see also "Foreign Labor Briefs," *Monthly Labor Review* (Washington, D.C.), December 1969, pp. 63–64.

46. "French Unions a Bit of the Old Concord," *The Economist*, September 26, 1970, p. 91.

47. Clyde H. Farnsworth, "Tactic of French Group Protests—Locking up Boss," *New York Times*, December 28, 1970.

48. Adolf Sturmthal, *Workers Councils* (Cambridge: Harvard University Press, 1964), p. 40.

of the work force, and technological change. Management is required to report annually on its activities in these areas. While there are some model consultative arrangements, "it is feared in trade union circles that employees, as has often happened in the past, may not give the works committees enough information for the consultation to have any effect, or consult them only after the relevant decisions have already been taken."[49] The "failure of the plant committees" evidenced in the "small number of active committees" has been attributed to the outlook of the French employer who sees the committees as "socialization without socialism," and to the CGT which holds the view that "works committees constituted a weapon in the class struggle" and should not be considered as an instrument of cooperation between employers and workers.[50]

A 1950 law permits plant agreements with unions (*accords d'enterprise*). Still "exceptional," these agreements pioneered by Renault have been concluded in several large-scale enterprises.[51] A model plant agreement formulated by the Inter-Union Pay and Productivity Study Center provides for a management commitment not to dismiss workers because of innovation. In return, provision is made to transfer workers after negotiation. An industrywide program has been negotiated for the textile industry which provides for joint union-management effort in modernization and productivity improvement in return for strengthened and augmented pensions and unemployment compensation programs and placement activities for redundant workers. In iron and steel, planned technological change is complemented by early retirement, severance pay, preferential rehiring of disemployed workers, and regional development for new employment and related retraining.[52] A number of recent agreements have established joint employment committees which, in the view of an FO official, "can be regarded as the start of a systematic forecasting policy concerning manpower needs."[53]

On balance, the network of worker representation in the undertaking has acted to fragment trade union influence by blocking direct access to the rank and file and by creating a multiplicity of competing and overlapping approaches to management without necessarily giving the worker a larger voice in the enterprise. The weakening of the union's shop floor influence can conceivably be reversed by Grenelle and post-Grenelle developments. The Grenelle agreement undertook to give the union's presence on the shop floor a measure of legitimacy. The February 19 agreement, as

49. ILO, *Labour and Automation: Manpower Adjustment Programmes, vol. 1, France, Federal Republic of Germany, United Kingdom* (Geneva, 1967), p. 67.
50. Adolf Sturmthal, *Workers Councils*, p. 44.
51. ILO, *Manpower Adjustment Programmes*, p. 72.
52. *Ibid.*, pp. 69–70.
53. Roger Louet, "Protecting the Workers against Adverse Effects of Technological Change," *Free Labour World*, May 1968, p. 14.

it related to the works councils, mandated a more effective involvement in manpower policy of the enterprise.

VI

Trade union influence on labor market administration is mainly exercised through the unemployment insurance system and, to a somewhat lesser degree, through a variety of social security, vocational training, and apprenticeship programs.

On the urging of President de Gaulle the four labor centers negotiated in 1958 an agreement with the CNPF for the establishment of a system of unemployment compensation. The government then made the insurance scheme compulsory "for all firms in any sector of industry or commerce for which there is an association affiliated to CNPF."[54] Before this the unemployment risk was covered only by a 1914 assistance program requiring a means test. The current scheme is administered through labor and employer representation in national and regional bodies. The presidency rotates between the labor and employer representatives. André Bergeron of FO, who served twice as president of the national body, played "a kind of mediatory or conciliatory role . . . and may have discussed current issues privately with all groups except the CGT. . . . He is an excellent technician . . . and has been intimately familiar with the institution since its inception." The CFTD has also been singled out for its "excellent staff work" and its pressure for extending the unemployment compensation system.[55] The experience has demonstrated, in Meyer's view as of 1965, "a history of effective and constructive relations between all the major trade union centers and the central federation of employers' associations." For its part the government has "exploited the plan. . . . Unwilling to establish a conventional State unemployment insurance scheme," it has "permitted the Ministry of Finance to call upon the reserves of the plan to provide for apparent social needs." This meant that "the plan was merely to foot the bill for new functions without adequate independence or control over policy formulation."[56]

Labor movement representatives are influential in the consultative bodies to the various social security programs and often serve as chairmen. But "the autonomy of the funds governing boards (Conseils d'Administration) has become increasingly theoretical under the strict regulations imposed by the trustee authorities."[57]

54. Frederic Meyers, "The Role of Collective Bargaining in France: The Case of Unemployment Insurance," *British Journal of Industrial Relations* (London), November 1965, p. 366.

55. *Ibid.*, pp. 379–80.

56. *Ibid.*, p. 387.

57. Jean Daniel Reynaud, "The Role of Trade Unions in National Political Economies," in *International Labor*, ed. Solomon R. Barkin (New York: Harper and Row, 1967), p. 411.

An "outstanding" example of collaboration by workers' organizations has been the vocational training system for adults, which is counseled by a coordinating committee at the ministerial level and in the regions.[58] Labor representatives, along with employer and public representatives, serve on (1) the Committee on Vocational Guidance and Training (Haut Comité de l'Orientation et de la Formation Professionelle) which "determines the needs for training and vocational guidance in the context of extended compulsory general education"; (2) national consultative trade advisory committees (Commission Nationelle Professionelle) which draw up the lists of apprenticeable trades, determine examination requirements and regulations, and establish syllabi for apprenticeship, further training, and retraining; and (3) area committees on technical or vocational education (Comité Departemental de l'Enseignement Technique) which advise on the areas in which related instruction and vocational schools should be established.[59]

VII

The policy areas which have engaged the trade unions have been economic planning, national wages policy, industrial relations reform (mainly to achieve a légitimate and crediblo union presence in the enterprise), shop floor participation in enterprise manpower planning, and labor market administration. The union involvement in economic planning serves a "public relations" function for the government, but its actual influence on the planning outcomes is peripheral. The union effect on industrial relations reform and national wages policy has been achieved mainly by confrontation and eruption.

Up to now "in the great majority of cases the work of the [councils] seems to have been a formality."[60] Whether the Grenelle and the February 1969 agreements will usher in a new day in works council involvement remains to be seen. Workable advisory relationships have been developed in the various institutions of the labor market but, with the possible exception of unemployment insurance, the trade union influence is not central.

The main reasons why French trade unionism is incapable of sustaining a viable negotiating posture are (1) the narrow membership base further fragmented by ideological divisions among the trade union centers; (2) the ideological conditioning which disparages compromise under capitalism; (3) the organizational shortcomings in staff, finances, and shop floor representation; (4) the state's preemption of employment regulation and the consequent dependence of the unions "on the state for the very conditions

58. ILO, *Manpower Adjustment Programmes,* p. 68.
59. ILO, *European Apprenticeship,* 2d ed. (Geneva, 1966), pp. 148–51.
60. Greyfié de Bellecombe, "Workers' Participation in Management," p. 88.

of existence and functioning";[61] (5) the revolutionary orientation of the trade unions which discourages employers and the government from coming to the bargaining table; (6) the traditional employer attitude that "complete authority is . . . the corollary of maximum efficiency";[62] (7) the "technocratic" approach of the higher civil servants who think of themselves as the embodiment of the true general interest—"The notion is straight out of Rousseau."[63]

Supplementary References

Delamotte, Yves. "Extension of Bargaining Objectives." Paper delivered at Trade Union Seminar on New Perspectives in Collective Bargaining, OECD Regional Seminar, Paris, November 1969.

Dessau, J. "Planning and Incomes Policy in France." *British Journal of Industrial Relations*, October 1963, pp. 310–17.

Gorz, André. *Strategy for Labor*. Boston: Beacon Press, 1967.

Gretton, John. *Students and Workers*. London: Macdonald, 1969, pp. 144–270.

Hayward, J. E. S. "Interest Groups and Incomes Policy in France." *British Journal of Industrial Relations*, July 1966, pp. 165–200.

---

61. Val Lorwin, "Labor Organization and Politics in Belgium and France," in *National Labor Movements in the Postwar World*, ed. E. M. Kassalow (Evanston: Northwestern University Press, 1963), p. 155.
62. Greyfié de Bellecombe, "Workers' Participation in Management," p. 58.
63. Cohen, *Modern Capitalist Planning*, p. 50.

CHAPTER EIGHT

Trade Unions and National Economic Policy in Western Europe: A Summary

We have examined here selected country cases of trade union involvement in national economic policy dealing with planning, manpower, incomes and wages, and industrial relations. The central theme which runs through these cases is a union undertaking to relate its protective demands in collective bargaining and legislation to specified national policy goals. We call this economic policy unionism. Unions which for varying reasons are not responsive to national policy goals may be termed, after Sturmthal, "pressure group" unions because the union "does not make an effort to integrate the interests of its group with those of the community of which it forms a part."[1]

The economic settings against which economic policy unionism has emerged have taken their main features from the successive phases of development which the postwar European economy has experienced; specifically, these are demobilization, recovery, full employment, structural change and growth, and currently "overfull" employment accompanied by the implacable inflationary pressures which seem to be a permanent feature of the post-full employment era. This post-full employment is in striking contrast to the depressed state of the European economy in the interwar years marked by, in Lundberg's admirable synthesis: "(1) the slow rate of growth, (2) the imprint of severe cyclical setbacks, (3) the U.S. economy as the engine of business cycles, (4) the high instability of international trade, (5) the deflationary tendencies, (6) the high rates of unemployment, (7) the disorganization and overcapacity problems, (8) the destabilizing conditions regarding international and national systems of credit and finance, (9) the low scale of government operations, (10) the weak role of economic policy."[2]

1. Adolf Sturmthal, *The Tragedy of European Labor* (New York: Columbia University Press, 1943), p. ix.
2. Erik Lundberg, *Instability and Economic Growth* (New Haven: Yale University Press, 1968), p. 23.

When demobilization and recovery had been achieved, "the main difficulty of the postwar economies was not slack demand, relative overproduction or insufficient investment, but an ungovernable tendency of demand to outrun the economy's capacity to meet it without inflation and price rise."[3] The touchstone of economic policy in Western Europe has in a generation thus shifted from preoccupation with mass unemployment to concern over the inflationary consequences of full employment and growth. The constraints on economic policy which the governments have had to grapple with in this post-full employment period have been aptly characterized by an OECD committee on fiscal policy as the "narrow band—the narrow room for manoeuver between, on the one hand, an unacceptably low level of employment and, on the other, a pressure of demand that creates an inflationary strain on resources";[4] or put another way, "the narrow band that lies between overheating the economy on the one hand and the loss of high employment on the other."[5] The important place of the trade unions in the making of economic policy in this period did not spring from a trade union push for power but rather from a kind of "coopting" of trade unions by governments to help moderate the inflationary pressures caused by labor stringencies.

The willingness of unions to be drawn into the making of economic policy with governments and employers brings into focus the other distinctive feature of postwar European society: the ideological readiness of mainstream socialism, with which most trade union movements are strongly identified, to believe that gradual modification of "reformist" capitalism can work and to collaborate with the "ruling classes" in making it work. This ideological conversion is the result of several lessons learned during the interwar and postwar years: (1) the enormous hazards to which ideological dogmatism subjects democracy and trade unionism, (2) reformist capitalism's ability to produce full employment and the welfare state, and (3) trade unionism's great stake in maintaining a stable and democratic order, even under reformist capitalism.

II

The most systematic effort at national planning involving the trade unions has been the French Plan. The union representation mechanism provided a hearing for union viewpoints but not significant involvement. This marginality of union power and influence in France is attributable to the intent of the Plan bureaucracy and the predisposition of the trade

3. M. M. Postan, *An Economic History of Western Europe* (London: Methuen, 1967), p. 19.

4. Walter Heller *et al.*, *Fiscal Policy for a Balanced Economy* (Paris: OECD, 1968), p. 10.

5. *Ibid.*, p. 28.

union movement which has neither the motivation nor resources to go beyond contesting and challenging.

The planning process in the Netherlands, Austria, and the United Kingdom, while not as structurally elaborate as the French Plan, has come closer to involving the trade union movements as partners. The United Kingdom's TUC was part of a tripartite National Economic Development Council for the brief period when the council was in the center of the planning effort. The Netherlands' Social and Economic Council with its strong union participation was not a planning body in its own right, but nevertheless highly influential in general economic policy. The Austrian Joint Council on Wages and the Advisory Council on Economic and Social Affairs, also with decisive union participation, are in effect instrumentalities for the negotiation of economic and social policy.

Union participation in economic planning has been viable in Austria and the Netherlands because (1) their smaller scale economies make the planning process more manageable, (2) the trade unions are integral parts of the mainstream, and (3) in the Austrian case the unions have been able to command adequate staff resources through the Chambers of Labor. In the United Kingdom, the trade union movement was initially very favorable to economic planning but the plan targets were thrown off balance by recurring payments crises and the sheer magnitude of the planning undertaking. As far as the British and to some degree the Dutch trade unions were directly concerned, their interest in planning was frustrated by—as they saw it—the bureaucrats' takeover of the planning process and the inability of their own meager staff resources to exert countervailing influence.

The concept of economic planning is ideologically agreeable to the unions but its administration cannot normally provide a meaningful role for union participants. The clash in Britain has been between the planning professional's approach through sophisticated economic analysis and the trade union view of planning "as a bargain between interest groups."[6] Even when union economists are available, planning becomes a staff not a leadership function. Planning at the industry level, as in the British EDC's which are mostly information exchanges, was able to enlist a more substantial union involvement due perhaps to decentralization and the practical orientation of the councils.

III

The most systematic and comprehensive involvement of a trade union movement in manpower policy is represented by the Swedish movement

6. Andrew Shonfeld, *Modern Capitalism* (London: Oxford University Press, 1965), p. 155.

whose economists conceptualized the "active manpower policy" for Sweden and subsequently through OECD made the active manpower policy the model for Western Europe. The Swedish movement has also played a decisive part in the administration of the active manpower policy through the National Labor Market Board. While no other trade union movement has put manpower policy at the center as the Swedes have done, the West German and the Austrian trade unions have been the major proponents in their respective countries of Swedish-type policy and organization. The recent enactments of extensive improvements in policy and administration in both countries owe much to the efforts of the trade union movements and their political and civil service allies. The West German trade union movement has been instrumental in transforming the national placement and unemployment compensation service into a comprehensive labor market agency including an institute for labor market research.

The education, training, and apprenticeship aspects of manpower have been a special focus of trade union interest. At the policy level, the trade unions have pressed for broader scope and longer duration. The Austrian and German trade union movements have maintained a continuing criticism of their traditional apprenticeship systems urging (1) a more systematic training component, (2) a reconstitution of the apprenticeable trades to arrest their deterioration into subterfuges for substandard employment, and (3) greater trade union influence in the determination of apprenticeship standards. In the United Kingdom, unions and managements, through the industry training boards, are combining to modernize apprenticeship in respect to training methods and duration. In Sweden, apprenticeship seems almost to have shed its restrictive features so that it can concentrate on training; this generally serves as a productive way both of alleviating the distress of unemployment for the worker and of improving his qualifications and hence his job choice.

Redundancy is another special area of manpower policy which unions, most specifically in the United Kingdom and Germany, have considered. IGM in Germany has stood out as the union which has most insistently agitated for and negotiated comprehensive rationalization agreements. Collective bargaining on redundancy in the United Kingdom has wavered between the more restrictive approaches of the shop floor and an attitude of toleration in the higher places of the union. The Contract of Employment Act and the Redundancy Payments Act which the unions helped to pass in order to ameliorate displacement effects have undoubtedly contributed toward a softer union approach to redundancy.

In general the manpower policy area appears to be most compatible with the union's interests as a protective institution. Manpower programs act to enhance the worker's security at the same time that allocation of labor resources is more efficient. Manpower policy can offer credible assurances of protection to workers who incur risks in behalf of national economic policy through the devices of income protection, relocation, further training and retraining, counseling, and job placement.

Incomes and wage policy has been the most contentious policy which trade unions have had to face. No movement has been able to escape involvement in one form or other. The Austrian and Dutch cases represented the most systematic and enduring union involvement in both policy and administration. The Austrian scheme applied to both wages and prices, and the Dutch scheme mainly to wages with prices subject only to intermittent control. Swedish wage policy functioned through the self-restraint exercised by the bargaining partners but with the possibility of state intervention never too far off. In Germany a wage policy effect was achieved by the self-denial of the trade union movement. In the United Kingdom, the TUC collaborated strongly with a postwar labor government in wage restraint, then rejected participation under successive Conservative governments. Under the later Labour governments the trade unions took a hand in shaping policy at first, but progressive disaffection with heavier doses of regulation brought trade unions and Labour government into open conflict. The Netherlands represents—at different times of course—both the most spectacular success and failure. In every country case, overt rank-and-file rebellion undermined trade union involvement.

Innovative contributions by trade union movements in aspects of incomes policy have been the various German and Dutch investment wage proposals and the Swedish solidarity wage policy. The investment wage proposals aim to moderate short-run inflationary pressures and at the same time achieve a distributive justice objective by inducing workers to make capital investments through wage allocations. The solidarity wage policy of the Swedish trade union movement seeks to favor the low-wage worker in the allocation of the wage-increase "kitty."

Trade union commitments to incomes and wage policy seem to yield positive results only for short periods and under urgent pressure. The trade union sources of incomes policy attrition are (1) incomes policy as mainly wage repression, (2) rejection of incomes policy restraints by the rank and file, (3) the inability to assure the rank and file a secure *quid pro quo* for the exercise of wage restraint, (4) the government's tendency to overstate the emergency, (5) the theory of unions and workers as scapegoats for inflation, and (6) the redundancy of the union as an institution under a scheme of external wage control.

Incomes policy becomes more amenable to union involvement when (1) the trade-off is more concrete, as in British productivity bargaining; (2) there is some room for maneuverability either explicit or implicit, as in reasonable wage drifts—unlimited wage drift is, of course, the negation of wage policy; (3) equitable income distribution goals, that is, "distributive justice", are recognized; (4) the incomes policy is intelligible (the Dutch incomes policy was not intelligible in its later stages); (5) the trade union leadership has been significantly involved in the discussion and negotiation of the policy; (6) there is strong awareness of the urgency of the economic situation which requires the incomes policy; and (7) the repressive features are of short duration.

In Britain, which furnishes the major case of industrial relations reform, the industrial relations system has been judged by a Royal Commission to be the major source of manpower inefficiency. Within the system, the inefficiency has been specifically located in "the largely informal, largely fragmented and largely autonomous bargaining"[7] in the factory, a condition produced by the multiplicity of unions, craft-conscious unionism, and an imbalance of steward-power.

The trade union movement supported the Royal Commission's investigation; union spokesmen participated in and joined in the findings and subsequently were appointed to the Commission on Industrial Relations—the agency established to implement the findings. But the Labour government's move in 1969 to legislate punitive sanctions for unofficial strikes brought it into open and bitter conflict with the trade unions which abated only when the government was forced unceremoniously to withdraw its proposals. The Conservative government's effort in a similar direction in 1970–71 has encountered even more militant union opposition. The government's pressure for internal union reform by law had the effect of pressing the TUC to come forward with its own measures of self-regulation of unauthorized strikes and of wage policy.

In the other countries, with the exception of France, centralization of bargaining structures and industrial unionism represent reforms which emanated from the bargaining parties reacting to the need for coherent collective bargaining responses to economic policy. In France, reform is in an earlier stage of evolution focusing on union rights in the enterprise. As this is being written, the rank-and-file membership throughout Western Europe may, however, be applying a corrective counter-reform against overcentralization.

IV

Thus far we have summarized the policy content of trade union involvement and suggested that some policy areas by their nature are more conducive than others to involvement. In this section we examine the processes and mechanisms of involvement.

7. Royal Commission on Trade Unions and Employers' Associations, *1965–68 Report* (Cmnd. 3623) (London: HMSO, 1968), p. 18.

Self-determination describes the situation where the trade union movement deals with national economic policy issues through its own internal
processes. The TUC commitments to "vet" the wage claims of its affiliates
and to avoid unofficial strikes, the self-imposed wage restraint of the
German unions during reconstruction, and, in a sense, the Swedish movement's solidarity wage policy are important examples here. Collective
bargaining or bilateralism in the negotiation of economic policy is
preeminently illustrated in the Swedish determination of economywide
wage policy and in the German IGM bargaining for adjustments to technological change. Tripartism, or even multilateralism, is the alignment of
interests found in the Austrian and Dutch high level councils and in the
German "concerted action." The most diverse alignment of interest
representation is to be found in the numerous "socio-occupational
categories" established under the French Plan. The bipartite or tripartite
forms of interest representation are more conducive to negotiating types
of interaction. The multilateral types of interest representation, as in the
French Plan, make negotiation more difficult—which may have been the
result intended.

The degree to which union involvement is expressed through formal
organization is most advanced in the Austrian Chambers of Labor, the
French modernization committees, the Dutch Social and Economic Council, and the British EDC's and Industrial Training Boards. Involvement
through confrontation is at the opposite pole wherein power is asserted
without formal organization, exemplified in the confrontations in France
in May and June of 1968 and in the aftermath of devaluation in the fall of
1969.

The structured forms of union involvement have the advantages of:
(1) conferring legitimacy on the union presence, (2) providing continuous
access to technical staff resources, and (3) developing representational
competence in the union leadership. Nevertheless, excessively bureaucratized procedures may, by a kind of Gresham's law, operate to overwhelm
the more meaningful interactions, which is what a TUC report may have
had in mind when it referred to "the many documents and technical
papers which had to be assimilated by trade union representatives" in the
EDC's;[8] another example of bureaucratized procedures is the practice observed in French planning of burying the trade union representative with
technical 400-page reports which he had neither the time nor the resources
to digest.

The strength of union influence depends on whether its consent is
essential to the implementation of the economic policy, as it is in wage
policy and in aspects of manpower policy or as it has *not* been in eco-

8. TUC, *1966 Report*, London, p. 334.

nomic planning. Union influence also turns on the quality of its participation. Union ineffectiveness is seen in both French and British economic planning. The Swedish and Austrian trade union movements continue to be strong because of their indispensability in economic policy determination and the high quality of their participation. In other contexts German trade union participation in the Federal Institute and the IGM collective bargaining are also of the strong and constructive variety.

Innovation and initiative are prominent features of the Swedish trade union involvement. The initiative of the DGB's representatives in the Federal Institute in Germany has been directed toward constructing a more comprehensive labor market policy and most recently toward the establishment of a research arm of the Institute. The French trade union posture of contesting and challenging represents the reactive extreme.

Swedish trade unionism makes its influence felt at all stages of the decisional process: opinion-making, legislative enactment, policy implementation, and administration. The German IGM has been notably skillful in the opinion-making stage of its program for rational adjustment to technological change. The opinion-making medium has been a series of widely publicized and well-organized conferences with a roster of international participants. The technical resources and consultative channels available through the Chambers of Labor have enhanced the legislative effectiveness of the Austrian trade unions. The German DGB has been particularly influential in the administration of labor market policies.

The locale of trade union involvement in national economic policy may be the shop floor, the enterprise, the industry, the national economy, and, although not explored here, the international economy. Examples of industry- and economywide involvement have been frequently alluded to here. Britain's industry training boards and EDC's are the best example of the former, and Swedish collective bargaining between LO and SAF are the best examples of the latter. No trade union movement has experienced more critical economywide influence than did the French in the 1968 general strike and its negotiation aftermath. German efforts in codetermination, IGM's rationalization programs, and the Swedish and German county labor market boards exemplify involvement at local levels.

V

Union effectiveness in the making of economic policy is associated with integration and rationalization in the industrial relations environment. Integration means the coordination of the diverse interests within the union, and between the union and other interest groups, so that a coherent policy response is feasible. Rationalization means efficiency in policy involvement made possible by rules, organization, and professionalization replacing ideology, hit-or-miss, and trial by struggle.

The decline of ideology as an integrating influence paves the way for the intellectual acceptability of the common interest concept which underlies trade union involvement in national economic policy. Second, the decline of ideology has been essential because bourgeois governments—or even social-democratic governments—and the business classes are not ready to accept trade unionism as a collaborator in national economic policy, or in anything else, if their own institutional survival is likely to be endangered. Third, the deemphasis of ideology has been necessary to keep the otherwise sectarian trade union movements—as in Austria, Germany, and especially in the Netherlands—under one umbrella. Fourth, the decline of ideology has been essential to deal with the major policy areas as *immediate* problems, and this has meant in a practical way coming to terms with capitalism. The deemphasis of ideology has been necessary, finally, to enhance the appeal of the trade union–related socialist parties to middle-class elements without whose support these parties cannot aspire to govern. Only French trade unionism, and especially the dominant CGT, has been substantially immune to these anti-ideological tendencies, which explains some part of the movement's virtual isolation from national economic policy-making.

The structural features of trade unionism which enable it to develop the internal organization for participation in economic policy are designated here as: (1) industrial unionism, (2) integrated unionism, (3) centralized bargaining, (4) trade union–party compatibility, (5) management acceptance of trade union legitimacy, (6) union effectiveness in regulating the terms of employment, and (7) union professionalism.

Industrial unionism has two advantages for the trade union performance in economic policy-making. First, it strengthens the union's bargaining position by minimizing sectional divisions; second, the industry unit represents a more rational basis for economic policy-making than the more fragmented units. The difficulties encountered by British and French trade unionism in adjusting to an economic policy-making role are in different ways related to the fragmentation of their respective structures. By the same token the industrial unionism of Sweden, Austria, the Netherlands, and Germany have been strengthening influences in their policy-making roles and represent historically, for the latter three, a deliberate restructuring of trade union jurisdictions.

Integrated unionism is meant to describe the degree of federation authority over affiliates as an element in policy-making effectiveness. The Austrian ÖGB and the Swedish LO are strong federation types which have been able to speak with unified voices in the nation's policy councils. But ÖGB as the most centralized federation, it should be noted, has a total membership smaller than any one of several industry unions in Germany, the United Kingdom, and the United States—a fact undoubtedly related to the manageability of such concentrated authority. In any case, the authority of powerful federations rests ultimately on consent and they have to be structured formally and informally to bring all relevant interests into play in the making of what ultimately emerges as a unified decision on policy.

Integrated unionism also relates to the extent of union penetration in the economy. The critical problem here is the weak role of the union in the enterprise and on the shop floor, as in Germany and the Netherlands and, in a special way, in Britain. In both Germany and the Netherlands the works council system has no organic relationship to the trade union movement and may in fact be considered a rival to it. In Britain the force of union representation in the enterprise is effectively inhibited by the multi-union steward system which, while being union-related, is psychologically conditioned to act as a permanent opposition to union influence from above. When this psychological opposition is combined with industrywide bargaining which has the characteristic effect of leaving plant employment terms to local determination by the stewards, there results a decentralized authority system which does not lend itself to participation in and implementation of commitments by union officials above the local level.

Integrated unionism also includes the problem of multiple unionism, that is, the existence of multiple and rival union centers. Unions which function in a rival union situation may fear that forbearance in behalf of a national economic policy commitment will expose them to reprisals from competing unions. The forbearance which the trade unions in Sweden, Austria, the Netherlands, and West Germany have demonstrated in wage policy was made easier by their relative freedom from rival movements. The Netherlands has three federations—Socialist, Protestant, and Catholic—but they act as one on trade union questions and on almost all social and economic questions. None of these countries, it is worth noting, has a significant communist influence in the trade unions. Rivalry is a major factor in the disruption of Swedish trade union unity where the LO's leadership has been challenged by TCO and SACO, the white collar and professional unions. The rivalry among the CGT, FO, and CFDT in France undoubtedly deters economic policy commitments.

Centralized collective bargaining, that is, where unions and management have the authority to negotiate inclusive agreements on an economywide basis, provides the optimal instrument for economic policy-making through collective bargaining. The Swedish collective bargaining system represents the ideal type in this respect, but Austria and the Netherlands have at various times not been far behind.

Union involvement in national economic policy requires a viable trade union–political party relationship. First, unions will be loath to make self-denying commitments if they lack trustworthy allies on the political front, because they will fear that hostile political forces will use the trade union concessions to weaken the union as an institution. Second, unions are more likely to make concessions for national economic policy as a means of supporting "their" party or "their" government. Third, the cross-fertilization of ideas between party and trade unions is an important source of ideas and technical competence. The TUC's rejection of the Tory government's overtures in the early sixties illustrates the first point; the TUC's straining to accommodate its policies to the Labour government's policies illustrates the second; and the interlocking directorate between the Swedish LO and the Social Democratic Party illustrates the third. But it must be noted that the stock of good will between a socialist party in power and the trade unions is not limitless. The party's broader constituency may force it to take on the trade unions, as in Britain, or to soft-pedal union demands, as in the SPD's treatment of codetermination. In terms of the historic relationship, the party has been the source of economic policy while the union has been mainly concerned with social policy, for example, housing, social security, etc.

Economic policy unionism requires receptive attitudes among employers and in government. Indeed, the spur to union involvement invariably has come from the government. Sweden and Austria demonstrate acceptance and legitimacy of the trade union's economic policy role by employers and government. In West Germany and the Netherlands the employers will not accept the *union* presence in shop floor and enterprise bargaining. In France, employers and the present government hardly concede the legitimacy of the union; they admit them to their important councils only when the unions seem to be on the verge of destroying the established order.

The ability of the union to participate effectively in the regulation of the terms of employment, whether through collective bargaining or through legislation, appears to be a necessary condition for effective participation in national economic policy. The main reason for drawing the unions into the economic policy orbit in the first place is their authority over the work territory. And the broader the base of union membership in the work territory the greater is its authority and the less likely it is to pursue a "narrow monopolistic policy" because "the consequences will affect its own members to a very great extent."[9] The narrower the base, the more likely the trade union movement can "safely pursue an efficient policy of group egotism."[10] There is a strong, if not perfect, association

9. Gösta Edgren, Karl-Olof Faxén, and Clas-Erik Odhner, "Wages, Growth and the Distribution of Income," *Swedish Journal of Economics* (Stockholm), September 1969, p. 135.

10. Gösta Rehn, "Unionism and the Wage Structure in Sweden," in *The Theory of Wage Determination*, ed. John T. Dunlop (New York: St. Martin's Press, 1957), p. 229.

between the union membership–nonagricultural labor force ratio and the degree of participation in national economic policy: Sweden and Austria with their 65–70 percent ratio are on the high side of involvement, while the United Kingdom (over 40 percent), Germany (about one-third), and France (about 20 percent) are on the lower side.[11] The union, in asking short-run forbearance from its constituents in the name of national economic policy, is credible only if it argues that this will strengthen the worker's longer-run position and only if the union is already established as an effective protective institution.

Unions which are not firmly established in their territory—where, for example, the state is the major dispenser of worker protection—are likely to view economic policy commitments (as in France) as "limiting their strength" and to see themselves as "becoming prisoner to commitments" which they cannot fulfill.[12] But on the other hand, unions may be so overwhelmingly established in their exclusive job control, as in the United Kingdom, that economic policy commitments are viewed as a threat to the union as an institution that must be rejected on principle.

Rationalization of union administration is expressed mainly as the professionalization of certain union functions. The effective involvement of Swedish and Austrian unionism is, by way of example, strongly associated with a high-quality research and technical staff performance: in the Swedish situation, through the LO's own staff; in the Austrian situation, through both the ÖGB and the Chamber of Labor technical staff. In the Netherlands, professionalization takes the form of an officer selection process which stresses intellectual ability. Technical staff work is a prominent feature of the German IGM's examination of and policy for technological change. Research is not a high priority function in the French and British trade union movements.

Trade union involvement in national economic policy typically begins with issues which pose "a clearly perceived threat to the nation's economic health."[13] Postwar Western Europe has produced three such issues: (1) postwar reconstruction, as in Germany, Austria, and the Netherlands; (2) inflation and its effect on the nation's position in the international economy, as in virtually every country under examination here; and (3) structural adjustment to economic growth objectives as in Sweden and, in a different way, in Britain.

11. E. M. Kassalow, *Trade Unions and Industrial Relations: An International Comparison* (New York: Random House, 1969), pp. 88–89.

12. Derek Robinson, "National Wage and Incomes Policies and Trade Unions," in *International Labor*, ed. Solomon R. Barkin (New York: Harper and Row, 1967), p. 240.

13. Lloyd Ulman, "Wage-Price Policies Abroad," *Industrial Relations* (Berkeley), May 1969, p. 211.

The forbearance exercised by the unions in the economies undergoing reconstruction has been a major element in the successful rehabilitation of Western Europe. The performance of the German trade unions is the most interesting in that the forbearance was unilateral and that, unlike Austria and the Netherlands, it was not consummated through bipartite or tripartite consensus. The willingness of the German trade unions to submit to rigorous internal discipline is, of course, related to the enormity of the economic and social holocaust so deeply imbedded in the consciousness of the German people. The vigorous effort mounted by the Dutch and the Austrian unions for collaboration is hardly a less prominent example of how short-run trade union priorities can be discounted in favor of an overriding general interest if the perception of adversity is intense enough.

Balance-of-payments instabilities and difficulties in the international competitive position replaced reconstruction as the dominant object of economic policy concerns. The sense of urgency which this problem stimulates has, however, not been sufficient to sustain support of the wage repression types of incomes policies for any substantial period. The extraordinary achievement of the Dutch unions consisted of their ability to sustain support of wage control long after the sense of urgency had begun to wane. The British TUC followed "with remarkable fidelity" the appeals of the immediate postwar Labour government for wage restraint. The post-1964 experience has been considerably less successful, with the TUC highly resentful of the villain's role in which the trade unions have been cast in the popular theory of international trade, and not a little suspicious that the crisis climate was synthetically contrived to further wage repression measures. Swedish trade unionism may be in a class by itself—perhaps Austria is in this class too—in having been able to sustain economic policy commitments not only in adversity but also for the more positive goal of structural change for growth.

VI

Sweden represents the most advanced expression of economic policy unionism marked by (1) an ability to sustain its commitments not only in adversity but for affirmative purposes of economic growth and structural change; (2) a scope and depth of involvement in economic policy expressed in (a) a broad range of policy interests even though labor market policy occupies the primary place, and (b) an effectuation of union influence at every strategic point in the policy-decision process from theoretical analysis to program administration; (3) the centrality of union influence in the decisional process; (4) the high level of technical competence; (5) the deliberate undertakings in innovation in organization and concepts; and (6) the "congruence" achieved over a long period between protective or "pressure group" interests and economic policy objectives. Sweden's accomplishment reflects, to be sure, an act of will, but also a receptive environment—namely, popular awareness of the economic situation, the relatively small scale of the economy, the maturation of democratic institutions, an even economic development, and avoidance of the costs of war.

Austria seems to be the next effective demonstration of economic policy unionism. Austrian trade unionism has had a longer road to travel—Marxian socialism, Nazi domination, war and devastation, occupation, reconstruction, and industrial development. Austrian trade unionism does not have the policy scope which Sweden has—the active manpower policy is just now emerging, in large part as a consequence of union pressure—but the magnitude of involvement and union influence has nevertheless been considerable. The technical resources in the trade unions and especially in the Chambers of Labor have been of high quality and have demonstrated how essential these are in working out complex economic policy issues and problems. Even though diverse political currents and ideologies exist within the trade union movement, the institutionalization of diversity has made it possible for trade unionism to function in an integrated way. Austria also illustrates smallness of scale as a favorable condition for central trade union involvement in economic policy issues.

Before the early 1960s, the place next to Sweden, if not closely rivaling it in realizing important national economic policy objectives, would clearly have belonged to the trade unions of the Netherlands. There too the Nazi-reconstruction syndrome generated an overriding motivation. Trade unionism proved to be indispensable in maintaining rigorous economic discipline over a longer period than elsewhere in Western Europe. The rigor was evidenced in the complex price-wage rules and the intricate organizational arrangements for collaborative decisionmaking. But the discipline has been in the process of deterioration since the early 1960s.

German trade unionism represents an effective involvement in labor market policy and administration. Beyond that, involvement has been rather limited. The causes are to be found first in the determination of the Christian Democratic governments, which ruled West Germany during much of this period, and of the employers to keep the predominantly socialist-oriented trade unions in their place—a place that was not in the higher councils of economic policy-making. Moreover, the theory of the social market economy and the trade union's self-imposed moderation minimized the pressures for involvement. The ascendancy of the SPD in the governments since the middle 1960s may usher in a larger scope for trade union participation in economic policy, but the unsettled state of the codetermination question introduces an element of uncertainty. Economic policy through collective bargaining has marked the IGM's approach to technological adjustment and the various efforts at negotiating wage investment programs.

The British trade union movement is interpreted as being in slow transition from protective sectional unionism toward economic policy unionism. The process of transition has been accompanied by tension and turmoil. There is a general acceptance of the legitimacy of common economic policy interests but with some important dissents. There are even significant beginnings in implementing national economic policy commitments, as in the training boards and industry development committees. But still very fundamental blocks exist: (1) the inability of the highly decentralized industrial relations system to organize effectively for economic policy objectives, and (2) the unsuitability of the government's policy mix with its strong emphasis on wage repression and union complicity in Britain's difficulties.

The French case illuminates the incompatibility in a modern industrial society between trade union involvement in economic policy and polarized, class-oriented unionism. The circumstances which produce this incompatibility are anticapitalist ideology and rhetoric, fragmented union power and effectiveness in regulating labor conditions, the rejection of or, at best, containment of union influence by government and employers, and the massive confrontation strategy of resolving interest conflicts.

VII

A wave of rank-and-file union militancy broke out in late 1969, and, as this is being written, has continued into 1970. The viability of the national economic policy model is in this way being threatened at its most vulnerable point—support from the membership. In fact, "there has been a widespread shift in the location of initiative and power from the central organization to the periphery, from trade unions to formal or informal work-place committees."[14]

The causes of this rank-and-file militancy have been different in different countries. In France the cause was dissatisfaction with the August 1969 devaluation and with the post-devaluation stabilization program adopted by the government. In West Germany the discipline of the German workers and of their trade unions—a "miracle" in its own right—has not been proof against the unprecedented wildcat strikes in coal, steel, and a variety of other metal-working industries, protesting the inferior position which the long-term contracts had put the workers in, relative to the price-and-profit boom.

In Sweden unauthorized strikes reflected rank-and-file disaffection with the leveling objectives of the LO's solidarity wage policy and the remoteness of the union decisionmaking authority. Earlier, serious strains had developed in the 1969 negotiations between the predominantly manualist

14. Michael Kidron, *Western Capitalism since the War* (Baltimore: Penguin, 1970), p. 69.

whole. . . . The very fact that the two sides were arguing about percentage points of national income rather than cents per hour, indicates clearly that they had become accustomed to think in terms of real income instead of money incomes, and to concentrate on longer run trends rather than the immediate past."[20] This concept is further developed in the report of an OECD-sponsored trade union seminar on planning. The trade union participants distinguished between "bread and butter issues . . . settled in terms of increases in hourly wage rates or fringe benefits, gained through well-understood mechanisms" and "collective bargaining issues of the future" which "may include questions of employment security, employee retraining programmes, labour force mobility and productivity. The unions will have to try to understand the correlation between specific wage and working conditions and the national interest. . . . It will become less and less conceivable that the two sides of industry and the government act in a unilateral fashion without first having gone through consultation, debate and perhaps negotiations on economic and social goals."[21] The economy-wide collective bargaining system has been analogized to an economic parliament in which "questions about the distribution of national income between wages and capital income, the international competitiveness of the economy and the significance of wage developments for prices have become the central subjects of discussion between the parties of the labor market."[22] Johann Böhm, the late president of the Austrian ÖGB, "believed that the power of the trade union movement carried with it so great a responsibility for economic development that wage policy could not be based on the bargaining power of the unions alone but must take account of the wider demands of the community as a whole."[23]

The British TUC addressed itself to the task of "creat[ing] a more constructive framework within which the trade union movement could discuss the whole issue of collective bargaining developments in relationship to the growth of incomes."[24] A leading DGB economist observed that the trade unions acknowledge that "trade union wage policy" can have "important repercussions" in a situation of "excess demand" and that moreover "an examination of actual economic developments shows quite clearly that the German trade unions have recognized their responsibilities in this matter and have framed their policies accordingly."[25] The French

20. William Fellner et al., The Problem of Rising Prices (Paris: OEEC, 1961), p. 389.

21. OECD, International Trade Union Seminar on Economic and Social Programming, Final Report (Paris, 1964), p. 46.

22. Edgren et al., "Wages, Growth and the Distribution of Income," p. 135.

23. Johann Böhm, quoted in Anton Proksch, "The Austrian Joint Wage and Price Council," International Labour Review (ILO, Geneva), March 1961, p. 232.

24. TUC, 1969 Report, London, p. 341–34 passim.

25. Heinz Markmann, "Employers' and Workers' Wage Policies and Their Effect on Inflation" in The Labour Market and Inflation, ed. Anthony D. Smith (New York: St. Martin's Press, 1968), pp. 94–95.

CGT-FO, by contrast, has been "opposed to any centralising policy which under the guise of an incomes policy would seek to limit the progress of wages and to hamper the development of collective agreements which are the special instruments of the trade union movement's action for social advancement."[26]

Trade union commitment to national economic policy does not mean the abandonment of particularist claims but an assessment that "the best method of forwarding these particular claims" is to relate them to their effects on national income, productivity, investment, and balance of payments.[27]

The economic policy commitment can be undertaken by the union internally, as in the TUC wage review procedure or as in the self-imposed wage restraint of the German unions. It can be negotiated with the employer, as preeminently in the Swedish case. Economic policy can also be negotiated directly with the government, as in the TUC negotiations with the Labour government over industrial relations reform. Finally, economic policy can be negotiated multilaterally among the trade unions, employers, and government (as in the Dutch Social and Economic Council). With or without direct government participation, national economic policy is most commonly conceived as reflecting some public consensus; most often, however, it is articulated by the government.

In return for the exercise of short-run restraint and forbearance in its money income demands, the union expects a compensatory or better real income return for its constituency. There are also "psychic income" returns for the union in this sort of transaction. If the union leader's sense of community is strong enough, he may at times even be prepared to accept a lower real income return for the "larger good," that is, for the strengthening of the economy and society as a whole, even if no part of the improvement will accrue to the union's constituency. "Taste for power" psychic income is involved when the options open to the union are either negotiated restraint or restraint imposed by direct state intervention, which is how the TUC formulated the alternatives.

The terms of the *quid pro quo* are likely to be more credible to the union leadership than to the rank and file and to the higher union leadership than to the shop union leadership. This is because the higher ranks of the union are more exposed to the pressures for "responsibility" and "reasonableness," and through experience and practical education they have a stronger appreciation of the broader economics of the situation.

For the government, the *quid pro quo* in enlisting union commitments is the economy of means. The union's influence with its constituents will

26. *CGT-FO Information Bulletin*, April 1964, quoted in OECD, Manpower and Social Affairs Directorate, *Non-Wage Incomes and Prices Policy* (Paris, 1966), p. 150.

27. H. A. Turner, "Trade Union Organization," in *The Labour Market*, ed. B. J. McCormick and E. Owen Smith (Baltimore: Penguin, 1968), p. 113.

achieve a better policy accommodation than the government can on its own power. For a trade union–related government, the union can only be bypassed at the cost of alienating allies, which can seriously endanger its survival.

The method by which the unions come to terms with the other parties represents in many cases a species of conventional negotiations, even when the policy commitments are not made through formal collective bargaining. Decisions are likely to be made in a face-to-face posture: offers and counter-offers are made and the parties may threaten to use sanctions against each other.

The ability of Western European trade unionism to negotiate a wide range of economic policies with employers and governments contrasts with the pre-war period when, as Adolf Sturmthal so powerfully argued in *The Tragedy of European Labor*, "the root of the breakdown of European democracy" was the labor movement's failure with some exceptions to develop an economic policy. The labor movements "had a social but no economic policy. They strove to defend wage rates and unemployment benefits as well as they could but they had no constructive program for dealing with the economic crisis itself." They "had too much the character of pressure groups and were not enough concerned with the fate of the community of which they formed a part."[28]

IX

Without stressing it too much, it might not be inappropriate to comment on how this study relates to some well-known theories and ideologies of the labor movement. Selig Perlman stressed job rights as the central concern of unionism. He is, I believe, fundamentally correct for most of Western European unionism. Unions are in their essential nature protective institutions which, to recall George Woodcock's way of putting it, "are not the agents of any programme which discounts the present in favor of the future."[29]

But what Perlman could not have foreseen, writing in his 1928 American milieu, was that unionism's unit of protection need not be limited to the shop floor. The union, under changing economic circumstances, may find it necessary to assert protective interests at the levels of industry and economy to the point where the trade union movement joins with employers and the state to negotiate economic policy in a kind of industrial parliament. Even so, the pressure of shop floor interests can never be disregarded as the current rank-and-file resurgence bears witness.

The Marxist-Leninist theory of trade union development, that is, the evolution from trade union economism to socialist consciousness, seems to

28. Sturmthal, *Tragedy of European Labor*, pp. vii, 4, 7.
29. TUC, *Trade Unionism* (London, 1966), p. 51.

have been turned upside down by post-World War II developments. Socialist consciousness appears to precede, rather than to follow, trade union consciousness. The contrast between West European unionism before and after World War II represents dramatic evidence of the transformation from socialism to economism, with the German transformation the most dramatic. To be sure, trade union economism in most of Western Europe is in the economic policy rather than the "shop rights" stage but this does not, it seems to me, weaken the force of the counter-Marxist drift.

The integration of trade unionism into the social structure which is associated with economic policy unionism has been identified by some with both syndicalist and corporatist tendencies. For the purposes of this sort of comparison, the important feature of economic policy unionism is its essential pluralistic—either bilateral or multilateral—character. But both syndicalism and corporatism acknowledge the legitimacy of only *one* interest: in the case of syndicalism, the workers or trade union interest; in the case of corporatism, the state interest. In reality, syndicalist or corporatist tendencies are paradoxically manifested mostly in the trade union situations which are *farthest* removed from economic policy unionism. There is thus a strong syndicalist overtone to the behavior of the British shop stewards and a corporatist quality to the assimilationist emphasis of the French Plan.

Finally, the theory of union oligarchy, as first formulated by Michels and given contemporary application most notably by Lipset and Herberg, is not supported by the "widespread shift in the location of initiative and power from trade unions to formal or informal workplace committees,"[30] which has occurred in Western Europe and in a somewhat different context in the United States.[31]

Supplementary References

Barkin, Solomon R. "Trade Unions Face a New Western Capitalist Society." *Journal of Economic Issues*, March 1969, pp. 49–65.

Caire, Guy. "Participation by Employers' and Workers' Organisations in Planning." *International Labour Review* (ILO, Geneva), December 1967, pp. 557–80.

30. Kidron, *Western Capitalism*, p. 69.

31. See Will Herberg, "Bureaucracy and Democracy in Labor Unions," *Antioch Review*, September 1943, pp. 405–17; V. I. Lenin, *What Is To Be Done* (New York: International Publishers, 1929); Seymour M. Lipset *et al.*, *Union Democracy: The Inside Politics of the ITU* (Glencoe, Ill.: Free Press, 1956); A. Lozovsky, *Marx and the Trade Unions* (New York: International Publishers, 1942); Robert Michels, *Political Parties* (New York: Dover, 1959); Selig Perlman, *A Theory of the Labour Movement* (New York: Augustus Kelley, 1949).

Cox, R. W. "Trade Unions, Employers and the Formation of National Economic Policy." In *Industrial Relations and Economic Development*, edited by A. M. Ross. New York: St. Martin's Press, 1966.

Edelman, Murray. "The Conservative Political Consequences of Labor Conflict." In *Essays in Industrial Relations Theory*, edited by G. G. Somers. Ames: Iowa State University Press, 1969.

Lipset, Seymour Martin. "The Changing Class Structure and Contemporary European Politics." In *A New Europe*, Special issue of Daedalus, Winter 1964, pp. 271–303.

"Participation of Workers and Employers in Economic and Social Planning: Some Introductory Remarks." *International Labour Review* (ILO, Geneva), April 1966, pp. 331–36.

Reynaud, Jean Daniel. "The Role of Trade Unions in National Political Economies (Developed Countries of Europe)." In *International Labor*, edited by Solomon R. Barkin. New York: Harper and Row, 1967.

Ross, A. M. "Introduction." In *Industrial Relations and Economic Development*. New York: St. Martin's Press, 1966.

CHAPTER NINE

Implications for the United States

The contemporary economy in the United States is dominated by two immediate problems: "(1) What can be done to curb our present inflationary movements without creating appreciable unemployment? (2) How can this kind of effort be related to a broadening of economic opportunities that would help bring an end to poverty."[1] Earlier in the postwar period, depressed areas, adjustments to technology, and recurring recessions occupied the center of policy concerns. The problems of a post-full employment economy create the backdrop for trade union involvement in U.S. economic policy as they did in Europe. But unlike the European economy, the American post-full employment economy includes an underclass whose disadvantaged condition is made all the more intolerable by the general affluence.

American trade unionism has been involved in four major policy areas relevant to this inquiry: (1) full employment and general economic policy, (2) wage-price policy, (3) adjustment to technological change, and (4) manpower policy for the disadvantaged. Collective bargaining continues to be the principal means through which the unions have asserted their interests in these policy areas. Law and its administration, although subordinate to collective bargaining, have become, however, increasingly important in union strategy.

II

In a generation, that is since the New Deal, the mainline trade union movement has broadened the scope of its public policy concerns from defensive reactions against anti-union measures, like the injunction and the "yellow-dog contract," to broad economic policy with major emphasis on full employment objectives. For the 1970 Congress, by way of example, the AFL-CIO gave the highest priorities to "rising unemployment, occu-

---

1. U.S. Department of Labor, Manpower Administration, *Assessing the Economic Scene* (Washington, D.C.: Government Printing Office, 1969), p. 1.

IMPLICATIONS FOR THE UNITED STATES

pational safety, environmental pollution, expanded health education, manpower training and anti-poverty programs, skyrocketing interest rates and monetary policy reform, true bargaining rights for farm workers and situs picketing rights for the building trades."[2] Only the latter two could be considered "pure" trade union issues. The following have been mainly responsible for the enlargement of trade union policy perspectives: (1) the demonstration, which began with the New Deal, that the state could serve as ally and not only as adversary in the advancement of labor interests; (2) the emerging awareness that the condition of the nation's economy has much to do with the effectiveness of the trade union performance; and (3) the ascendancy of the industrial union interest in the American trade union movement and hence the broadening of the trade union base in the working population. At the present time, the support mustered by the AFL-CIO and assorted national unions may constitute the single most powerful political influence behind the broad range of full employment and welfare legislation.

President Johnson has provided a measurement of AFL-CIO influence. "I have met with Mr. Meany and his assistants many times, but with Mr. Meany himself, 49 times, in personal meetings either in my office, the Oval Room or in the mansion. In addition . . . he has called me, or I have called him, 82 additional times." Meany's intervention usually dealt with "minimum wage bills and things of that nature that applied to labor," but he was also concerned with "education of the young, medical assistance for our old, conservation of our resources—human and natural. . . ." President Johnson knew "of no living single group that . . . has been more responsible for the advances in this field in the last five years than the AFL-CIO headed by George Meany. . . ."[3]

III

The formulation of collective bargaining approaches to a national wage-price policy in peacetime bears the special imprint of the UAW and Walter Reuther, its president. In 1945 Reuther argued the proposition that to raise wages without increasing prices was indispensable to the maintenance of a full employment economy. "We are not going to operate as a narrow economic pressure group which says 'we are going to get ours and the public be damned.' "[4] In the 1957 negotiations Reuther proposed a price reduction for the 1958 car models in return for which "the UAW promised to give full consideration to the effect of such reductions on each company's financial position in drafting our 1958 demands and in the

2. AFL-CIO, *Labor Looks at Congress, 1969* (Washington, D.C., 1970), p. iii.
3. *AFL-CIO News* (Washington, D.C.), January 18, 1969, p. 7.
4. *New York Times*, December 29, 1946.

negotiations." The UAW offered to abide by an impartial review of whether "the granting of our demands would necessitate restoration of part or all of the $100 per car price reduction."[5] But automobile management rejected the appropriateness of the union interest in price policy and the UAW proposals were never put to the test.

For several years the UAW has proposed a notification and hearing procedure for price and wage increases which "envisage a Review Board for conducting the necessary hearings and a Consumer Counsel representing the public interest. Advance notice would have to be given of any price increase proposed by the corporation that functions as the 'price leader' in any major industry. . . . The Consumer Counsel would be able to initiate hearings in cases where he believed prices should be reduced. . . . Unions would be required to participate in the hearings and to justify their demands in cases where the corporation involved claimed that granting those demands would necessitate the proposed price increase or would prevent a decrease."[6]

The wage-price guideposts instituted by the Council of Economic Advisors in 1962 set a ratio between permissable wage and price increases and productivity. The trade unions have faulted this guideposts policy for: (1) the lack of effective consultation, (2) the arbitrariness and inflexibility of the productivity standard, (3) assuming as given the existing distribution of income, (4) the "disparate treatment of wages and prices,"[7] and (5) the scapegoating of wage increases as the source of inflationary pressure. The guideposts were abolished with the settlement of the 1966 airline machinists' strike when stability via guideposts became incompatible with industrial peace, and the choice was made for the latter. The strike made the essential point, which dominated the labor scene for several years thereafter, that wage-restraint policy could not stand up against the rank-and-file's discontent with a worsening real wage position.

The current trade union position on wages and prices takes the form of a defense against the scapegoating of wages as the prime mover in inflation and an attack on the Nixon administration's "blunderbuss, general form of restrictive economic policies, tight money and sky-high interest rates." The AFL-CIO favors "selective measures aimed at restraining the specific causes of inflationary pressures . . . since the inflation of 1969 was largely a profit inflation."[8] It has indicated its willingness to cooperate in an

5. Report of UAW President Walter P. Reuther, United Automobile Workers Constitutional Convention, 1959, p. 12.

6. Nat Weinberg, "The Death of the United States Guideposts," in *The Labour Market and Inflation*, ed. Anthony D. Smith (New York: St. Martin's Press, 1968), p. 44.

7. *Ibid.*, p. 28; Circular, AFL-CIO Department of Research, June 22, 1970.

8. AFL-CIO, *The National Economy* (Washington, D.C., 1969), p. 6.

incomes policy as it has "reiterated on many occasions, if the President
determines that the situation warrants extraordinary over-all stabilization
measures . . . so long as such restraints are equitably placed on all costs,
prices and incomes—including all prices, profits, dividends, rents and
executive compensation, as well as employees' wages and salaries. 'We are
prepared to sacrifice,' the AFL-CIO Executive Council has repeated, 'as
much as anyone else, for as long as anyone else—so long as there is equality
of sacrifice.' " The federation specifically rejects "a voluntary guideline
approach . . . as an unfair and one-sided pressure on workers' wages, as
well as unenforceable in a country of continental size, with no nationally
centralized business or labor institutions."[9]

IV

The trade unions have had a major impact on policies for adjustments
to technological change through both collective bargaining and legislation.
By common practice rather than by concerted policy, collective bargaining
seems to have established the general principle that employees have an
equitable interest in the stability of the job situation; in the event of
material impairment of that stability due to technological change, the
employer is obligated to offset in some degree the losses attributable to
that change.

Union obstruction of technological change is the exception rather than
the rule. A more characteristic union strategy is first to slow down the
pace of displacement. When displacement inevitably occurs, the union acts
to ease the burden of change on the displaced worker. Job and income
protection for current employees is a characteristic first line of union
defense. In one form, unions negotiate explicit productivity gain-sharing;
for example, an "annual improvement factor" where wage rates rise in line
with a predetermined rate of productivity increase. More broadly, any
increase in real wages and wage supplements (such as negotiated health,
welfare, and pension programs and supplementary unemployment
benefits) and reduction in hours without loss in earnings may represent an
explicit sharing in the gains of productivity.

Layoffs due to technological change are frequently slowed down by
contract requirements (1) prohibiting reduction in the manning schedule
for the performance of a given task, (2) guaranteeing current employees
against job and income loss so that the displacement operates to reduce
future job opportunities, and (3) offsetting net job and income losses
through job and income gains as in the reduction of weekly hours and in
increases in paid leaves (holidays, vacations, "sabbaticals," etc.) of one sort
or another.

9. *Ibid.*, p. 7.

When worker displacement does come, specific provisions act to (1) induce voluntary separations by raising pensions for early retirees, (2) authorize dismissal or separation allowances to tide workers over to the next job, (3) aid the displaced worker to find another job in the same company by enlarging the seniority unit within which the worker can legitimately claim employment rights or by a relocation allowance to permit the displaced worker to move to a company plant in another area, and (4) provide effective retraining opportunities. Procedures to encourage advance planning of technological change have been incorporated in contract provisions requiring (variously) advance notice of major labor-saving changes and consultation between unions and management in planning the displacement. Joint study committees, with participation by neutral outsiders, have been negotiated to explore the problems of work displacement long before the climate of crisis sets in.

This sort of bargaining policy for adjustment to technological change is "programmatic bargaining ... characterized by agreement on limited mutual goals and the willingness to bring in a sufficient number of variables to insure mutual commitment." This is distinguished from "concessionary" bargaining which "is characterized by unilateral goal-setting and concessions. Because neither party is committed to the other's goal, it is fair game to seek to minimize the costs of the concessions. Concessionary bargaining elicits a series of adaptations, mainly via variables outside the bargaining, which erode the other party's gains" and "tend to frustrate problem-solving."[10] The limitation of collective bargaining under any circumstance has led the unions to legislation as a method of dealing with the disemployment effects of technological change.

V

The trade union movement continues to be a prime mover in manpower legislation as it has evolved from one dominant theme to the next, specifically: depressed areas, technological unemployment, youth, the "competitively disadvantaged, and the need to coordinate and consolidate our manpower programs."[11]

The trade unions have been under great pressure to make a more intensive effort in behalf of the disadvantaged low-wage worker, especially the ethnic disadvantaged (here the strongest pressure is exerted in behalf of the Negro worker, somewhat less urgent concern is shown for the

10. Melvin Rothbaum, "Economic Dilemmas of Collective Bargaining," in *The Crisis in the American Trade Union Movement*, ed. Solomon R. Barkin, The Annals of the American Academy of Political and Social Science, Philadelphia, November 1963, pp. 103, 95.

11. *Studies by the Staff of the Cabinet Committee on Price Stability* (Washington, D.C.: Government Printing Office, 1969), p. 24.

Puerto Rican and Mexican-American worker). The pressure on the craft unions, particularly the construction trades, has come from civil rights activists and the federal government. The pressure on the industrial unions has come not only from these sources but also from the internal union "black caucus" groups. The target of pressure on the craft unions has been their restrictive entry practices with a special emphasis on apprenticeship. In the industrial unions the targets have been post-hiring disadvantages caused by (1) restricted opportunities for advancement under a seniority system, (2) the denial of fair representation, and (3) an unfavorable imbalance of Negro participation in union leadership.

The methods of pressure have consisted of threats of disruption by civil rights activists and the threat of litigation by the federal government under the Civil Rights Act of 1964 and federal contract compliance standards. The remedies sought against the craft unions and construction trades contractors have been commitments to employ specified numbers of Negro workers by crafts in a fairer proportion to their numbers. Against the industrial union the main thrust of the government has been to modify restrictive seniority and promotion systems to allow fuller participation by Negro workers in promotion opportunities. A more representative distribution of Negro members in the union leadership has been the objective of the "black power" groups in and around the trade union movement.

The trade union response to the pressures begins with the emergence of viewpoints which come to grips with the critical problem. Nowhere is this more apparent than in the building trades unions which have moved from what amounted to denial that discrimination exists to "affirmative action" and "outreach" programs where "a more intensive effort [is exerted] by paid personnel to recruit, train and place minority youth."[12] Symbolic of the new level of perception is the so-called Chicago Plan which commits an operations committee composed of representatives from the craft unions, contractors, and a coalition speaking for civil rights activist groups "to obtain employment at once for 1,000 qualified journeymen who possess the necessary skills of their respective trades and look to the coalition to supply . . . such journeymen. Each respective craft union will accept such journeymen within the time period called for in the pertinent collective bargaining agreement, and each craft union will accept its initiation fee or required fees on a partial payment plan. . . ."[13] Standard apprenticeship requirements as a condition of entry are relaxed in the Chicago Plan and supplanted by the standard of "journeymen who possess the necessary

12. Statement of Policy on Equal Employment Opportunity, AFL-CIO Building and Construction Trades Department, Washington, D.C., September 22, 1969, pp. 1–10 *passim.*

13. The Chicago Plan, An Agreement for the Implementation of Employment of Minorities in the Chicago Building and Construction Industry, AFL-CIO Building and Construction Trades Department, Washington, D.C., January 12, 1970.

skills." Those with less skill or no skill may work up to journeymen status through combinations of apprenticeship and training substantially below conventional standards.

The Chicago Plan makes, as noted, the Coalition for United Community Action a party to the agreement and thereby recognizes the legitimacy of a third party, civil rights interest. The Philadelphia Plan is the prototype of the Chicago Plan but with the difference that the federal government, relying on its procurement authority, is the immediate third party.

Trade union involvement in the administration of manpower programs for the disadvantaged have included: (1) on-the-job training contracts with the U.S. Department of Labor, Manpower Administration, under which "the unions agree to recruit, train and place men and women who are unemployed and who meet the Labor Department's specifications as hard-core"; (2) the "buddy-system" component of the National Association of Businessmen's JOBS program (Job Opportunities in the Business Sector) which trains union workers to act as "buddies" to hard-core workers; (3) upgrading programs "to encourage workers hired at entry-level jobs" to move up the ladder; (4) Job Corps training, as in the Operating Engineers, to train for heavy equipment maintenance and to undertake to place those who have completed training; (5) "outreach" programs "to develop special programs to recruit, motivate and prepare minority-group youngsters to become apprentices in skilled trades."[14]

The method of "social enterprise" is meant to describe the establishment of union-sponsored organizations outside of the union structure which engage in research, education, training, and community organization to improve the conditions of life for the disadvantaged. The AFL-CIO's Human Resources Development Institute, financed largely by government grants and trade union contributions, aims to "mobilize and utilize the vast resources of skilled talent and experience available within the labor movement to plan, develop, coordinate and operate manpower programs for the hard-core unemployed . . . with emphasis on developing necessary support and problem solving services to obtain and maintain sound employment for such workers."[15] The Center for Community Change, manned and conceived by former staff of the Industrial Union Department of the AFL-CIO and financed by the Ford Foundation, aims to "provide technical assistance, leadership training and interpretation of legal and governmental rights necessary for local residents to negotiate social change."[16] The A. Philip Randolph Institute aims at "the preparation of far-reaching social and economic programs, serious school integration

14. Julius Rothman, "A New Look at Manpower Policy," *American Federationist* (AFL-CIO), August 1969, pp. 4–6 *passim*.
15. AFL-CIO, *Executive Council Report, 1969*, pp. 132–33.
16. Jack Conway, "Challenges to Union Leadership," *Proceedings of the IRRA* (December 1968), p. 185.

plans, nonviolent strategy, community organizing . . . to extend the basis for united mass action by the civil rights organizations on the national level."[17] The distinguishing marks of the social enterprise method in its current settings are (1) the commitment to social rather than to particular union or class interests, (2) the organizational separateness from the union, (3) the reliance on expert personnel rather than on trade union leadership, and (4) the collaboration with government, employer groups, and private foundations.

VI

The trade unions have relied on interest representation in government as the major vehicle for involvement in public policy. Interest representation is used in the sense of a pressure group "acting in concert to influence public attitudes or to obtain specific policy decisions from legislative bodies and administrative officials."[18] The leverage for interest representation is general electoral activity made possible by trade union manpower, money, and activity.

Interest representation operates outside and inside the government. The personnel outside the government consists of full-time legislative representatives—"lobbyists"—and technical policy specialists of the AFL-CIO and the national unions who work directly with sympathetic legislators and their staffs for or against specific pieces of legislation. Under mandates established by the governing bodies of the respective unions, this corps participates at all stages of the legislative process and follow-up, including the influencing of public attitudes, bill and speech drafting, lobbying, research, compromise, grass roots pressure, and surveillance of administration.

A variety of methods is utilized to achieve interest representation *within* government. The Department of Labor is viewed "as a department for labor [which] looks to its labor constituency to provide it with continuing sustenance."[19] Appointments to policy-making posts in the department, including the Secretary, have in recent years been made in consultation with the AFL-CIO—more typical in a Democratic administration—or on the basis of a general sympathy for worker interests. It is customary for one assistant secretary to be chosen from unions ranks—in Democratic administrations, by nomination from the trade union movement. Where an agency's activities impinge directly on union and labor interests, special

17. "Randolph Forms Institute to End Negro Poverty," *New York Times*, March 12, 1965.

18. Avery Leiserson, "Organized Labor as a Pressure Group," *Labor in the American Economy*, The Annals of the American Academy of Political and Social Science, Philadelphia, March 1951, p. 111.

19. *Ibid.*, p. 166.

units or personnel are recruited from union ranks or with union approval to assert union viewpoints. The advisory committee method is widely utilized to secure counsel from unions and other interest groups on specific programs which are affected with a strong labor interest. When advisory committee participation is supported by a substantial research effort, union viewpoints can be highly influential in molding the administration of programs and new legislation. There is also the "window dressing" type of advisory committee participation in which all there is, is a union presence. Interest representation is most influential when union participation is integral to the administration of policy, as in the tripartite disputes settlement procedures during World War II and the Korean War.

The form of trade union policy involvement with the broadest scope is the labor-management advisory committee, conference, or assembly at the executive branch level. There have been seven such undertakings beginning with a conference convened in 1918 by President Wilson. President Kennedy established a President's Advisory Committee on Labor-Management Policy on the urging of his Secretary of Labor, Arthur J. Goldberg, "which was the first *permanent* tripartite advisory committee to the President of the U.S."[20] The executive order which created the committee is still in effect but President Johnson utilized the committee in a "desultory" fashion[21] and President Nixon has not used it at all. The common features of the labor-management committee include tripartite representation, advisory status, nonbinding authority, and "summit" level participants. Of the six bodies prior to the Kennedy committee, "four met at the call of the President to deal with problems growing out of U.S. involvement in World Wars I and II and the conclusion of these wars. The other two were convened during the administration of President Eisenhower at the beginning and toward the end of his two terms in the White House. Only the conferences called at the outbreak of the two great wars were successful; the others broke up in recriminations among labor and management or were permitted to die without a formal burial."[22] The major source of recrimination are issues raised on the management side which in the union view appear to be aimed at weakening union power—for example, the union shop in President Roosevelt's 1941 conference, the management prerogatives question in President Truman's 1945 conference, and union monopoly in President Kennedy's committee.

The Kennedy committee made "some significant contributions largely in the form of reports and statements of agreement between labor and management: automation, collective bargaining, unemployment, foreign

20. Jack Stieber, "The President's Committee on Labor-Management Policy," *Industrial Relations* (Berkeley), February 1966, p. 4.

21. *Ibid.*, p. 19.

22. *Ibid.*, p. 1.

trade and fiscal and monetary policy." A tax statement exercised "an important influence" on administration legislation. The meetings helped create a "close and friendly relationship" between the labor and management participants. "A particularly close relationship existed with the Council of Economic Advisors . . . [which] met with the committee to give its members a preview of forthcoming annual reports."[23] As a CEA member recalls it, however, the committee made no "constructive contribution" to the CEA's guideposts. "In contrast with a specific bargaining situation, there were no clear economic or other pressures on the contending parties to arrive at a constructive policy solution."[24]

The committee work could have been strengthened if (1) its role were clarified, (2) its advice were sought before issues were "acted on by the Administration," (3) appointments were made on a staggered basis, (4) a full-time staff were available to develop position papers "free from the inhibiting influence of established policies and vested interests" when staff members are "seconded" from other government agencies, and (5) if it had been "maintained as an ongoing organization at all times and not permitted to lapse into long periods of inactivity."[25]

From time to time, variations on the labor-management committee approach have been proposed by trade union spokesmen. In 1944 Philip Murray, president of the CIO, urged a National Production Council "composed of representatives of labor, industry, agriculture and government" which in collaboration with government agencies would "be responsible for taking the country through reconversion and keeping it prosperous," and select industry councils "in the great basic and mass production industries, composed of representatives of labor, management and government."[26] In 1958 Arthur Goldberg, then a union attorney, urged "a labor-management assembly, modeled after the United Nations assembly, as an instrument for bringing together the leading figures in American industry and the leading figures in the American trade union movement for a periodic examination and discussion of the issues which affect us all. . . ." Government, through the secretaries of labor and commerce as chairman conveners, would supply "facts and . . . bring together a secretariat. The rationale was the need for a better "place to discuss and think about important issues than is possible in collective bargaining."[27] Reform from within the trade union movement was the aim of Solomon Barkin's

23. *Ibid.*, pp. 18– 19 *passim*.
24. Gardner Ackley, "The Contribution of Guidelines," in *Guidelines, Informal Controls and the Market Place*, ed. George P. Shultz and Robert Z. Alibu (Chicago: University of Chicago Press, 1966), p. 77.
25. Stieber, "Labor-Management Policy," pp. 18–19 *passim*.
26. Philip Murray, *Re-Employment Plan* (Washington, D.C.: CIO, 1944), p. 1.
27. Arthur J. Goldberg, "Labor-Management Relations 1958–59," *Labor Law Journal*, June 1959.

suggestion "for a full dress examination . . . by its own leadership assisted by the counsel, research, and penetrating understanding of the American environment and the trade union movement of its professional friends." Barkin singled out as urgent agenda items for the examination: the "obsessive" fear of technology, "an economic program built on the potentials of a society of abundance," and incomes policy. [28]

The union in America employs law and its administration mainly as an auxiliary strategy. It is subordinate to collective bargaining because, by comparison, (a) its effects on the terms of the employment relationship are less clearly perceived by union people, (b) it is necessarily not as responsive to union influence, and (c) it is not as adaptible to *particular* union interests. Strategy of law and its administration represents a species of bargaining because effective utilization requires the union to engage in negotiations with politicians, legislators, and administrators based on the union's ability to give or withhold material and moral support.

VII

American trade union involvement in economic policy differs from the mainline European experience in its policy scope and methods. The salient difference in policy scope is the "macro" reach of European trade union interests—the European word is "global"—compared with the characteristic "micro," program-oriented terms of reference of American trade unionism. Where the Europeans tend to think in terms of the economy and social policy, the Americans characteristically think in terms of specific programs and pieces of legislation—for example, manpower, civil rights, technological change, wage-price inflation, and disputes settlement.

As to methods of involvement, American trade unionism gives greater weight to bilateral collective bargaining and interest representation from without than European trade unionism which is more likely to favor tripartitism, interest representation from within, and integration. Here integration means that the major decisions in the European cases are more likely to arise out of (a) interest representation within the government structure, (b) a "problem-solving" atmosphere, and (c) a process in which the union movement exerts a central influence. The major decisions in American industrial relations are made through decentralized collective bargaining with individual managements, and involvement in public economic policy is mainly through interest representation external to the government. Where the American trade unions are involved in tripartite processes in peacetime, the union influence is typically peripheral. This is in contrast to the high involvement situations in Austria, the Netherlands,

28. Solomon R. Barkin, "The Road to the Future" in *Crisis in the American Trade Union Movement*, pp. 140, 142, 143, 144.

and in a special sense in Sweden, where variants on the multilateral economic and social councils are the forums from which major decisions are likely to emerge.

The classical American model of bilateral collective bargaining is now undergoing great stress and strain, unable to contain all the interests which are clamoring for recognition. The "public" or "general" interest demands recognition of the inflationary consequences of collective bargaining in a period of full or high-level employment. The civil rights interests which include both the activists and the government are demanding redress of the disadvantaged position of the black worker. In a sense, the civil rights demand reflects the position of the low-wage worker who has been largely excluded from the benefits of collective bargaining, not so much by deliberate act as by the characteristics of low-wage employment which tend to frustrate unionism and collective bargaining. Within the union the strain on the bargaining system is coming from the rejection of settlements made at the top which, in the rank-and-file view, do not take enough factors into full account, including the inflationary erosion of wages.

Many of the differences in the patterns of trade union involvement between the United States and Europe can be explained by differences in external circumstances. The greater complexity and size of the U.S. economy make a manageable macroeconomic policy more difficult. Moreover, the idea of economic policy in the United States as a continuing government responsibility has yet to achieve the acceptability that it has achieved in Europe. The United States has, finally, not experienced the sense of national urgency arising out of reconstruction, payments crises, and growth which proved to be so potent in bringing the European trade union movement into common purpose with other elements in the society. The civil rights upheaval shows some signs of serving this common-purpose end for the United States.

American trade unionism and industrial relations are unsuited to wholesale involvement in economic policy because of: (1) the relatively narrow base of union membership, that is, as of 1968 about 23 percent of the total labor force and 27.8 percent of nonagricultural employment—narrower than any European trade union movement except France; (2) the absence of important unions—for example, auto workers, teamsters, NEA teachers—from the largest national labor center; (3) the decentralization of collective bargaining authority; (4) the absence of a strong trade union–political party link, and hence the strong emphasis on pressure-group-from-without methods of influencing national economic policy; (5) the insufficiency of union technical staff resources, particularly in the research area; and (6) employer resistance to union recognition for purposes of dealing with national economic policy questions—this, it should be noted parenthetically, is the reverse of the European situation where employers are willing to deal with unions for economic policy but tend to resist enterprise bargaining.

American trade unionism also brings several assets to involvement in national economic policy: (1) The movement is not ideologically alienated from the mainstream of the society and therefore accepts the legitimacy of common purpose with management and government. (2) Union effectiveness in collective bargaining makes possible the achievement of important policy objectives through negotiations with management. (3) The importance of collective bargaining in regulating the terms of employment makes union participation in national economic policy-making essential. (4) While the union leadership, we know, cannot take the shop floor reaction for granted, neither has the shop floor been institutionalized as a permanent opposition to the union leadership as it has in many countries. On the contrary, the steward system, the grievance machinery, and the local union are integral parts of the union and collective bargaining structure and therefore permit, perhaps, a more unified response. (5) The American union is relatively well-financed and can apply substantial resources to support its involvement if it chooses to. (6) Interest representation within the government, while not on the European scale, is nevertheless sufficiently established to serve as a base for expansion.

VIII

The circumstances of Western Europe are different enough, we have argued, to preclude the grafting of the Western European model in its full Swedish or Austrian panoply on American trade unionism. The American and European experiences are, however, converging in the area of concern with the substance of bargaining. After a generation of state intervention directed essentially to the *procedures* of collective bargaining, public policy in the United States is having to intervene in the *results* of collective bargaining. The Wagner, Taft-Hartley, Landrum-Griffin types of regulation were largely concerned with redressing imbalances in power relationships—union vs. management, union leader vs. union member. The guidepost policy marked for the first time during a period of peace a concern with the economic terms of bargaining and, as this is being written, the concern has assumed the highest policy priority. The present stage of government antidiscrimination policy also represents intervention in the *terms* of collective bargaining, as the government and the civil rights movement are undertaking to modify union control over the hiring process in the building trades and seniority systems in industry. The American trade unions have not yet set the specific terms for their acceptance of an incomes policy but they are likely to be along the following lines:

1. Incomes policy standards should be subject to effective consultation and possibly to negotiation.

2. The wage policy must be part of a general incomes policy enforceable also against nonlabor incomes.

3. The standards for wage policy cannot, as under the Council of Economic Advisors' guideposts, be tied solely to productivity because this will perpetuate inequities and injustices in the wage structure.

4. The *quid pro quo* for wage restraint has to be the achievement of a measure of price stability without substantial unemployment.

5. Wage restraint has to be of a temporary and emergency character because rank-and-file opposition cannot be held in check for more than a brief period.

6. Scapegoating of the unions as the dominant influence in inflation must be avoided.

7. Economy must be exercised in the use of compulsion and restraint.

8. "Politicization" of the economic experts in the sense of a systematic bias of the economic analysis in favor of restraint—the Dutch experience is in point here—should be minimized if the economic analysis which supports restraint is to be credible.

The strong type of economic and social council as in Austria and the Netherlands is not feasible nor desirable for the United States, but the advisory committee established by President Kennedy does appear to be the closest approximation feasible in the American situation. The reconstitution of that committee at a time when the need for "reconciling private and public decisions" has never been greater would seem to be in order.[29]

With respect to trade union involvement in incomes policy and broad economic policy, the European experience is very instructive regarding the importance of quality research support. Trade union research in the United States could not now meet the demands which extensive involvement in incomes policy or general economic policy would make on it. Research in American unions is understaffed: the AFL-CIO, with an affiliated membership of about 16 million, has a smaller research staff than the Swedish LO whose membership is only one-tenth as large as the AFL-CIO's. Research in American trade unions is almost exclusively preoccupied with servicing immediate needs in collective bargaining and legislation. The utilization of trade union research for serious analysis of broad trends and policies is uncommon. Employment in the unions consequently offers little appeal to the talented university economist trained in the techniques of modern economics.

The limited scope of research in the unions reflects the leadership's judgment of its limited relevance rather than a general antipathy to tech-

29. G. W. Taylor, "Labor-Management Relations and the Balance of International Payments," *Proceedings of the IRRA Spring Meeting* (May 1962), p. 502.

nical competence; this idea is supported by the example of the relatively influential role—albeit in a service capacity—of the union lawyer. No union would think of getting along without lawyers, but most unions think they are able to do well enough without economists and research. Reflected also is the second order priority of economic policy in union calculations. This is seen not only in research but in the way union personnel is "seconded" for government service; if a high union official is selected, he will function only part-time on his government post. Only lower ranking officials are released on a full-time basis to a government post.

Both European and American experiences suggest some newer approaches to organizing research in the union commensurate with an important union involvement in economic policy. The DGB's economic research institute and the American examples of "social enterprise" cited earlier suggest the efficacy of the semi-autonomous organization as a method of professionalizing the research function. The research carried on by the Austrian Chambers of Labor suggests further that economic policy research in the interests of the trade union movement may be carried on within a quasi-government framework without trade union independence being compromised. In an American application of this principle, trade union representation in an agency like the President's Advisory Committee on Labor-Management Policy could be appropriately supported by a research staff paid out of public funds. In both instances, the public interest in informed partisan representation would seem to justify the use of public funds.

Education in economics is also part of the process of effective union involvement in economic policy. In this area, the American trade unions have taken the initiative to offer courses and have also collaborated with universities, but the subject matter has been largely trade unionism and collective bargaining and the audience has been largely shop-floor leadership. The scope of the subject matter needs to be enlarged to reflect the higher priority of economic policy concerns and the clientele needs to be extended to include the top-most leadership. The AFL-CIO Institute for Labor Studies is already available as the vehicle for an enlarged program of this sort. J. B. S. Hardman has put the nub of the educational problem incisively:

> True as it may be that organization is itself education, "the school of hard knocks" is not the total source of union wisdom. At some point in the unionist's empirical educative process, the acquiring of actual knowledge, the kind that comes through learning, is needed to supplement orientation through experience. With every day of our time, the business of being a responsible unionist grows in complexity, calls for exercise of judgment, for possession of a sense of values. Yet labor education has not recognized the importance of formal learning. The union as a whole is getting even more deeply involved in the main-

stream of the intellectual contests and encounters international life as well. And the individual unionist worthy of his membership card cannot in safety stay out of intellectual contact with the realities of twentieth century labor life. It is the function of labor education to achieve the "holy wedlock" of theory and action—or it just isn't education.[30]

On the whole, the posture of American trade unionism on the effects of collective bargaining on economic policy has been defensive and reactive. Only Walter Reuther's unsuccessful attempt to tie wages to prices represented a trade union initiative. The issue which this raises is whether the importance of union power in the society does not "carr[y] with it a partial trusteeship for the system . . . imply[ing] a responsibility to perceive the problems confronting the society and . . . an obligation to *lead* in their solution."[31]

Is the defensiveness, which was understandable when the unions were isolated enclaves, altogether appropriate to the modern union condition of prestige and influence? That the trade union movement does not have the concentrated power to assert and enforce a direct relationship between collective bargaining and economic policy should not preclude it from engaging in analysis beyond polemics to illuminate the question. It is here, perhaps, where the AFL-CIO as a federation is in a good position to mediate the issue, so to speak. Not having its own rank and file or employers with whom it bargains, it can take initiatives which may not be available to the constituent unions. It can, for example, provide a forum for internal discussion among the unions freed from the constraining influences of the bargaining table and the legislative hearing.

In effect, it is this sort of mediating role which the federation has assumed in the civil rights question between the civil rights activists and the government on the one side and its affiliates on the other. Supported by a headquarters technical staff, the federation has been influential in improving affiliates' civil rights practices which no direct government intervention could probably have accomplished as well, although the ultimate sanction of litigation undoubtedly reinforced the federation efforts. The federation's role in conciliating economic policy and collective bargaining need not be so much to urge a particular policy as to create a climate of union responsiveness to economic policy where, in George Taylor's words, "analytical processes" would be partially substituted for "the old testing grounds of force and power."[32]

30. *The House of Labor* (Englewood Cliffs, N.J.: Prentice-Hall, 1951), p. 476.
31. David B. Truman, "Labor's Responsibility in Public Affairs," in *Labor's Public Responsibility*, National Institute of Labor Education, Madison, Wisconsin, 1960, p. 111.
32. George W. Taylor, "Collective Bargaining," in *Automation and Technological Change*, ed. J. T. Dunlop (Englewood Cliffs, N.J.: Prentice-Hall, 1962), p. 87.

The European experience with union involvement in rationalizing the construction industry would appear to offer promise for the United States. Such problems as seasonality, organizational fragmentation, production techniques, and training have apparently been amenable to collaborative effort. The U.S.Department of Labor has launched an undertaking in this direction but it is too early yet to judge its results. The undertaking will, of course, have to involve local unions and employer groups as a basic condition of effectiveness.

Some part of union defensiveness comes from the fact that the unions are usually invited in to discuss national economic policy under crisis circumstances when all the available options lead only to union self-denial. Union participation becomes more viable when the unions are brought in before crisis develops and when presumably it is the union leaders' competence and insights which are being solicited and not only their power and influence.

Supplementary References

Barbash, Jack. "The Causes of Rank and File Unrest." In *Trade Union Government and Collective Bargaining*, edited by Joel Seidman. New York: Praeger, 1969.

_____. "The Impact of Technology in Labor-Management Relations." In *Adjusting to Technological Change*, edited by Gerald Somers. New York: Harper and Row, 1963.

_____. "Trade Unions and Social Justice—The Case of the Negro Worker." Paper delivered at Conference on Labor and Migration, Brooklyn College Center for Migration Studies, March 1970, New York; discussion paper, University of Wisconsin Poverty Research Institute, 1971.

Index

UNIVERSITY LIBRARY
NOTTINGHAM

THE JOHNS HOPKINS PRESS

Composed in Press Roman text and display
by Jones Composition Company, Inc.

Printed on 60-lb. Sebago, MF, Regular
by Universal Lithographers, Inc.

Bound in Columbia Fictionette
by L. H. Jenkins, Inc.